CHILDREN AUSTRALIA

Children Australia

Edited by

R.G. Brown

GEORGE ALLEN & UNWIN

Sydney London Boston

in association with

THE MORIALTA TRUST OF SOUTH AUSTRALIA

First published in 1980 by
George Allen & Unwin Australia Pty Ltd
8 Napier Street
North Sydney NSW 2060

National Library of Australia
Cataloguing-in-Publication entry:

Children Australia.
Index
Bibliography
ISBN 0 86861 186 7
ISBN 0 86861 194 8 Paperback
1. Children—Australia. I. Brown, Raymond George, ed.
305.2'3

Library of Congress Catalog Card Number: 80-68644
Set in 10 on 11 pt Plantin light by
Asco Trade Typesetting Limited, Hong Kong
Produced by Graphic Consultants International, Singapore

Contents

Foreword: On Human Potential—The Australian Child 7

Contributors 8

Introduction 10

PART 1 Children and Society 17
Jacqueline J. Goodnow and *Ailsa M. Burns*
Children and the State 35
David Brous, David Green and *Donna Jaggs*

PART 2 Children and Families 41
Peter Eisen
Every Girl's Dream 62
Denise Bradley

PART 3 Ethnic Children in Australia 67
J.J. Smolicz with *Roger Lean* and *Margaret Secombe*
Aboriginal Children 86
Anne-Katrin Eckermann
A Faint Ray . . . 107
Jim Giles

PART 4 Children and Values 114
Graeme W. Speedy
Practical Possibilities for Parents, Teachers and Planners 132
David R. Merritt

PART 5 Children's Health 138
Basil S. Hetzel and *Graham V. Vimpani*
Children's Health, Parents and the Community 166
Deane Southgate

PART 6 The Child and Education 173
Malcolm Skilbeck
The Unending Challenge 190
Roy F. Smallacombe

PART 7 The Economic Costs of Children and Child Poverty in Australia 197
Peter Saunders
Economic Relationships and Social Values 218
Barbara Spalding

PART 8 Children and the Law 225
Richard Chisholm

Afterword: Policies for Children 246
R.G. Brown

References 262

Index 279

Foreword

On Human Potential—The Australian Child

The idealism that should be one motive of the human services will not become a reality unless those services can work together thoughtfully and effectively for the common good. One condition for that is that the literature to which they may turn for knowledge and inspiration is sensitive to the diversity of problems and issues they face.

In 1979, the International Year of the Child, the Morialta Trust in South Australia agreed to give substantial support for the development of a book on Australian children. A sub-committee of the Trust was formed, the Foundation for Social Responsibility, to plan a project to produce the book. A theme was decided: the rights and responsibilities of children, parents and the community and in relation to that the responsibilities of the human services. Authors were commissioned to write from their specialized knowledge about particular aspects of children's lives, and administrators and practitioners in the human services were asked to comment from their experience on the application of this in practice. The contributors met in Adelaide over a weekend to discuss the first drafts of papers and commentories. This book is the outcome: it provides material for further debate and study.

As an administrator in community welfare I think the contributors have come to terms thoughtfully with problems facing the human services; as a family man I believe they have taken up issues that are important for children and families. These matters demand more attention. The book should stimulate discussion and action. I hope the issues raised in it will be studied more deeply and taken into the wisdom of the human services in their responsibilities for children, and that this will contribute to furthering the aims of the International Year of the Child.

I would like to thank the Morialta Trust of South Australia for their continued support and Bronwyn Halliday of the Department of Community Welfare in South Australia for all her efforts in proof reading, reference checking and general co-ordination and organisation throughout the preparation of the book.

Adelaide, July 1980

Ian S. Cox
Foundation for Social Responsibility

Contributors

Professor Jacqueline Goodnow and *Dr Ailsa Burns* are with the School of Behavioural Sciences at Macquarie University.

David Brous, *David Green*, and *Donna Jaggs* are with the Victorian Department of Community Welfare Services.

Dr Peter Eisen is Medical Director of the Department of Child and Adolescent Psychiatric Services at the Austin Hospital in Melbourne.

Denise Bradley is Women's Adviser to the South Australian Education Department.

Dr Jerzy Smolicz, *Roger Lean* and *Margaret Secombe* are with the Department of Education at the University of Adelaide.

Dr Anne-Katrin Eckermann is with the Centre for Multicultural Studies at the Armidale College of Advanced Education.

Jim Giles is Deputy Director-General of Education in South Australia.

Dr Graeme Speedy is Director of Sturt College of Advanced Education.

Dr David Merritt is Executive Director of the Joint Board of Christian Education of Australia and New Zealand.

Dr Basil Hetzel is Chief of the CSIRO Division of Human Nutrition.

Dr Graham Vimpani is Coordinator of Maternal and Child Health Services in the South Australian Health Commission.

Dr Deane Southgate is Director of the Clovelly Park Community Health Centre and Associate Professor in Primary Care and Community Medicine at the Flinders University of South Australia.

Dr Malcolm Skilbeck is Director of the Curriculum Development Centre in Canberra.

Roy Smallacombe is Assistant Director of Curriculum in the South Australian Education Department.

Peter Saunders is with the Economics Department of Sydney University.

Barbara Spalding is Executive Director of the Victorian Council of Social Service.

Richard Chisholm is with the Faculty of Law at the University of New South Wales.

Professor Ray Brown is with the School of Social Sciences at the Flinders University of South Australia.

Introduction

We set out to write about children: but in a particular way. From our different experiences and expertise we wanted to bring together what we knew about children and what is happening with children in modern society. All of us are concerned in some way with the work of the human services—those public services which provide social and other assistance to people on behalf of society. We decided that we should try to do two things: to set down what we believed to be the present state of understanding about children in Australia; and to consider the implications of this for the work of the human services.

We thought we should write for people who are concerned for children—parents and others who are significant in their lives, students, practitioners and administrators in the human services—who want to understand children, their needs and problems, and to understand the response that the Australian community, through its human services, is making to them. Some of the questions we hoped to consider were these: Is the status of children changing? Is our understanding of children changing? What are the assumptions that are determining our attitudes to children and the ways we respond to them?

Our intention was to try to capture, for thoughtful people who may not have the time to read the specialist literature, something of what is known about children in Australian society; something of what we in Australia are currently doing—what assumptions we are making, and how we are going about responding to children. And we wanted to look to the future, to how things might be, with particular reference to the tasks of the human services.

What emerged as we worked on this was the sense of change and uncertainty which now surrounds our understanding of and our relations with children. Children may not have changed much. Perhaps they are maturing earlier and learning to assert themselves more strongly at an earlier age. What have changed are our attitudes to children and our assumptions about relations between children and others. As we have begun to understand these things, however, we have become more uncertain about what we should do about them. The new understanding has been less about the relatively firm matters of the physical maturation and psychological development of children than about the changing nature of children's relations with others. In human relations we may know more, but what we have learnt has shown us how much more we need to know. And what we think we need to know about children is bound up with what we believe are the right ways to act toward them.

Nowhere is this more obvious than in those complex relations that are at the centre of this book—those between the child, the family and the state. Notwithstanding the interest taken in other life styles, almost all children grow up in some nurturing relation with one or two adults—in a family. It is clear that those people have strong but not necessarily predictable influences on children. And most children from an early age have dealings with the state through its human service agencies. It has long been accepted that the state was entitled to intervene in the relations between children and adults, although the assumptions on which that intervention may rest are changing. The uncertain nature of that uneasy compromise between child, family and state is one of the main concerns of this book.

Those relations are explored in what follows. Each section consists of two parts: an account of the current understanding of children with respect to a particular aspect of their lives, and a response to that from the viewpoint of the operating human services. In this way we have attempted to bring together not only something of what is known about children but also something of how that knowledge is applied. The book falls into two parts, the first concerned with more general aspects, the second with some particular fields of human services response. The first section deals with some general issues of the relations between child, family and society, beginning with a consideration of those changing relations in an historical context, then looking more particularly at the child in the family. This is followed by a discussion of children in a multicultural society. It concludes with a consideration of children's values. The second section deals with four areas of the human services' response to children—education, health, economic security and the law. The dominant theme of the book is the rights of children and in relation to that the responsibilities of children, families and the wider community.

While there are continuing uncertainties in the changing human relations that surround children, which we have attempted to address, some changes were accepted by us as bases from which our discussion should move. These include the geographic distribution of our population, its changing age structure, changing patterns of work, and changing patterns of family formation. Most Australians—

most Australian children—live in urban coastal centres. Nine main centres together account for some two-thirds of the Australian population. Only in Queensland and Tasmania is less than half the state's population found in the capital city. The two conurbations of Newcastle-Sydney-Wollongong and Melbourne-Geelong account for nearly three-quarters of the population of their states and together for almost half the population of the country. There are some indications elsewhere, for example in the United States, of a reversal of this trend toward urban agglomeration. Whether it will also be seen in Australia is not clear, in the light of the probable slowing down in the rate of population growth over the next quarter century. For the forseeable future there seems no likelihood of any substantial development of new regional centres of population and no diminution in the flow of people, of young people in particular, from the country to the larger towns and the cities.

Settlers and their children, those who are now sometimes referred to as ethnic-Australians, have made a substantial contribution to Australia's population growth and its prosperity since the end of the Second World War. About half the increase in population since 1947 has come from new settlers and their families. But despite the apparent diversity of their backgrounds, the majority of people in Australia are of European origin and of those almost half have come from the British Isles. While that may have reduced the effects of migration on new settlers it has not eliminated it. For some settlers there have been problems of transition and resettlement, and these have been felt by their children. These cultural problems can be expected to continue with the recent migration to Australia of significant minorities of people from different ethnic backgrounds, and from the doubling of the Aboriginal-Australian population which can be expected by the end of the century. The pattern of settlement of ethnic-Australians, but not of Aboriginal-Australians, has shown much the same tendencies as for the European-Australian-born. With the exception of their considerable contribution to some inland developments, particularly in mining and construction, most settlers have concentrated in the capital cities and their industrial hinterlands where there was employment in building, manufacturing, textiles and the service industries.

Patterns of work have changed and, along with these, patterns of education and of marriage and family formation. These trends Australia shares with other industrially developed countries. The most pervasive trend, related to the growing predominance of urban life, has been the shift of people from primary to secondary and to tertiary (or service) industries. At the same time children have been staying longer in education and have been coming to work with higher formal qualifications. Nevertheless, there are large numbers of children who leave school at the minimum age, who have little or no formal qualifications, and whose future is uncertain in the present changing economic times.

To what extent changing economic conditions will reverse well-developed trends of work-force participation is unclear. Australians have shared with people of other Western industrial and urban societies some well-defined tendencies which might have been expected to continue. More women have been working outside the family, so have more women with children, and so have more women with pre-school age children. The last has perhaps been the most publicly debated aspect of family life after the issues of divorce and abortion. The trend has been for more people to marry, for them to marry younger, for both partners to work outside the family for a few years to establish and furnish a home, then to have a small family, two or three children close together, and then for both parents to return to outside work.

Patterns of family formation are reflected in the age distribution of the population. Almost two-thirds of the population are in what are considered the working ages: 15–64. This is not expected to change much by the end of the century. What will happen is that the proportion of young people below working age will fall, while the proportion of people above working age will rise, leaving the balance between those inside and outside the working ages much as it was. Whether these trends will continue in the long term is less clear. They are volatile because they depend upon habits of child bearing that have changed sharply in the past and because they can be affected by immigration policies. Immigration aside, what can be expected is that Australia will move toward a demographically stable population, with near zero population growth, an average family size of about two children, and an age and sex distribution of the population which will be much as it is today.

That general account masks some significant variations. There are still many large families and some of these, particularly those with a single earner on a low income, are amongst the most disadvantaged in the country. We were not primarily concerned with disadvantaged children so much as with those situations where children in general are at risk. Nor were we concerned with children with problems as such: we did not set out, for example, to understand the particular situations of physically, intellectually or emotionally-handicapped children, or of children who have become delinquent. Our concern was with the needs and status of all Australian children, while recognizing that some of them have particularly pressing problems, some are especially needy and some are grossly deprived.

Our account does not set out to examine some divergent trends in family life. More children are growing up in families that differ from the ideal family of the past. More married people are divorcing and more divorced people are remarrying. More people are entering into unions that do not involve a formal marriage contract and more single parents are bringing up children. For the children this may mean that while they are in a relatively stable relationship with one or more adults at a particular time, this relationship may change as marital unions form and reform. What has become more unusual is not the existence of family-like arrangements but the picture of the family as a stable institution of man and wife legally joined in perpetuity where the husband is breadwinner and the wife is home-maker.

Generality is inevitable in an account of this kind which attempts to put together what is known and understood and about which there is some agreement. It is uncomfortable to write in such general terms without reference to the many qualifications which could be added. But to have done that would have defeated the purposes of the book.

This, then, is not a book by children about how they see their world—that is another, a different, and perhaps a more difficult task. It is a book about how we think children are seen, by adults and by the community, by those who see themselves as responsible for children, who take actions on behalf of children, who make laws affecting children, who for better or worse are influential in children's lives. The task we set ourselves was to consider the needs of and the public response to children within the existing political and economic assumptions and in relation to prevailing family life-styles. We have limited ourselves to considering children to the end of primary schooling—roughly to age 12. We have done that mainly on the ground that relations between child, family and state begin to change sharply at that time, and new assumptions emerge about the rights of children and the role of family and community in relation to them. They demand separate consideration.

Inevitably in many respects we have done less well than we hoped. There are gaps. Country children and outback children have not been considered in their own right. Nor have children living under alternative life-styles. The emerging issues of family and sexual politics have not been considered explicitly. Nor has the question of whether the Australian political economy can hope to guarantee to children the things it purports to and on which in part at least it bases its expectations of them. It is perhaps not enough to say that we did not regard these as unimportant. It may be a partial defence to say that we were attempting to write from what was known and was substantially agreed upon for the benefit of the majority of people concerned with children in general.

In the end, of course, there is no complete defence against the criticism that some important issue has been overlooked. There has not been a tradition of writing in Australia on the public assumptions about and the response to people's needs and problems. We think we have made something of a start in attempting to consolidate some of what has been done. There is room for more.

PART I

Children and Society

Jacqueline J. Goodnow and *Ailsa M. Burns*

We usually think of children within the setting of a family. But children—and families—are also part of a larger setting, and they look to people and organizations in this larger setting for a variety of services: for schools, recreation facilities, medical care, day care, legal aid, child endowment, and emergency help, to name just a few. The kind of service looked for may vary from family to family and from time to time. And the part of that larger setting turned to may also vary: it may be neighbours for emergency help, the local council for recreation facilities, volunteer groups for legal aid, and the state for schools, child endowment or subsidized day care. Some form of interaction with the larger world is almost always present.

The focus in this chapter is on interactions—between children, parents, and the state.[1] By 'the state' we mean that part of the larger setting which has an official status, which has some legal responsibility for providing services and some legal rights of control over what children and families can do.

To look at such interactions, we shall use the concept of an 'eternal triangle' as this analogy, more than any other, captures the dynamics, the push-and-pull that actually exists between children, parents, and the state. Each member of the triangle interacts with the others, forming agreements and alliances that are far from constant. Sometimes the alliances themselves may change, as may the extent to which the parties are happy with them.

At times, for instance, parents may welcome an alliance with the state in meeting children's needs. Let us take the example of schooling. Few people nowadays object to compulsory schooling, although many—at the time it was introduced—were strongly opposed to it and actually combined forces with the children, abetting their 'truancy'. At times, however, parents may find little to approve of in the system, perceiving the state as either not fulfilling its part of the bargain (not providing the kind of schools expected, for example) or—at the other end of the scale—as being excessively zealous, perhaps taking-over a prerogative of the family.

In its turn, the state may at times interact with children only through the parents to whom the children 'belong'. One or both parents are thought of as the ideal conduit for all dealings with children. Parents, for instance, receive financial assistance to be used for children; parents have the deciding say about custody; parents are informed without question if their children ask independently for medical advice or other help. At other times, the state interacts directly with children. Children may, for instance, be taken from parents and made wards of the state; they may be asked directly about their preference in custody; they may be granted independent legal aid and privacy in medical consultations; and discussions may centre around 'children's rights', rather than 'parental rights' or 'state's rights'.

What is involved in being part of this eternal triangle? How is it that we shift from one alliance to another, from one idea about the best relationship to another? Why do we sometimes follow one social policy for children and sometimes another? What determines the boundary line between 'family support' or 'child welfare' and 'intrusion' or 'take-over'? What are the consequences of shifting the line?

To explore such questions, we shall concentrate on two aspects of interaction—goals and resources.

Goals

Each member of the triangle has certain objectives in mind, objectives that are usually easiest to spot in discussions about the 'needs' and 'rights' of the various parties: children, parents, and state. The state may have as its primary objective, for example, the development of citizens who will be sober, industrious, educated in a fashion or to an extent that fits the labour market, willing in times of crisis to place the needs of the state or nation above their own, and—perhaps above all else—who with not be 'a burden'. Parents and children may have a different set of needs, or a different set of priorities.

Asking about goals helps us to become aware of the way objectives may be different for each member of the triangle. It also brings us face to face with other aspects of variation. Take, for example, the questions: What do we want children to be? What kind of life do we want them to have, as children and as adults? The answers have been different with each generation and with each historical period. And they still vary because of the children people have in mind when they answer the questions: this for our daughters; this for our sons; this for children in general, this for the 'deserving' but not for the 'undeserving', etc. Small wonder, then, that no clear-cut directives can be laid down for setting objectives for children.

Resources

To meet any set of objectives, we need to use resources of various kinds: money, buildings, goodwill, people. What we do may vary according to the resources that are actually available, or—a more subtle but critical point—that are perceived to be available. The state, for example, may not look upon a particular parent (a father, for example) as a feasible resource in bringing up children. And it may not agree with the parents' perceptions of young children as useful labour resources. Generally speaking, we all carry around with us ideas about the 'raw material' we have to work with: the 'natural' or 'given' qualities of children or parents. We also have ideas about 'extras'—about the resources that need to be added to the raw material. We do not always agree, however, on the extras that are needed, on whose responsibility it is to provide them, on the underlying 'quid pro quo' for any extras, or on who has first call on extra help (who is the most 'in need' or the most 'deserving').

Terms such as 'goals' and 'resources' may seem abstract to an off-putting degree. Suppose we start with a little history, some English but most of it early Australian. This will bring 'goals' and 'resources' to life, making clear how the 'eternal triangle' has changed over the years in accordance with ideas about what should be achieved and how. We can then turn towards an expanded and more contemporary look at goals and resources, using the perspective gained from looking at where we have been. "The fish is the last to discover water", according to an old proverb. And we may need to look backwards to become aware of the assumptions we take for granted, the ideas that seem so 'natural' and 'right' that we find it hard to see how anyone else could look at things in any other way.

Some selective history

Suppose we start with a specific 'modest proposal' for children—a proposal from Locke—and then proceed to a look at what conditions were like in early Australia.

> The children of the laboring people are an ordinary burden to the parish, and are usually maintained in idleness, so that their labor is also generally lost to the public, till they are twelve or fourteen years old. The most effectual remedy for this ... is that working schools be set up in each parish, to which the children of all such as demand relief of the parish shall be obliged to come. By this means the mother will be eased of a great part of her trouble in looking after and providing for them at home, and so be at more liberty to work; the children will be kept in much better order, be

better provided for, and from their infancy be inured to work which is of no small consequence to making them sober and industrious all their lives after.... It may reasonably be concluded that computing all the earnings of (such) a child from three to fourteen years of age, the nourishment and teaching during the whole time would cost the parish nothing; whereas there is no child now which before the age of fourteen, cost the parish fifty or sixty pounds.[2]

Locke's proposal involves some particular *goals* for children and for the parish: children should grow up to be sober, industrious and inured to work; the parish should be responsible for helping but should be as free of financial burden as possible. His proposal also involves some particular ideas about *resources*. The main resources are to be self-help and one's own labour, from the age of three on, without regard for the separation of children from mothers. In effect, the children in the working schools and the parents are treated as separate and almost equal individuals, all holding work contracts with the parish. Certainly the parish does not attempt to form a partnership with the parents in raising children.

Some of Locke's ideas are evident in the early development of centralized social services in Australia. There were in the beginning, however, some particular difficulties in encouraging self-support. The new land was harsh and alien; neither convicts nor the accompanying military personnel possessed much in the way of agricultural skills; and for the first two years the infant colony was threatened by famine. Governor Phillip placed his private stock of food in the communal store and the community, bond and free, was kept alive on government rations. By the time of Phillip's departure in 1792 the worst was over, but the colony was still far from being self-supporting.

Nor were prospects good for an early transformation of the first white settlers into stable, self-supporting family units. Among the arrivals in the First Fleet men outnumbered women by more than 3:1; by 1819 the ratio of males to females in New South Wales had reached 6.02:1 and by the 1830s 8.35:1; in Van Diemen's Land it was 6.6:1.[3] Even if the ratio had been better, however, the situation probably would not have been much different because the convicts seemed little disposed towards family life. Contemporary observers were "all but unanimous that the convicts who made up the vast majority of the first white Australians were generally speaking a demoralised, dissolute, drunken and lazy ... set of men and women".[4] By the end of Governor King's period of administration in 1806 only 395 of the 1430 adult women in New South Wales were married.[5] Births, however, had boomed. The vast majority of women convicts were aged between twenty and thirty-five years, and, mainly by natural increase, the number of children rose from 36 in 1788 to 200 in 1792. The ratio of children to women rose from 1:10 in 1788 to 1:3.5 in 1792 and 1:2 in 1795, and reached 1:1 in 1799. Two-thirds of the annual number of new births were reported to be illegitimate. Illegitimacy did not necessarily mean that a child was unwanted, or that the parental union was unstable (permission to marry was often difficult to obtain); but it did mean that many children were neglected, leaving the colonial authorities with the burden of supporting "a miserable progeny, nursed in the lap of vice; and inoculated with the virus of parental depravity'.[6]

What resources and measures did the colony's administrators see as appropriate to use in such a situation? And where did their ideas come from? The colony's officials came from a society long accustomed to the presence of large numbers of poor, neglected and delinquent children. And they were heir to centuries of welfare and reformatory philosophies and programmes which did not always agree on the measures considered appropriate or on the distinctions drawn among the children who were to be 'a charge' upon them (orphans, delinquents, 'poor but honest', etc.).

The most consistent tradition during those past centuries was the ideal of labour. Labour reduced the burden placed on the rest of the community by those who were both needy and idle. And labour was also a virtue in itself, a point brought out particularly well in 1720 by a citizen who cautioned against expecting too much economic benefit from the labour of the workhouse poor. "Give me leave to warn you", he wrote to fellow parishioners who were planning a workhouse in Kent, "not to promise yourselves too much from the produce of the labour.... The Men and Women are generally old and helpless, and the children perfectly new and inexperienced in everything." Nonetheless, the task itself was worthwhile:

> If you keep them employed tho' the Produce be no more than what will pay for the Articles of Firing and Candles ... it is something not to be despised. And what is still of greater Consequence is, that by keeping them employed you keep them in Health and from Idleness, the Parent of most Disorders in Society.[7]

A second recurring feature was the search for some acceptable balance between labour and education. The two were often seen as opposed: poor children who spend all their time "in play or poring upon a book", wrote the philanthropist Firman in 1678, "by such means ... get such a habit of idleness, that many times they will never take to any labour at all ...; whereas, if whilst young they were taught to work, they would fall in love with it, and when old would not depart from it." Firman advised against teaching all children of the poor to read, "except for some few who might be destined for more liberal employment'.[8]

What we have, then, is a see-saw effect between the notion of state help (together with education according to ability) and that of self-help (together with education only to the extent that under-educated labour is a drain on the nation). In Tudor times, for example, some orphan institutions had provided grammar school education for the cleverest of their boys, thus providing a route to social mobility. In subsequent centuries, however, the Puritan emphasis on work and thrift, together with the general impoverishment following the Civil Wars, produced increasingly negative attitudes towards *all* poor people, along with an insistent demand that even children be made to support themselves. John Locke's "Report on the Reform of the Poor Law", cited above, gives the flavor of this philosophy. By the late eighteenth century the Puritan approach was in turn being questioned, as knowledge of the suffering and corruption of 'innocent' and 'delinquent' children alike in workhouses, orphanages, reformatories, and gaols became known to the English middle classes through the work of reformers like John Howard.

Governor Phillip and his successors thus were acquainted with a range of ideas regarding the education and support of poor children. The special circumstances in which they found themselves, however, demanded some new applications of these ideas. In England, the growth of industry and mining had thrown up a demand for child labor which (for a while) strengthened traditional patterns. In Australia, by contrast, no such occupations were available for the rapidly increasing child population, and the prospect of a new generation heir to their "abandoned parents' profligate infamy" was not a happy one.[9] As early as 1794 the Chaplain to the new colony, Rev. Richard Johnston, had concluded that "If any hopes are to be formed of any Reformation being effected in this Colony, I believe it must begin amongst those of the rising generation". Schooling was chosen as the means of intervention. The rationale is explicitly set out in a memorandum to Governor Bligh, which states that:

> In a settlement where the irregular and immoral habits of the parents are likely to leave their children in a state peculiarly exposed to suffer from similar vices, you will feel the peculiar necessity that the Government should interfere on behalf of the rising generation and by the assertion of authority as well as encouragement, endeavour to educate them in religious as well as industrious habits . . . you are authorised to make such advances as you may deem requisite to afford the means of education to the Children of the Colony.[10]

Government in Australia thus committed itself from the beginning to a policy of major intervention in the lives of children, as a counter to the influence of parents, and as a means of improving the quality and industry of the next generation of citizens. Before the colony was a decade old about half the children were in school (including three-, four-, and in some cases two-year olds) receiving instruction in the three Rs and the scriptures, at a time when it was estimated that only one English child in sixteen was in school.

For a special group of children even further provision was required. These were the offspring of destitute mothers and fathers unwilling or unable for various reasons to provide support. The colony's leaders agreed that residential institutions were needed in which these children (and in particular the girls) could be secluded from corrupting influences and brought up in "habits of religion and industry". Official action was in this case supplemented by the philanthropic work of a group of élite women aware of the new educational and social thinking now gaining ground in England. These women, led by the wives of Governors King, Macquarie and Darling, involved themselves in the management of the Sydney Orphan School and School of Industry. They themselves instructed the girls in practical household skills, took an interest in their nutrition, health, and hygiene, and found positions for them when they reached an appropriate age (generally 12 to 14). But, as an article in the *Sydney Gazette* of 1836 indicates, their aim was to benefit others too, not only the girls.

> If the female part of our Community—the humbler sort too—is reared with proper attention, and duly instructed into all the simple yet complicated duties of industrious housewifery, just in proportion will the male part of the colonial population become benefited, since it will be utterly impossible to separate the interest and happiness of the one from the other—so that Mrs Darling's School (The School of Industry) will not only be the asylum and academy for producing "virtuous wives and pious mothers" but this lady will also have the enviable felicity of making good husbands and tender fathers.[11]

Institutions such as the School of Industry also adopted a very firm attitude towards the role of parents as a resource or as an influence in the rearing of citizens. Parents were allowed to visit the school only on the day of the general meeting of the committee, and then only in the presence of the matron. In effect, the family was ascribed a powerful influence, but this influence was seen as a negative one. Without community intervention it would damage the young through bad example, lack of attention to moral, religious and useful training, and the over-arching lower class habit of 'idleness'.

Modern psychology stresses the importance of a strong emotional bond between the child and the parent or other caretaker for healthy personality development; but nineteenth-century philanthropy seems to have had no such concern. Nor was there concern for the provision of substitute 'attachment' figures. For the religious philanthropists, attachment to God was probably seen as filling a similar role, as perhaps providing a secure anchor, a reliable model, and a degree of personal interest not to be found elsewhere.

From 1832 government-assisted passages were available from England to New South Wales, and a little later to other states. The population grew rapidly, occupations diversified, the huge surplus of men declined, and a more 'familist' life style took hold. Nevertheless the problem of abandoned and delinquent children remained a major one. In 1870 alone, 2498 children passed through the charitable institutions of New South Wales, 0.5 per cent of the whole population of the colony.[12] In Victoria the situation was rather wores. The gold rush of 1851 had left many children abandoned or orphaned, and a large number of these were in gaols simply because there were no other places to send them.[13]

So many children in need meant great public expense and, perhaps inevitably, public policy moved back towards the self-help Puritan philosophy. The Victorian Neglected and Criminal Children's Act of 1864 provided for a number of self-supporting industrial schools, where each child was to have a fruit tree, and silk spinning and castor oil industries would be developed. The children would be trained for apprenticeship into the trades of general service and farm labouring, and in the meantime were to defray expenses by taking in work. Although instruction in the three Rs was part of the training, it was likely to be given lower priority than money-earning occupations: "The elder girls go to their lessons when they can be spared from their washing."[14]

In practice, conditions in the institutions, as in the British workhouses, were often very poor, due to shortage of money and staff. Disease and death ravaged the inmates, and by the mid-1870s the mass institutionalization programme was written off as a failure. Boarding-out in private homes—colloquially known as 'baby farming'—was adopted as an alternative, and 100 supervisory ladies' committees were set up in Victoria alone. As the country moved towards the twentieth century a new conception began to enter public thinking—the idea that the lower classes, however apparently coarse and ignorant, might be educated into parenthood, and treated as collaborators in the goal of turning out healthy and productive children. The infant welfare movement and the kindergarten movement were amongst the new developments which stemmed from this philosophy. The state, however, continued to display a sturdy reluctance to picking up more of the tab than was absolutely necessary. The Royal Commission on Child Endowment or Family Allowances in 1929, for instance, recommended against endowment on both economic and social grounds:

> Involving, as it would, a high increase of taxation, almost certainly of direct taxation ... the result would be to check progress, to increase unemployment, and to reduce the sum of human welfare in the community.
>
> On the *social* side the main objection is, that if the State relieves parents of all financial responsibility for every dependent child in the family, the sense of parental responsibility and the incentive of parents to do their best to prepare their children for the full life of citizens in a free State would be seriously weakened. That incentive is so invaluable, and if removed, so irreplaceable, that any course likely to have the effect of destroying it, in whole or to a material degree, would be a sacrifice of one of the best elements in the character of the people.[15]

We have chosen these relatively colourful aspects of Australian history—with an emphasis on the first settlements and on the times before the major bulk of free settlers arrived—as a way of illustrating shifts in ideas about goals and resources. Let us now take a closer look at this change in ideas, and pay particular attention to questions that could apply to any time or to any country. Where possible, however, we shall continue to use examples from the Australian scene.

Goals: needs and rights

Any discussion of goals involves a consideration of the needs that should be met and of the rights that should be guaranteed. In each instance we might ask four questions. We shall treat the first pair very briefly and concentrate instead on the second pair, since these have a particular importance in the dynamics of the eternal triangle.

When are needs or rights most likely to be in jeopardy?

'Needs' and 'rights' are usually ascribed to those people we regard as being part of the mainstream. The people most vulnerable are those who are somehow set to the side, or those whose ideas about their special needs and rights are consistently ignored. Within Australia, Aborigines provide a particularly poignant case. They are constantly confronted with a tradition that defines the land as 'empty' and of 'no significance' until it was ploughed or mined, that defines them as 'primitive' and as 'colonized' and 'improved' rather than 'conquered'. In addition, they face the view of many white people that their children are incapable of learning and that the help families are given amounts to an unearned handout, given at the expense of a more deserving poor. The gap between such terms of discourse and any terms starting from pride in oneself is enormous.

Can rights be forfeited?

Indeed, they can. Children can be declared 'incorrigible', parents 'incompetent', minorities 'uneducable', governments as having 'no claim on my loyalty'. What changes from time to time is not the *presence of forfeit* but the conditions used to justify it. We still class children, for example, as 'neglected' or 'incorrigible', but few of us would agree with the reason given by a mother who, in 1867, asked for her eight-year-old to be committed to a reform school because he habitually "wandered about with no ostensible lawful occupation."[16]

Whose needs or rights come first?

As soon as we talk about children's needs and rights, we are inevitably also discussing the relative claims of mothers, fathers, neighbours, communities, and the country at large. What keeps the discussion lively is the fact that the claims are not always compatible. Take the issue of rights. Your right to leisure or a child's right to leissure—or to education for that matter—does not always fit in with the demand of the family of the state for immediately productive labour. Your right to self-expression may conflict with mine for peace and quiet; your need for independence or individuality with the goal of a 'collective good'.

Within this context, the notion of children's rights is a relative novelty. It appears as part of a general sensitivity to the legal and human rights of each individual, displayed in a concern for the rights of women, minorities and children. Even more than women, children have traditionally *belonged* to someone else. It has not often been said that "the child *belongs to himself*, in the care of his parents", a statement that, not surprisingly, is made in the context of physical violence against children.[17]

At a less dramatic level, the 'proper' balance of individual claims against the 'collective good' is also open to debate. The ladies who established Sydney's School of Industry, for example, were careful to insist that the education they provided would not disturb the social order. They recognized that:

> There are indeed some persons who ... imagine mischief must arise from enlightening the lower orders of society, because while

imparting knowledge, a spirit of discontent is apt to be aroused in the mind.

But, they affirmed, the school would not permit this to happen. It would instead:

render them in every respect better qualified for their condition in life; not, as some would erroneously have supposed, to raise them above, or to make them discontented with it.[18]

The most ready examples of debate over 'individual' and 'collective' good, however, seem to stem from the interactions of children and parents. The oldest daughter in Australian families, for example, was frequently the sacrificial lamb, remaining uneducated so that she could help with younger children, and then unmarried so that she could look after aging parents. Such arrangements seem to be becoming less frequent; their decline seems unlamented. Where the shift in the order of rights still seems poignant, however, is within ethnic groups that place a strong emphasis on the good of the family, and on the subordination of individual interests to the family good. Soccio's account of change within his Italian-Australian family is a superb emample.[19]

Which needs or rights are important?

Albert Ellis devotes a large amount of his time to pointing out the dangers of expecting to have 'every need fulfilled', an expectation he sees as leading us into frustration and a readiness to complain about our lot. He has provided recently a parody of this position:

I cannot have all my wishes filled—
Whine! Whine! Whine!
I cannot have every frustration stilled—
Whine! Whine! Whine![20]

Given that not all needs can be met, what shall be the order of priority? Suppose we limit our discussion to the needs of children. The earlier Australian priorities were largely physical and often expressed in negative terms: children should not starve, should not be beaten, and should not be exploited as labour or as sexual objects. Later expectations have been somewhat more positive and encompassing.

The need to develop good physical health is a considerable advance from the baselines of not starving or not being neglected. In current times, an equal advance has occurred in the area of psychological health. It has often been said that the prime psychological need for children is a sense of being loved, growing out of a strong attachment to the parent, usually the mother. In addition, it has often been said that attachment—to be effective—must begin at birth and be sustained by the relatively constant presence of a responsive adult during the early years. This set of ideas grew out of concern for the sterility and coldness of the care given to young children in child-care institutions and in hospitals, with children in the latter suffering both the trauma of both hospitalization and separation from a known and caring world. The concern—spearheaded by Spitz and by Bowlby—led to a considerable amount of reform in hospitals and institutions. It also led to the simplistic notion that all separations from the mother were in themselves harmful, were a form of 'maternal deprivation'. The result was a suspicion of any form of child care outside the home, and a considerable anxiety about the effects of prematurity and the chances of successful adoption for children other than very young infants.

Among psychologists at least, the steam has gone out of discussions about 'attachment'. The theory seems to have suited a particular period when servants and nannies were disappearing; it both exempted fathers from child care and sugar-coated the fact that one person was now expected to take over work once divided among several. More finely, attachment theory is now thought to be rather narrow in its application. It says relatively little, for example, about the psychological needs of older children or about their needs in contexts other than the close confines of home: in school, for example, or in their general encounters with society.

We would like to sketch briefly three current suggestions about the needs of children, needs that seem to go beyond early years and to have particular relevance to interactions between children, parents, and 'others'.

The first is the need for *continuity of experience*, a need often invoked in discussion about relationships between home and school, between care by parents and care by others, or between home and an outside world where a language and a culture prevail that differ from those found at home. The difficulty in all these discussions is that we cannot say how much continuity is needed or how much discontinuity (or what type) can be readily coped with. The easiest assumption to make is that children faced with discontinuity will experience culture-conflict and that this in itself will be damaging: the children will feel torn between two worlds.

The second is the need for a *sense of worth*, for the feeling that one matters or counts. This is a particularly 'social' need, in the sense that it requires affirmation from others, both from parents and from the larger social world. It is difficult to maintain a sense of worth, however loved by parents, if one's image of oneself finds no echo or no reflection in the larger world, or if what the world reflects is a devaluing image: you are 'just a dole-bludger', 'only a child', 'just a housewife', 'one of those wogs', etc.

The third is for a *sense of effectiveness*, the feeling that we have some say in our fate, that what we do will have some impact on what happens to us. This notion is often discussed in its negative form, under the term 'learned helplessness', a phrase expressing the idea that we start with a sense of competence but acquire a sense of helplessness when our actions lead nowhere and when most of the decisions made about our lives are made by others. The concept is linked to another called 'locus of control', which describes the way individuals differ in the extent to which they see themselves as 'movers' or as 'pawns' in the game of life, controlling what happens to them or being swept along by external forces. The sense of effectiveness is thought to be affected not only by our experiencing successful actions, but also by the explanations that others provide, and we absorb, for success and failure.[21]

These three needs—continuity of experience, a sense of worth, and a sense of effectiveness—reflect a society where a number of physical needs have already been met. They also express a concern for psychological health as requiring more than a rewarding family life, more than only two parts of the triangle. These 'new' needs demand attention to all three parts of the triangle, arguing for an increased recognition of the importance of experiences outside the family and of the images reflected by others in informal interaction or in official policy.

Resources: raw material and extras

In the earliest days of Australian settlement, the leading members of the community—the experts of the time—felt little uncertainty about what children needed, or needed to be. The question rather was how to achieve this with the resources that were at hand and were perceived as feasible to use.

Their concern would have fitted easily into the area generally known as 'resource theory', a framework often used in psychological and sociological analyses of relationships between parts of our triangle. Burns and Goodnow provide a number of examples of its use—in such contexts as residential care, day care, unemployment, working mothers, inequality, and violence against children.[22]

For our present purposes, we shall concentrate on two kinds of resources. One kind consists of the raw material. We expect, for instance, to work from the base provided by the 'natural' or 'given' properties of people: the 'natural' disposition of children, the 'natural' or 'instinctive' feelings and skills of parents, the 'natural' ties between children and parents. Actions by the state seem closely tied to views about the 'raw material': the state moves in, for example, at times when it regards—either in truth or in a rhetoric that justifies its actions—parents as incompetent, unwilling, or as 'abdicating their responsibility'.

The second kind of resource consists of additions or changes to the raw material. It is when we come to these 'extras' that we are faced with a number of questions such as.

What should be added? Is the most effective addition, for example, fresh air or better medical care, separation from the family or support to the family, more jobs or more leisure?

Who should provide any further resources? We have already seen, for example, some divisions of opinion about the relative use of self-help, community help and state help.

Who should do what part of the job? When both home and school are expected to provide resources, for example, the division of responsibility is not always agreed upon. The boundaries that mark 'neglect' on one side and 'intrusion' on the other may vary significantly.

Who is thought competent to help? We can find examples of different answers to this question in discussions about the role of 'consumers' and 'experts': ex-addicts may be presented as the most competent to help addicts, parents who have abused their children the most competent to help those currently in trouble, etc.

Who is allowed to help? Competence aside, 'ladies committees' or 'professional committees' may insist on various kinds of credentials, leaving some available resources unrecognized or untapped.

What is the expected response to help? What is owed in exchange? Most services can be regarded as an exchange, with the terms of the bargain shifting from time to time. To choose one example, the 1929 commission on child endowment proposed (but did not achieve) a very specific *quid pro quo*:

> If however public funds are to be applied for the establishment and maintenance of a scheme of child endowment, and especially if such endowment is designed to provide the full cost of maintenance of dependent children, *eugenic considerations which have not hitherto been regarded must be taken into account.* The children who would be beneficiaries by such a scheme would, by that fact, become in an important sense of the term 'wards of the state' and 'assets' entering in a somewhat direct fashion into the national balance-sheet. The authorities responsible for the expenditure of large sums of public money in building up such assets could hardly fail to attempt some form of eugenic control over the recipients of the national bounty.[23]

In this case, the expected exchange was quite explicit. It went beyond the vague expectation that the recipients of help would be grateful, would turn over a new leaf, would return the favour when help was needed, repay the debt with interest, etc. Some sense of exchange underlies many of our transactions with others—parents, children or organizations, with difficulties arising whenever the terms of the exchange are not agreed upon or are thought to be inequitable.

We cannot obviously hope to cover all of the questions about resources listed here but they are important and need to be raised if nothing else. Instead, we will concentrate on one idea that surfaced early in our discussion: How is the 'raw material' perceived?

The 'raw material' most often discussed consists of the properties expected to occur in children and in parents. Let us look at some English and some Australian ideas about such properties.

Conceptions about the 'expectable' properties of children have undergone considerable changes from one period to another, changes well documented by Pinchbeck and Hewitt in a study that concentrated on the English situation.[24] Few 'modern' parents or educators, for example, would accept without comment this grandmother's view of children, expressed in a story by Katherine Porter. The grandmother relied

> on the dogma that children were conceived in sin and brought forth in iniquity. Childhood was a long state of instruction and probation for adult life, which was in turn a long, severe, undeviating devotion to duty, the largest part of which consisted in bringing up children. The young were difficult, disobedient, and tireless in wrongdoing, apt to turn unkind and undutiful when they grew up, in spite of all one had done for them or had tried to do.[25]

Ideas about the 'expectable' properties of children often vary with the sex of the child—'Boys will be boys', for instance—but an even more important division by sex may occur in the properties expected to occur in mothers and fathers. Twopenny, in 1883, felt that Australian marriages showed great promise, each spouse concentrating on one sphere:

> Domestic occupations so occupy the thoughts of wives, and business those of husbands, as to leave few moments of vacuity for Satan to introduce mischief into.[26]

Within this division of labour, there is the strong expectation that women will be competent and practical. That expectation undoubtedly occurs in many countries. In Australia, however, our impression is one of a particular pattern: women are counted on to display 'reserves of strength', rising to the occasion with considerable managerial skills, and then retiring again to a more 'cared for' role once the emergency is over or a male partner returns. The examples are numerous: Lady Macquarie managing Merinos for the many years her husband was in London and Mrs Bessie, in the novel *Coonardoo*, are only two. The 'expectable' pattern appears to be not a continued display of competence beyond the domestic scene, but a reserve to be drawn on only when needed.

If Australian women are regarded as the natural allies of the state in raising children or in keeping families intact—once past that first small group of "damned whores" and into the ranks of "God's police"[27]—the same can not be said of fathers. The payment of child endowment directly to the mother and without a means test appears to be a uniquely Australian alliance of the state with mothers, an alliance which bypasses fathers. This third feature—the reluctance to expect much of fathers—may reflect an early history of a high incidence of deserted wives, drunken husbands and de facto wives. The reluctance to rely on fathers is certainly not something which only happened in the distant past, however. The expectation that fathers cannot be readily counted on to cooperate with the state in supporting their children recurs, for example, in the debate on child endowment in 1929. Both parents were thought likely to weaken in their efforts to support their children, but:

> The effect on the father would be evident in a probable slackening of energy more than in the case of the mothers. It would be dangerously easy for many fathers to slacken off in their own efforts, and to pass into a condition of careless acquiescence in a system which made the children, at least from the financial point of view, wards of State. The price of this easy acquiescence would be the loss of much of the virile and strenuous independence of character, and ready acceptance of the whole responsibility for his children, which are among the most admirable characteristics a man can possess.[28]

In still more recent times, even fathers who had taken over primary care for motherless children were seen as being poorly informed about past aspects of the health or education of their children. All in all, they still do not appear to be regarded as allies or resources to be readily counted on in any partnership between parents and the state.

Do ideas about the 'raw material' matter? Ideas about natural resources are not purely of historical interest. At state or family level, such ideas may be used to justify action. They may also shape the way we bring up children. If we believe in 'original sin', for instance, we try to cleanse, cure, or stamp out the original vice. If we believe in original innocence, we aim at protection from corruption. Our ideas also shape legal decisions: decisions about awarding the custody of children—girls especially—to fathers, for example. They shape our perceptions of what is happening. At the 1975 Perth conference on child abuse, for instance, Gurry noted that it was difficult for physicians to be suspicious of parents and start 'playing detective' when all their medical training stressed the role of being a facilitator or helper to naturally loving parents—and to mothers especially.[29] Finally, ideas about nature shape the attitudes people hold about asking for help. Gurry, for example, noted with feeling that both physicians and mothers were "victims of a myth": the myth that parenting comes naturally, that motherhood is a state of unalloyed bliss. Such beliefs make it difficult to ask for help when one so clearly falls short of the 'natural' state.[30] Assumptions about natural strengths and natural responsibilities—about the 'givens' of human nature—can give rise to interactions between children, parents, and the state that are the opposite of what we wish to achieve, that diminish rather than strengthen effective relationships among the three parts of the triangle.

We have been considering relationships between children, parents, and the wider social world represented by neighbourhood, community, or state. This tri-partide picture is a shift from our usual image of the child within the bosom of the family: of the child as part of a self-sufficient unit to which he 'belongs' in many senses of the word, in need primarily of love and 'attachment'—needs which are met by people linked to the child by biological ties.

Such a picture is only partly true. Like it or not, children and their parents are part of a larger world. This larger world can grant or deny the help parents need, can affirm or negate the image parents present of themselves to their children, can provide continuity or a sharp break with the life at home, can intervene and over-rule the decisions of parents. The reality is a constant working-out of shifting alliances, unwritten 'contracts', and implicit agreements, sometimes to the satisfaction of all, sometimes to the satisfaction of no one.

Interactions between the parts of the triangle, we have proposed, vary from one historical period to another and, even on the contemporary scene, from one person or setting to another. More specifically, the elements that change may be regarded as related to (a) objectives (goals, needs, rights); (b) resources (the means we use to achieve any goal); and (c) rhetoric (the justifications we present for taking action or for refusing to intervene). When all these are agreed upon, people exist in harmony. When they are not, the result is a sense of frustration, of not being understood, of being 'wronged' or treated 'unfairly'.

Objectives, for example, may be defined very differently by

children, parents, and the state. They may also vary in the way they are phrased and the groups they are applied to. Shall we speak, for instance, of a 'right to learn' or of a 'duty to be educated'? Does the right or the duty apply to all, to the élite only, to the majority, or to the 'deserving'? For minority groups especially, there is a special need to insist on certain objectives being as appropriate for their children as they are for the children of those who have more say in defining 'proper' objectives for varying segments of the population.

Resources, and ideas about their proper use, may vary even more widely. We have defined the term 'resources' broadly, using it to cover everything that helps us to achieve objectives: from time and money to patience, willingness, and enthusiasm. We have also drawn a distinction between resources that are our 'raw material' (the 'natural' qualities we perceive in children, parents, and 'others'), and resources that are 'extras' (the things we need to add to what is given). Historically, we have suggested, Australia started with little official doubt about objectives: what was needed was the development of sober, industrious citizens. The doubts expressed were over the raw material (officialdom saw little good in the parents of the first generation), and the provision of 'extras'. The initial solution was to bypass parents, thereby establishing a direct line of contact with children and deploying resources—such as schooling or residential care—to the young and the very young with little regard for parents' 'rights'. Of social policy, we have proposed, see-saws between perceiving the 'raw material'—children or parents—as impossible or promising, between emphasizing self-help or state help, between distributing assistance directly to children or distributing it only through the parents (or only through the mothers who are perceived as the natural ally of the state).

All told, we gain a clearer sense of our contemporary policies when we locate them in a section of these several see-saws, and when we ask about the expectations with which children, parents and state turn towards or away from one another, asking for help, asserting obligations, or drawing boundary lines. Equally, we shall be helped if we become alert to the changing rhetoric we use to justify inaction or action. We have said little directly about changes in rhetoric, but the quotations from early Australian documents have surely made the point for us. Society always has an interest in children, often a self-interest. We speak now of the 'rights of the child' rather than the 'inalienable rights of parents' or the need to avoid 'burdens on the state'. And we express our concerns in secular rather than religious terms. Beneath the changing rhetoric, however, lies the constant reality of a larger social world of which children and their immediate families are all part.

Children and the State

David Brous, *David Green* and
Donna Jaggs

"People seldom agree on their ideas about what life should be like and how to make it happen. . . ." Goodnow and Burns's claim is increasingly valid in Australian society, as reflected in relations between parents, children and those representatives of the state who determine and administer policies affecting children. Despite demands for public intervention in the interests of children, there is confusion about the objectives to be achieved and the processes to be used in achieving them. The International Year of the Child has provided a forum for these debates, and has highlighted long-standing uncertainties about the roles of parents and the state in the development of children.[1]

The last decade saw a great demand on governments in Australia to respond to the diverse interests and traditions of our society. Expansion in the machinery of the state—its departments, agencies and instrumentalities, serviced by professionals and technocrats—was unprecedented. Almost co-incident with these pressures, however, has been a decline in the community's confidence that the public sector can meet the needs for which it was established. The political and administrative structure appears increasingly isolated from the community to which it is expected to be accountable, and less in control of the outcomes of its strategies. The ethical and ideological bases of the actions of the state are no longer apparent, for they are more and more difficult to delineate and communicate. Consequently there is less confidence that the state serves the common interest.

The problems of legitimation of policies and actions in the interests of children are manifold. The state tends to respond with lofty and generalized statements of aims and objectives which are vague and idealized and incapable of meeting specific and practical demands. Is it clear when parents forfeit their rights to be guardians of their children, or when the state ceases to have a strong claim on the parenting of children? Yet the state is attempting to answer these questions, and even to respond differently yet equitably to the varied cultural and ethnic groups within society. The answers are difficult to comprehend when the interests of the various actors—the family, children and the state—are at odds and power is distributed unevenly between them.

Goodnow and Burns demonstrate how the 'good' society, and the means to achieve it, were so much clearer in nineteenth-century Australia. The state developed two major tools of social management: poor laws designed to relieve gross physical poverty, and vagrancy acts to deal with wanderers and individuals of bad reputation who were likely to undermine the social order. Legislative intervention by the state in the interests of children derived from these mechanisms and the assumptions upon which they are based. Colonial legislation for the protection of children in Australia conveyed the prevailing idea of the 'good' society and the means for its achievement, while specifying the state's responsibility for the care and control of children found in undesirable circumstances.

The poor law origins of the state's initial intervention in the interests of children is even more clearly demonstrated by comparison with another important area of intervention in personal relations between adults—namely marriage and divorce. Until the mid-nineteenth century divorce was an upper class prerogative requiring a Private Member's Act of Parliament. From these origins divorce action developed as civil proceedings. Child welfare provisions, on the other hand, have always favoured quasi-crminal proceedings, the allocation of blame, or fault, and the 'punishment' of the parties. Furthermore, having effected judicial orders, they allowed the ongoing decision making regarding the child to be transferred to the administrative arm of the state, i.e. to departments which sometimes had the least trained categories of officials. Divorce provisions, on the other hand, allowed for ongoing responsibility of the court to make requirements on both adult parties and to use the highest levels of trained practitioners.

So while the political functions of child welfare legislation and divorce legislation were basically similar, they operated in different ways, and generally affected different categories of people. The provisions of child welfare were directed towards the children of the poor, while the provisions of divorce were directed to the adult rich. Neither provision was ever particularly directed towards the needs and interests of children themselves, although both were directed towards maintaining order and cultural security upon which the future of social relationships depended. Both areas of intervention have been subject to investigation in all states in Australia, and at the national level in the adoption and current review of the Family Law Act. Many of the debates arising from these reviews demonstrate the problems of defining what kinds of relationship should exist between the child, family and society, and how those relationships should be achieved.

While new legislation in the field of family law expresses something of the changing relationship between child, family and society, the changing patterns of child socialization represent a more primary and basic guide to the uncertainty in these relationships. Sociologists have studied the decline of traditional, stable socializing institutions—the family and extended family, the neighbourhood and the church. These institutions provided the child with a stable base for personal development. Now a vacuum has been created into which have moved bureaucratic institutions, supported by legislative contracts and staffed by professional and administrative corps. The state, acting through a multitude of agencies, has become a force which determines the ideals and directions of society's children.

Christopher Lasch describes the process with dramatic style and vitality: "The citizen's entire existence has now been subjected to social direction, increasingly unmediated by the family or other institutions to which the work of socialization was once confined."[2] Yet there is something of a contradiction. While the state has come increasingly to intervene in the affairs of children and families with the decline of the traditional institutions, the state's own authority is being questioned, as is the legitamacy of its intervention. This is not due simply to abuse of power or malpractice by officials, but also to the unprecedented rise of therapeutic ideologies and an excessive preoccupation with private rather than public concerns, which have fostered the corruption of familial and public authority. As Lasch says,

> Those who wield authority—fathers, teachers, magistrates and priests—have all suffered loss of 'credibility'. Unable to inspire loyalty or even to command obedience, they have had to allow their subordinates a greater range of pleasures—and also a greater range of crimes and misdemeanours—than they would once have tolerated.

Debate over the propriety of the state's intervention in the affairs of children is profoundly relevant for all those engaged in administration and policy formation in state organizations. But it is also intellectually hazardous. Concrete goals of an economic or technological nature provide measurable standards of achievement; the development of children's services, on the other hand, depends on interpretation of needs and selection of objectives from a vast range of possibilities about which there can only be uncertainty.

The bases of developmental social policies for children

The last decade will be long remembered for its development of an awareness about social policy—if not the development of social policy itself. Just as Australia learnt more about ecological system, the nation also began to learn about the ecology of social systems—although almost always after the disruption had occurred and the costs had begun to show. The decade saw the development and acceptance of environmental impact statements. Perhaps the next decade could see the beginning of child impact statements.

Child advocacy and child impact statements

Modern social policies generally are predicated on the supposition that they are in the best interests of the child, family, migrant, handicapped person or other intended recipient. Yet all too often, implementation of such policies reveals conceptual confusion and professional bias, and the pursuit of sectional political interests. There are no child advocates at the level of the individual, or at the level of the impact of social policies on children. Consultation on public policies directly affecting children is usually attended by groups representing parents, professionals, local councils, pressure groups, political parties, and almost everybody except children.

There are many skilled and sensitive people who can think ahead for the child, who understand children and their differences and can relate that understanding to the actions of society. Such people should be valued and recruited to assist in assessing the impact of society's actions on its children. It is not difficult to imagine many of the issues which would be raised on behalf of children, but it is difficult to rise above the vested interest of professional and pressure groups and project those issues into the political arena.

Family impact statements are now being developed and reaching some sophistication. There is a new consciousness about the complex ramifications of policies, and a recognition that social policies for children must consider the heritage of the past in order to cope with a changing present and an imagined future. The development of both children and society depends upon a balance of the past and the future, an understanding of traditional values and certainties, and the base they provide for advances in the future. So why not 'Child Impact Statements' as a requisite for law-makers to consider before policies are translated into programmes?

Social policies which affect children must be meaningful to them, not in terms of the children's own immediate spontaneous feelings, but in so far as the policies prepare them for an adult life which is satisfying and in which they can expand their consciousness in an effective manner. James Paul described this process as class advocacy—where there is understanding of the problems which occur in the exchanges between children and their environments.[3] An impact statement for children would be a general statement regarding a problem or set of problems that children, or groups of children, have in common. Advocacy, on behalf of children as a class, describes action derived from this statement. One of the critical reasons why there has been so little class advocacy on behalf of children is a lack of clear statements about transactions between children and their environments and about the problems arising from those transactions.

Class advocacy cannot represent the individual except in so far as the individual shares the problems, needs and disadvantages of the group. To support the needs, rights and differences of the individual child society turns to the advocate. Paul emphasizes the need for children to be 'represented', particularly since the assumption in almost any situation is that the 'trouble' is the exclusive property of the child. Once this trouble has been identified the processes of labelling commence, with a consequent stigmatizing of the child. Paul defines stigma as a process of cultural quarantine, whereby the child who is different is labelled, isolated and dealt with in the interests of the group rather than in the interests of the child. The process of stigmatizing generally involves moral and ethical issues, and once a child is stigmatized it is extremely difficult for that child to recover in his social setting and existing group.

Within social contexts which have seen erosion of the cultural continuity of home, school and community, the child is even more vulnerable—and even more in need of an advocate. The child experiences such diversity and such disunity that the prospect of continuity is left very much to chance. "There is no effective alliance among child-socializing agents either in the strategy and rules of child-rearing or a shared commitment to the desired outcome of such a process."[4]

Socialization for freedom in a changing world

As Goodnow and Burns point out, social policies which promote continuity of experience and a sense of worth and of effectiveness are rare. It appears that those agents of the state responsible for policies and programmes which effect children have done little to foster the development of skills that allow for the growth of autonomous persons, and that promote the freedom which fosters motivation and self-esteem.

It is not difficult to define objectives of social policies for children when we talk of fostering their capacity to work at their own intellectual level. It is more difficult to define the ends and the means when we talk about children with mastery, self-confidence, initiative, responsiblity, and respect for other. Having recognized a child's individuality, it is necessary to create a relationship which is special to the particular child, paying attention to its strengths and weaknesses. When intervention is geared only to the child's weaknesses, the process of labelling is started, and children recognize their reduced value and significance more quickly than they do their enhanced worth.

Policies and intervention which deprive children of order, and which foster competition between family, community, school and church, or denigrate these institutions, destroy the child's opportunity to enjoy the freedom and security of continuity. Constant changes in the meaning and purpose of policies which affect children split the child from the family and other significant groups, and foster isolation, not freedom. However it is in promoting effectiveness that social policies and their implementors are probably most lacking. Children are concerned with skills, mastery and effectiveness, solving problems and asking questions. Their focus may differ, their zeal may fluctuate, but the push is always there, waiting to be fostered. Solving problems and mastering new skills provides the motivation for the next question.

In our health, welfare and education systems the development of effectiveness in the practitioner is often the dominant issue—not mastery for the child. Yet this statement is too broad, for teachers in particular are developing highly sophisticated skills not previously considered possible in young children. In the field of community health, children in a few instances are beginning to participate in the processes of gaining some control over their own diet, health and well-being. Knowledge, once the prerogative of the professionals, is being shared, and sometimes with children.

It is not too much to suggest that there are many skills which experts can give back. There is much knowledge which can be made available to families and children. Social policies which are concerned with children's experiences of continuity, effectiveness, self-worth and freedom must develop from the premise that they give back to parents, children and others control over knowledge and skills relevant for today's children.

PART 2

Children and Families

Peter Eisen

All children share the experience of living in a complex world, but within their individual experience there are many different patterns of living. These patterns are woven by their interaction with families and friends, with the community in which they live, and with the institutions of society at large. This chapter focuses on one arena of experience—the interaction of children and their families. It is assumed that readers are familiar with these interactions: what they are and how they are formed are not described. Instead, I am concerned to explore the state of debate on some of the significant issues which confront families and children in Australia, including the consequences for society of an increasing diversity of family structures and roles, the likely effects of various forms of stress on children and families, and the significance for child-rearing practices of changes occurring within society at large. These issues are examined by use of a conceptual model of some characteristics of the interaction between children, families and society. These characteristics are the universal presence of stress and its consequences, the multifactorial nature of human interaction, and the necessity for coping strategies, particularly those of problem-posing and problem-solving.

The effects of diversity, stress and change are shaped by recent, rapid alterations in society's response to children and their needs—thus these alterations are placed in an historical context. An operational definition of 'family' is proposed and then explicated by discussion of the diversity of family structures, roles, tasks and rights found in society. The major theme of family-centred stress is taken up in terms of its significance for children's development, the factors that may protect children from the damaging effects of stress, and the diverse modes of utilization of stress-coping strategies. This theme is developed by questioning assumptions about the nature of relationships between children and their families, and about the influences on these relationships brought about by society's attitudes and interventions. Predictions are made about emerging problems for children and families. Suggestions are advanced about the principles that need to be embodied in legislation which might avert the potentially deleterious effects of these problems.

The orientation of this chapter is well expressed by the following quotation:

> Our culture is in conflict about its children. We sentimentalize about childhood, but we do little for children, especially for those children who need help. At all levels, health, educational and welfare programs for children are inadequately funded, and yet we piously speak of children as our "future" and our "legacy". Our bequest to them, however, is symbolized by the welfare shelter, the dole, the detention centre, and the state institution. Children do not vote, and lobbying efforts on their behalf frequently eventuate in too little, too late. Contrary to the popular aphorism, children are neither seen nor heard.[1]

Despite this viewpoint, there is within every culture concern and endeavour by adults on behalf of children. Throughout history, the family has provided the crib where children are nurtured and where they develop. Still, it is pertinent to inquire into the past, present and future roles of families in relation to children. This raises questions about our culture's attitudes towards children, historical changes and trends in child–family relationships, current assumptions about the interdependent roles of families and their children, and the stress factors which influence these roles. Is it a fact that "of all our institutions, the family is the most influential in terms of human relationships. It is universal, being found in both sophisticated and primitive societies as far back as our knowledge takes us. Though it has had and will have many different forms it is unlikely that it will ever disappear, nor would we wish it to do so."[2]

Historical perspectives

A brief historical resumé of the roles of children within families provides a time-perspective which emphasizes the rapidity of present and anticipated future changes. "The history of childhood is a nightmare from which we have only recently begun to awaken. The further back in history one goes, the lower the level of child care and the more likely the children are to be killed, abandoned, beaten, terrorised and sexually abused."[3] Children have not been recognized as such till relatively recent times. Although by the sixteenth century children in Western cultures were accorded a social identity subserved by the name 'child', there was little if any functional distinction between them and adults.[4] "An examination of family diaries, letters and journals suggests that both in families of means and those less well off there was no clear demarcation between responsibilities and behaviour expected of adults and those expected of the young—once the time for indulgence generally allowed to infants had passed."[5] Many factors have contributed to changes in attitudes towards children. Some of these arose from adults' preoccupation with the hazards and opportunities for new societies in an expanding world. Increased concern for the maintenance of societies was expressed through an emphasis on development of the character of the children who were to carry the society into the future. This moral emphasis existed alongside a high mortality rate in children from disease and injury, which did not diminish significantly until the second decade of the twentieth century. Against the background of the long history of adults' neglect of children, it is interesting to look at how attitudes towards children are currently expressed.[6]

Anthony questions the state of the world with regard to its provision of a safe, happy, skill-enhancing environment in which competent parents care for children, and says, "it does not seem as if utopia is around the corner; life around the planet still appears to carry an inordinate amount of risk for the developing child."[7] In his view, although "we are much less openly murderous than our predecessors in antiquity ... we are covertly more ambivalent and balance somewhat uneasily, positive and negative attitudes and behaviour".

This ambivalence towards children is often expressed through services provided for children and families. Tizard, commenting on nursery services in the United Kingdom, says, "Today's decisions to cut back the expansion of nursery services for young children are being presented—and very largely accepted—as based on economic grounds. They are, however, in a deeper sense, political—as the rescue of the motor industry and the continuing support of Concorde should remind us."[8] It may be difficult to discern the basic attitudes and underlying philosophies that govern service provision. There is a complex relationship between the needs for services of children and families and the activities of the bodies that deliver services. This is well expressed by the Family Services Committee in its 1977 Report to the Minister for Social Security:

> Attempts are made to draw distinctions between the role of the family as a social institution, and the role of governments. Historically, most social welfare programmes were developed as residual support services. The prevailing philosophy was that poverty was the fault of the individual and intervention should only take place when the resources of the individual or a family

(which was seen as the basic social support unit) had completely broken down. More recently, this approach has been replaced by a belief that government should assume more direct responsibility for the basic social and economic well-being of its members who are frequently confronted by factors or situations beyond their control. In general, the Committee takes the view that there is a strong interdependence between the individual, the family, the wider community and the social welfare system. The ambivalence expressed in many quarters about the role of government vis-a-vis the family, can only be resolved in an evolutionary way.[9]

Within the report one can discern an ambivalence towards children, at the same time as it is promoting their needs. In commenting on the "changing place of children in society", it sees them as "economically and socially dependent on the family", and as exposed to "alternative behavioural models to parents", while also noting a "growing recognition of children's rights". Yet, it is claimed that "the new emphasis on the child as an individual is also apparent in the increasing provision of children's shelters and drop-in centres." It is still barely recognized that all children have a need for optimal development.[10]

Though there are changes in our world, there remains a curious and consistent familiarity about the pleas made on behalf of children. Child advocates have long pleaded for the recognition of children's particular needs, and of their individuality, vulnerability and their reliance on an understanding, empathic and tolerant adult-determined world. Recently a note of urgency has pervaded the oft-repeated pleas, based on a recognition of the rapidity of environmental and social change. There are different viewpoints about the genesis of world change and about our prospects for survival. Toffler says that "Change is life itself. But change rampant, change unguided and unrestrained, accelerated change overwhelming not only man's physical defences but his decisional processes—such change is the enemy of life."[11] Erikson accepts that change is inevitable, though he sees it more in terms of generational perspectives and challenges. He says, "the world wars and world revolutions as well as worldwide industrialization have made historical change unilinear, irreversible, and permanent", and thus there is "a determined tradition cultivating the continuous emergence of a New Man, whether characterised primarily by a national, political, economical, or technological type–or all of these".[12]

Irrespective of the basis for change and the various views about its significance, there is agreement that rapid world change threatens the stability of social institutions, and in particular, the various factors that maintain the family. "Rapid socio-cultural change will have a major effect on most of these factors that enhance or limit the capacity of the family to act optimally as a support system."[13]

Definition of the family

"The nuclear family does not represent an end product, a high point of development: the climax of successive stages of advancement from lower to higher, or from primitive to civilized. The fact is that people have always lived in families, and the nuclear form of family organization appears to be as old as any other. Moreover, it is only one of many types of family structures that have coexisted throughout man's history."[14] Although there have been changes in the form and distribution of families in our society, a number of these continue as dominant patterns. Many definitions have been given of the term 'family'. The Royal Commission on Human Relationships used "the term 'family' very broadly to cover not only the conventional nuclear family grouping of mother, father and children, but also one-parent families, families where there is no legal marriage, extended families and communes".[15] The United Nations has defined the family as "those members of the household who are related, to a specific degree, through blood, adoption or marriage".[16] The Family Services Committee found three types of definitions to be in accord with its terms of reference. "Families may be defined: (1) as groups (primary and institutional) which support children; (2) in terms of broader kinship relationships which often imply social and emotional support; and (3) in terms of common use of resources." Every definition of family depends on the context and use of the concept. As the focal point of this chapter is the relationship between children and families, the term 'family' *is taken to include all groups of people who occupy the same household, where a part of the groups' continuing activities is an involvement in child rearing*. This operational definition is essentially of a structural and functional nature, and deliberately excludes finite, temporal and legal considerations. Though it is acknowledged that both direct and indirect influences emanate from many generations, and include vital roles in child rearing, it is assumed that the criterion of continuity of care is a paramount consideration. This enables the inclusion of 'families' without blood or marriage relationships, such as foster families and other surrogate parenting groups.

Even when operationally defined, application of the concept of family has many problems. What does 'family' mean to a child when "the child might be born into a three-generational household, then live in a nuclear family when his or her parents set up their own household, then live in a single-parent family after the parents' divorce, and finally live in a reconstituted family when the parent he or she lives with remarries"?[17] The basic family unit may also change through transitory separations or prolonged illness and hospitalization of members. Numerous developmental changes and tasks affect the family and its individual members over its life-cycle. Social, economic and accidental factors may drastically alter a family's functioning as well as its structure over a period of time. Thus, any discussion of families' roles in relation to children needs to remain open to interpretations of the ever-changing nature of families and their different life environments.

Roles, tasks and rights of families

Given these limits to a precise delineation of family structure and functions, we can tentatively discuss the central roles, tasks and rights of families in relation to children. There are many recorded statements of family roles. The Family Services Committee identified "a minimum set of four interdependent and complementary functions of the family, namely: (a) population replacement; (b) socialization of children and other members; (c) social and emotional support for individual well-being; (d) immediate economic support." These are seen as representing "those needs of individuals and of society as a whole, which the family meets or is expected to meet". Such an analysis is predicated on a theoretical position wherein the family is seen as the basic unit of society operating within a complex societal system.

Lidz sees the family's primary roles as consisting of three sets of functions—"for the society, for the parents, and for the children". The family "fosters and organizes the children's development by carrying out a number of interrelated functions".[18] These are to nurture the children's development; to develop a family structure which to properly assist the child's integration requires that "the spouses must form a coalition as parents, maintain the boundaries between the generations, and adhere to their respective sex-linked roles"; and to provide socialization and enculturation of the child. That may be appropriate to some families with a traditional nuclear composition, but many families would not adhere to this structure and yet they fulfil similar child-centred roles.

From a more practical viewpoint, Pringle defines ten 'Child Care Commandments' as meeting the needs of children.[19] In essence, these concern the giving to children of continuous loving care, time and understanding, new experiences and language, encouragement to play, praise for achievement, ever-increasing responsibility, recognition of uniqueness, age-appropriate dispproval, continuing acceptance and avoiding the expectation of children's gratitude.

Pringle warns that as all parent–child relationships are unique, it is not reasonable to generalize this definition of roles to a prescription of roles for all parents (or families).

Thus, keeping within Pringle's warning, and bearing in mind our operational definition of 'family', we can posit a general statement of the central roles and tasks of families in relation to children. These include the fostering of development, and the education, socialization, protection, nurturing, and the enculturation of children. Obviously, many of the family-centred, interpersonal, societal, economic and educational activities of the family which are not primarily child-centred may enhance or interfere with these roles.

A brief look at the question of families' and children's rights will help place the general roles of families in a moral-ethical perspective. Although in 1959 the United Nations promulgated the Declaration of the Rights of the Child, there is no comparable statement of the rights of the family. It could be assumed that the rights of the family are covered by the Declaration of Human Rights. It is more likely, however, that separate and definitive rights of the family have not been formally recognized and proclaimed by any authoritative body. Even if they were, there is no guarantee that any declaration of family rights, or of those of children, would necessarily become embodied in legislation giving effect to them.[20]

Both Commonwealth and state legislation in Australia is ambiguous in its enactment of the issues pertinent to the rights of children and families.[21] Moreover, "nowhere in Australian law is there a clear enunciation of what the rights and responsibilities of the States and the Commonwealth are with respect to child and family welfare. Nor is there a readily accessible overview of the basis for regulating parental rights. Further, it is difficult to extract from legislation and case law, a simple statement of what the legal rights of parents and children are."[22] Fortunately, the Law Reform Commission is working towards clarification of the basic principles underlying the provision of legislation.

It is not within the scope of this chapter to elaborate on the implications arising from the absence of a coherent set of laws which give effect to families' and children's rights. I believe it likely that, in the absence of coherent legislation, the whole field of human services for children and families will continue to function in its present inequitable manner.

Questions about child–family relationships

In this discussion, the terms 'child–family' and 'parent–child' relationships will be used interchangeably, though it is recognized that this is a limiting and incorrect assumption. As so much has been written about child–family relationships, it is often assumed that we have a fairly complete knowledge of this vital area of human experience. This may well be a false assumption. According to the World Health Organization,

> It has been well demonstrated in studies in both developing and developed nations that variations in the psychosocial development of children are strongly associated with qualities of parent–child interaction. In particular, it is known that when children are reared in homes where there is a lack of conversational interchange, where parents do not interact positively with their children, and where there is a lack of play opportunities, the development of language, intelligence, and scholastic skills is likely to be impaired.[23]

Though there is fairly widespread agreement about such broad propositions, there are still many questions that need to be posed about the particular factors which influence the outcomes of parent–child and family interactions. It is suggested that there are three key interrelated areas towards which questions need to be directed.

1. Although much is known about the adverse effects on children's development of exposure to numerous types of stressors, far less is known about factors which influence the progressive and adaptive growth and maturation of children within families. Many assumptions used as the basis for child-rearing advice to families are derived from the known effects of adverse influences, and are directed towards the avoidance of such experiences. This advice may not always be soundly based. We need to know much more about what enhances development, so as to frame advice, education and services on the basis of knowledge rather than speculation.

2. Many children develop normally despite exposure to stressors, deprivation and multiple forms of disadvantage. Yet it is often assumed that all children exposed to such influences are 'at risk' or are likely to show deviations in development. It seems that there are protective factors within children and their families, and in the social environment, which enable some children to escape from or overcome stressors, deprivation and disadvantage. These factors are poorly understood. Knowledge of them may be potentially of more benefit to children than is an understanding of various disorders from which they suffer.[24]

3. It can be argued that all children and families are repeatedly exposed to various stress-provoking experiences, and to both normative and accidental crises. Some children and families appear to

cope effectively and adaptively with those experiences to which others occasionally or repeatedly show maladaptive and self-defeating responses. Little is known of the origins and diversity of coping styles and strategies used by individuals or families. It is possible that the coping mechanisms used by children are predicated by those which their families utilize. It is often assumed that such coping mechanisms depend on factors such as 'constitutional' strengths, and past experiences with stressors and support systems, but such beliefs are questionable in the absence of definitive knowledge. Given the never-ending need to cope with life's stresses, knowledge of how coping mechanisms develop and can be enhanced should have high priority in research into families and child–family interactions.[25]

These general propositions will be explicated through discussion of examples where there is a frequent use of questionable assumptions about child–family relationships. Before embarking on this, however, it is pertinent to emphasize "that to understand parent–child interaction, it is not enough to categorise parents in some way and then compare their children's attributes, though such studies do provide useful information. Rather, a complex situation exists in which there is a child who has relatively enduring attributes, but who is also changing with development; and there are parents with relatively enduring attributes, who must accommodate to the changes in the child, and who may be changing themselves."[26] Although the complexities of child–family relationships are emphasized, they are not discussed in depth, as the aim here is to pose questions that require further study.

The stability of child–family relationships

Is there, in fact, any stability in child–family relationships? Do they, and should they, change over time? Reference has already been made to the changing nature of the family's structure, roles and functions, and to the changing needs of children over the stages of their development. It is not yet clear if the changes that occur over time are of a continuous or a discontinuous form. It is a matter of debate whether the development of individuals and groups (including families) is essentially continuous or discontinuous,[27] just as there is disagreement on whether human development does occur in definable stages or phases. Despite the work of Sigmund and Anna Freud, Piaget, Erikson, Kohlberg and their colleagues and students, it cannot be stated unequivocally that there are universal, stable stages of development. However, it is likely that enduring changes in family roles and functions, and the influence of developmental progression, must at least alter child–family relationships over time.

These germinal theoretical issues are not widely appreciated and are not used as the basis for assumptions about the need for stability of child–family relationships. Rather, it seems that there is a widespread adherence to a loosely-based belief that only static, solid and stable relationships with families are 'normal' or 'healthy'. "Love together, live together: fight together, live apart."

Both popular and scientific 'theories' about child–family relationships tend to carry a peculiarly inviolable flavour. The following propositions about dependency and independence are examples of oft-repeated dicta. "All children are dependent on their parents throughout their lives"; "Children's development depends on their having a continuous and stable contact with their mother"; "Parents who separate must both remain available to their children". And conversely, "The sooner children learn to be independent, the better for them when they are adults"; "It is not possible to be really independent unless children have a reliable family to depend on"; "If children don't learn to be independent, they'll only marry someone to depend on".

If we question the assumptions on which these comments are based, we find we have considerable difficulty in sustaining any of propositions. We do not know whether the capacity for dependence is critical for human development. Bowlby has convincingly challenged this through his work on attachment and bonding.[28] Furthermore, it is unclear whether an ability to develop independence from significant 'others' is a protective factor against psychosocial disturbance. In fact, workers such as Erikson and Sullivan have adduced evidence about the protective function of 'intimacy' and 'chumship'.[29] The development of coping mechanisms is relatively unresearched; thus it is not possible to conclude that enhancement of dependency or of independence would facilitate the establishment of efficient coping styles and strategies. However, Lipowski and others suggest that a loss of dependent relationships may adversely affect coping behaviour.[30]

To summarize, the particular dicta about elements that contribute to stability in child–family relationships are not tenable. Similar arguments can be mounted about other factors that purport to demonstrate the central importance of stability in child–family relationships. These arguments should not be seen as indicating that this stability is of no significance. It has been demonstrated, for example by Rutter, that stable child–family relationships protect against the development of psychiatric disorder in childhood, adolescence and adulthood.[31] However, in our present state of knowledge, any foreclosure on the question of the necessity for stability in child–family relationships is premature. The facts suggest that for some children stability in their families is vital; for others it may be detrimental to have a stable, yet rigid family.

The universality of child–family relationships

In many ways, society at large and our legal systems appear to support the belief that biological parenthood bestows absolute rights and knowledge on parents. Moreover, biological parenting is often equated with psychological parenting.

> For the biological parents, the facts of having engendered, borne, or given birth to a child produce an understandable sense of preparedness for proprietorship and possessiveness. These considerations carry no weight with children who are emotionally unaware of the events leading to their births. What registers in their minds are the day-to-day interchanges with the adults who take care of them and who, on the strength of these, become the parent figures to whom they are attached.[32]

Our laws often appear to assume that children and adolescents are somewhat inferior or incomplete beings. No doubt, infants cannot remain alive unaided, children cannot entirely care for themselves, and adolescents are often unable to make critical decisions about life without support. Accordingly, the law assigns total responsibility to biological parents, or, if necessary, to alternative care-takers. Too often the law, parents and people working with children and families "view the child as a mere adjunct to the adult world, a passive recipient of parental impact".[33] The family is commonly seen by society as the unit responsible for and capable of child rearing: a responsibility and capacity firmly endorsed by legislation.

This view of adults' rights and of their parenting capacities is based on an odd form of logic. Children are not recognized as different from adults by virtue of their developmental needs, their immaturity and vulnerability, or their resilience. They are functionally different, and have needs that differ from those of adults. When children are seen as different from adults, by virtue of their size, age and abilities, it is then assumed that this difference is the same as unequal or inferior. The children are primarily recognized as being in need of control and protection. This establishes a hierarchy of rights, and society and the law assume that children's rights should not be compared with or equal to those of adults. In practice, parents' rights have precedence over children's rights, even when the Family Law Act and Children's Adoption Acts espouse a paramountcy of concern for the child. The issue is not of equal or comparable rights but of different rights, based on a recognition of children's different needs.

How does this inquiry into responsibilities, capacities and rights relate to the question of the universality of child–family relationships? There is a widespread assumption that parents and families are able to form judgements and make decisions in the best interests of their children. It may be that for the majority of children this is correct; but we simply do not know whether it is or is not. There is evidence that many families have an influence which is prejudicial to their children's optimal development. The adverse effects on children of parental divorce and separation,[34] of adoption,[35] of child abuse,[36] and of parental psychopathology[37] are very well documented. It is not just the gross disruptions to and distortions of child–family relationships that may have a deleterious effect on children. Some children are significantly disadvantaged by the apparently more minor influences of poor parent–child 'fit', by the fact of being a twin, and by maternal anxiety.[38]

It is not unreasonable to ask how any child survives into adulthood without developing considerable psychosocial defects. Rutter has discussed some of the protective factors that exist. A World Health Organization report on child mental health and psychosocial development, lists as possible protective factors female sex, adaptable temperament, isolated rather than multiple stress, coping skills, a good relationship with one parent, good experiences outside the home, and improvement in family circumstances. We know very little about these and other protective factors, about how families protect their children's development and about what coping mechanisms children need to overcome adverse family influences. It is not tenable to believe that all families can and do provide optimal relationships for their children. It is more realistic to assume that anthropologist Jules Henry may have been correct when, in discussing pathogenic family features, he said, "I worry that we have here, perhaps, a sudden discovery of the contemporary family rather than the pathologic family, unless, of course, we urge that in our culture most families are pathogenic in some sense".[39]

Family and community attitudes towards children

In any debate on attitudes towards children, there is a dilemma concerned with conflicting rights. When rights are in contest, should the family or the community be the final arbiter of whose rights will predominate? In pursuit of understanding, it is pertinent to extend our questioning of family and community attitudes.

Two problems are at issue. The first concerns a basic attitude towards child rearing—should this be child- or parent-oriented? The popular press often reports that parents are increasingly alienated from their children, that parents are more concerned for their own welfare than that of their children, and that the nuclear family, with its traditional child-rearing orientation, is at worst disappearing and at best changing. Given a world of rapid change, and a suggestion that the single most urgent preoccupation of communities is with their survival, it would not be surprising to find that parents are also increasingly concerned with their own needs. It is interesting to speculate whether community acceptance of the increasing rates of divorce and remarriage, social mobility and migration reflects such a quest for survival in an increasingly complex and uncertain world. Many social attitudes may influence the orientation of child rearing and the direction of responsibility. Do we need to be concerned about this apparently widespread phenomenon of parent-centred rather than child-centred care?[40]

It could be assumed that this is a new issue. However, study of the history of childhood suggests that the needs of children have always rated well behind those of parents when decisions are made about the use of resources and time, and the structuring of the living environment. This is despite the many people in the world who place the needs of their children uppermost, to the point where they would sacrifice their own life to save their children. Even if this is not a new issue, it might be that it has new dimensions. Anthony supports such a proposition when he says:

> The growing disinterest in childrearing among young adults in our society and the trend towards the postponement of having children is increasingly evident. Not only are fewer children being produced in almost all the developed countries, but these are turned over to the care of others while parents go to work. Some have seen this as questioning the existence of an innate drive toward parenthood or of a developmental phase of parenthood, but it may well be that social and cultural factors have a much greater impact on our innate behaviour than we have hitherto realised. It may even be that in our child-rearing methods we are raising children who no longer care to raise children.[41]

This questioning of adults' commitment to child care, leads into the second problem—should child-care services be predominantly family-oriented or child-centred? There are various practical, economic and theoretical components to this question. An underlying assumption that appears to be gathering momentum, deserves some assessment. In the provision of various forms of therapy, and also in the supply of support services, it is often assumed that the family needs and benefits from services more than do individual children. This attitude takes different guises. At times, as the family system is assumed to be the source of children's problems, it is said to need investigation, intervention and support, so as to benefit the child who may be identified as disturbed or distressed. At other times, it is assumed that the most disorganized and disruptive children imaginable can be managed within their families, if only sufficient assistance can be provided to the family.

To take up just one aspect of this problem—it is pertinent to ask whether children have a right to psychotherapy. This problem involves matters of attitude and professional orientation, of professional training, competence, and availability, as well as of therapeutic outcome and cost benefit. Until recently, there has been a rift between those who practise family therapy and those who undertake the individual therapy of children. Some therapists espouse a family approach to treatment, not only as an alternative technique, but as the imperative technique for all children and their families. These therapists avoid direct contact with children, and thus offer a cursory assessment of children's problems and a limited recognition of their individual needs. At times this approach leads to dangerous consequences for children.

> There is ample room for the development of various theoretical and treatment propositions, but also room for rivalry, envy, mutual disparagement, as well as a mutual working together. It is the task of those who espouse and practise various forms of treatment with children and their families, to develop test and evaluate the theories and techniques they use . . . ultimately, children's rights to treatment can only be met by people competent in their treatment.[42]

Children will only be protected from family and community interference with their development if there is a continual questioning of the priorities, assumptions and attitudes that underpin all child- and family-centred services.

Special types of families: stress, vulnerability, resilience and services

Australian families are changing in many dimensions. There are reasonably persistent trends towards an increase in family groups which differ from the traditional nuclear and extended types, including single-parent families, adoptive families and foster families, as well as non-traditional groupings with a diversity of compositions and structures, such as communal families, homosexual families, parent-less families and child-less families where pets replace children. Special types of families also differ, not because of their structure, but because of their particular circumstances. These include isolated families who mostly live in distant rural areas, though some live within densely populated cities; mentally-ill families, where one or many members suffer from a significant psychiatric disorder; families with chronically-ill or handicapped members. We do not know how many families are in these categories, where they live, how they function and what happens to their children. That there are many such families, and that they are often disadvantaged and handicapped, is attested to by many who work in welfare, health and education and in services concerned with housing, unemployment and legal aid. These special types of families are often relatively hidden and are poorly represented in official publications. This may be a function of the difficulties they pose, as much as of their relatively limited numbers when they are categorized into separate groups.

Devotion of much time and space to discussion of each of these special family types could be readily justified. Some generalizations will have to suffice, however, even whilst acknowledging this as an injustice on the grounds of the unique problems presented by each family type, and the importance of their need for recognition, understanding and services. Comments about some of the special family tupes will give a flavour of the issues they represent.

Single-parent families

The Royal Commission on Human Relationships reported on lone-parent families being exposed to isolation, poverty, limited work opportunities, anomalies and delays in obtaining welfare benefits, housing crises, child-rearing problems, and a lack of social support. The Family Services Committee states that:

> Becoming a one-parent family often means entry into a vicious cycle of disadvantage from which escape is difficult without substantial support or a relatively high income. The principal needs of income, adequate accommodation and suitable employment opportunities are not confined to the one-parent family. What is particularly characteristic of such families is the way these needs interact and impinge upon the families concerned at a time when their emotional resources are likely to be at their lowest ebb.

Adams describes some single-parent families as lower-class partial families, defining these as suffering from "poverty combined with fatherlessness". The partial family has characteristics shared by all single-parent families. They differ from nuclear families in key aspects of sexual, economic, political and emotional functioning. Single-parent families are sometimes said to be an inevitable outcome of societal change. However, "if the lower-class partial family does perform necessary social functions, then it merits subsidy and supporting services so that, at least, it can function under reduced economic burdens."[43]

Adoptive families

Adoption is a well-established measure which provides substitute families for unwanted children, and children for childless families and families who want more children. Adoptive families are often at considerable pains to ensure that they are not distinguishable from non-adoptive families. Though such an attitude is understandable, it is not necessarily realistic. For the majority of adoptive families and adopted children it is not possible to avoid some of the consequences of the fact of adoption. Although "the principle underlying adoption theory and practice is that the child's welfare and interests, rights and needs are paramount, and that these are best served in a family situation", adoption practice does not necessarily follow this principle. Probably as a direct result of this, adoptive families and adopted children do have special problems and needs.[44]

"The whole area of adoption, whether the child originates from in-country or inter-country sources, is a highly emotionally-charged issue. Adoption practice is increasingly seen as dependent on governmental legislative action. Accordingly, issues relating to the 'paramountcy of concern' for the interests of the child, over and above those of the prospective adoptive parents, create considerable tension with consequent stressor effects for the children."[45] Despite these stressor effects, resulting at times in adverse outcomes for adopted children, research findings confirm that adoption is the best possible placement for unwanted children. Adoption provides a greater likelihood of good outcome for children than does fostering, institutionalization, or their staying with parents who cannot care for them. However, adopted children are at increased risk for psychiatric disorder when compared with non-adopted children.[46] In consequence, there is a need for adoptive services to provide pre- and post-adoption education and counselling, as well as adequate screening of prospective parents.

Communal families

The growth of communes is a relatively recent phenomenon, though communes in some form have probably existed throughout human history. Communal families consist of groups of adults who are unrelated by blood or marriage, who form an organization separate from the mainstream of society, and share their household, their resources and work. They often have a commitment to a particular shared belief. The commune also tends to share its children.

> In theory, the child belongs to the commune rather than to the mother or the mother and father. The child has a variety of relationships with adults, and all the older members of the commune may serve as role models. Sex roles that are experienced are different from those in traditional families, since the mother and father roles are redefined with an emphasis on the sharing of child-care task.[47]

Several authors who have studied the communal family suggest that it has some distinctive child-rearing practices in contrast to practices in the traditional family. There appears to be a reversion to a pre-modern conception of children not being a special concern of adults, and consequently there is less distinction between children and adults. Children progressively become less the concern of their mothers, pass through a period of being cared for by the commune members on a shared basis, and by the age of 4 or 5 years are given less attention than in conventional family systems. They tend to behave, and are treated, as a member of the commune.[48] These forms of child rearing are different from those found in the kibbutz of Israel.[49] Though there are some similarities to the practices of some extended family groups, as well as some families living a loose community life in high-rise flats, over-riding allegiance to a shared belief system creates unique qualities of child care. There has been little research into what becomes of children reared in communes. It is possible that these children fare poorly on their return to society at large, and it is also possible that their special family experience may prepare them to cope with a diversity of lifestyles and a changing social environment.

Families with chronically-ill or handicapped members

There is a considerable literature on the problems of families which have a member with a gross and longstanding psychiatric disorder. Such families are under constant stress; their children are at high risk for psychosocial disturbance; and they require extensive service resources if they are to be given treatment and support.[50]

Families with members who have a chronic physical illness or a handicap are also seen as a special type of family. The number of such families in Australia is unknown. Conservative estimates suggest that between one-third and one-half of all Australian families contain a chronically-ill or handicapped member.[51] Not all of these qualify as special families: some would not see themselves as such, some would have adequate resources to cope with the problems of the ill or handicapped member, and some would have the member living outside the family in an institution or alternative household. For children who have a chronic physical illness or handicap, there is considerable evidence of interference with their developmental progression. "There are indications that vulnerability to the stressor effects of chronic physical illness is related to age, family relationship, and to social factors, more than to the severity of the physical disorder."[52] These children present enormous problems for their families, particularly those that are already disadvantaged or handicapped by other factors.

The Family Services Committee has paid particular attention to families with a chronically-ill or handicapped member, and what they say is highly relevant.

> The family with a disabled member has to make adjustments within its own functioning both for the sake of the disabled individual and the long-term health of the family unit. ... The disablement of a parent, particularly the bread-winner, is likely to be accompanied by a drop in income, and if the disablement is severe, the family may have financial, child care and home-management problems akin those of a one-parent family. The disablement of a child, although not directly affecting the family's income, may mean greater demands on that income for treatment and care, and may modify the parents' pattern of work and social life.

There are many ways of analysing the problems presented by these special families. Perhaps to do so at present would detract from the proposition that all children and all families, in all places and all cultures, need to be clearly understood. Whether they are currently facing problems is less important than the fact that they are certain to do so at some point in the future.

Predictions about emerging problems, current solutions and future services

It is difficult to define adequately the problems which currently affect children and families. It is much more difficult to predict future problems. Despite this, planning for the future of Australian society needs to include predictions about emerging problems and the possibilities for their solution. I believe that knowledge and understanding of the current lives of children and families may provide a framework for the establishment of policies which could safeguard their future—even a future that cannot be accurately predicted.

It is imperative that equitable child and family policies be formulated and that these policies provide guidelines for action. To be effective, policies need to meet a number of criteria. They must be clearly stated, based on knowledge, and be comprehensive. It must be acknowledged that the family is not the only institution responsible for shaping the future of children. Too often the family is seen as the sole progenitor and guardian of children's behaviour, attitudes and values. For instance, I do not believe that social issues such as sexual and class role determination could be the single responsibility of the family. Were the total responsibility for children's social development vested in the family, this would inevitably discriminate against those families whose social functioning is already under pressure and vulnerable to disruption or disintegration. Further, it is vital that policies are based on established facts rather than on what purports to be fact. Perceived notions of what is good for children and families are too often a means of ensuring the continuation of powerful, entrenched, governmental and service departments. Under the guise of espousing the good of children, it is the good of experts, legislators and administrators that is protected.

Discussion of the current and future problems that families may have in rearing children should not be taken as an indictment of 'the family's' capacities in this role, and thus used as a justification for experts to take over these responsibilities. Though many families have and will continue to have difficulties in caring for their children, there is a vast difference between supporting and facilitating a family's coping mechanisms, and taking them over.

On the basis of our knowledge of the current diversity, stresses and change to which 'the family' is exposed, the following predictions bear consideration. It is likely that the trends towards a greater diversity of family and societal structures, functions amd roles, will continue. There will be a related diversification of social institutions required to deal with an increase in the type and number of vulnerable social and ethnic groups. These trends will enforce an increase in the provision of human services. Resulting from these trends, further changes will occur in the established triadic relationships between children, families and the state. These changes will probably be in several directions: firstly, a greater involvement and at times intrusion by governments and bureaucracies into the decision-making processes of 'the family'; secondly, an increase in families' competition for child care and family support services, which will lag behind demand and need in their availability; and thirdly, a greater emphasis on children themselves having to take responsibility for their own welfare. This somewhat gloomy scenario is predicated by may doubts that society and its governments will modify quickly enough in anticipation of change.

It is difficult to compare the stresses that do and will exist with those of previous centuries. Such comparison is never straightforward. Perception of stress and responses to it are highly dependent on past experience, the environmental context in which stress occurs, and the availability of support systems. Whether the stress of high infant mortality compares with that of an increased likelihood of divorce is probably unanswerable. Some claim that families are under no more stress now than they were three or four centuries ago. Perhaps the problem is not one of comparability but one of predictability.

It seems that many families will be increasingly exposed to stresses arising from the widely publicized questioning and restatement of the rules and guidelines for child rearing. With a diversity of experts and services concerned with child care and family support, and when there exists a plethora of child-care theories and practices, it is hard for many families to know which advice applies to them. Given a diversification and specialization of many services, an increasing number of families will not meet the explicit and implicit criteria for admission to any service. In consequence, the more common and less complex problems of families will no longer be catered for. There are potent dangers that will arise from an increasing adherence to currently fashionable viewpoints. These include an expression of certainty about what all children and families need, and the belief that all people are fully responsible for their actions and for the consequences that flow from their behaviour.

Recent experience in a research project with families under stress suggests that many families find it difficult to state their needs, and they repeatedly experience the inability of services to hear and understand their imprecisely stated needs. Families who are traditionally regarded as stable and self-sufficient, as well as the special types of families, report these difficulties.[53] With the accumulation of detailed knowledge of family functioning and family disorder, it is already likely that services tend to focus on what might be called the esoterica of family problems. This will leave the majority of families who need help with the mounting problems of coping with everyday living bereft of the services they require. As stresses become more complex and protracted, and less predictable, the range of coping strategies and problem-solving skills that families need will increase.

There are some established historical certainties, particularly in the biological, psychological and social spheres of our functioning, which predict continuity and repetition of much of human behaviour. However, the most certain of predictions has to do with uncertainty. A realistic stance towards the future could be constructed from a cautious mix of curiosity, open-mindedness, optimism and trust in human ingenuity and resilience, welded together by respect for those with the capacity to live with uncertainty. Unfortunately, that capacity is in relatively short supply. Children reared by parents to have a reasoned expectation for the world into which they will grow, have not been exposed to techniques for dealing with uncertainty. There is now doubt that the 'average expectable environment'—a predictable set of known environmental conditions—has any validity.[54] Children are trained to live in a world that will not exist when they reach adulthood. The average environment of the year 2000 is not predictable. If this is so, then what can children be prepared to cope with in the future? Of a number of possibilities that deserve serious inquiry, I would suggest that today's children need to be tutored in a wide range of strategies for living and coping with uncertainty.

From these predictions come a number of principles that may enhance a future generation's capacities for coping with emerging and inestimable problems. If these principles were embodied in legislation which facilitated the development of these capacities, the child-rearing tasks of Australian families may be considerably lightened. They are:

(i) widespread recognition of the diversity, stress and change affecting families
(ii) recognition of the need to promote optimal rather than marginal development in children and families
(iii) acceptance of children's rights to be heard and treated as children
(iv) endorsement of families' roles in child rearing
(v) sequential preparation of children to be first children, then adolescents, and ultimately adults—with their perspectives for the future not being wholly subservient to the realities of the present
(vi) training children in problem-posing and problem-solving skills commensurate with their individual learning potential
(vii) commitment to enhancing children's capacity to tolerate uncertainty
(viii) promotion of human services that balance children's needs for protection and control with those of freedom and discovery.

Endorsement, acceptance and then conversion of such principles into political and social realities depends on our recognition of and understanding of continual change in the human condition. This leaves us with a final dilemma. "To understand change takes time, but what is understood about change is already dated by the changes that have already taken place since we took the time to understand change.[55] Hopefully, Australian children will deal with this dilemma better than do their parents.

Every Girl's Dream

Denise Bradley

Question: When you were a girl, did you expect some time that you would have children?

Answer: I think it is every girl's dream.[1]

This response, quite simply, reflects conventional aspirations which are both romantic and unrealistic. Such views of one's future usually encompass a husband, a house, and financial security. Any glance at statistical data, reports of government enquiries or social research findings quickly reveals that many Australian children live in quite different circumstances; circumstances which are not cosy and rosy. Mothers lack husbands, or homes, or a reliable income; and even when such elements are present, there seems no guarantee of happiness for the child. Many children are being raised in family situations which differ markedly from those which have traditionally been seen as ideal. A major problem is to determine whether we should be seeking to change our current child-rearing practices or whether we should be questioning the traditional criteria of a successful family unit.

This paper argues that there is in Australia diversity of family structures, a lack of consensus about what best serves children's needs, and a profound gulf between what people think having children is like and what it actually is like. It suggests that policy formulation and programme development in human service organizations can only take place within structures that accept diversity and develop flexibility to deal with people's expressed needs.

Unresolved issues seem to be:

1. Is there any kind of social consensus on what kind of children we want? Do we want strong individualists or good group members? Do we want dominant males and submissive females? Do we want people who, regardless of sex, are able to nurture children?
2. Should we operate on the belief that children are resilient creatures? Or should they be seen as fragile beings?
3. Do we create policies which serve children as children or children

as potential adults?

4. Is poverty a result of bad luck, bad breeding, lack of the ability to work, or structural inequalities in our society?
5. Are the biological parents always the best people to rear children? How much should the community interfere with the rights of biological parents over their children?
 Is the biological mother always to be preferred to the biological father in cases of disputed custody?
6. Must children have an opportunity for identification with both male and female role models during their early years?
7. What is the cost to adults of a child-centred focus by service agencies?
8. What should be the contribution of children to the family?

Such issues are difficult to resolve at present when there is greater awareness of differing family structures and when the traditional role of women as nurturers of children is being challenged. Lack of agreement about which family structures best serve the needs of all family members and evidence of apparent role conflict for Australian parents[2] have led some people to believe that all this heralds the demise of the nuclear family—its supposed passing welcomed by some and mourned by others.

The origins and role of the nuclear family have been examined and debated at length in academic journals and the popular press over the last few years. It has been argued that the nuclear family, which some see as the cornerstone of our social institutions, is a phenomenon which followed the Industrial Revolution, and that before then an extended family, with different generations living together and sharing the care of children, was the common pattern. People who believe that are inclined to view the nuclear family with which we are all familiar as a fairly recent invention. Others argue that the nuclear family has always been with us. Both sides see the apparent threats to its survival as of enormous consequence to our society.

Interesting as the details of this debate may be to participants and observers, it is not these details which are necessarily as significant as the fact that the debate is taking place now. It highlights the deep concern that is felt about apparent changes in the social structures within which children are raised. There is both discomfort about what appears to be happening and a search to find new structures and patterns which will provide children with effective care while allowing adults more choice.

In spite of the differences, there seems to be some agreement about one thing—that early this century the care and upbringing of children became the only and only the major responsibility of mothers. This was influenced by many changes. These included the shift in the production of goods from the home to the factory, the introduction of legislation to improve working conditions in factories and the movement of women and children out of them, a falling birthrate from the 1890s, the advent of compulsory schooling, and a new concern about children who were seen as potential adults—people who would shape society in the future.

More recently, the insights of psychoanalysis strongly supported the view that mothers had a critical influence on children's development. That development was best served by devoted and constant 'mothering'. The most influential proponent of that view has been John Bowlby.

> Just as the baby needs to feel that he belongs to his mother, the mother needs to feel that she belongs to her child and it is only when she has the satisfaction of this feeling that it is easy for her to devote herself to him. The provision of constant attention day and night, seven days a week and 365 in the year, is possible only for a woman who derives profound satisfaction from seeing her child grow from babyhood, through the many phases of childhood, to become an independent man or woman, and knows that it is her care which has made this possible.[3]

The extremes of the child-centred view about the responsibilities of parents, as expressed for example by Bowlby, placed great emphasis on the role of the mother. To be a good mother meant an unceasing commitment to the care of the child, an abdication of all expectations for personal fulfilment in other roles, and the acceptance of total responsibility for the child.

There has been growing rejection of this view over the last twenty years. Its detrimental effects on women and children have been noted and, in particular, women themselves have begun to question a life which offers them so few choices, which condemns so many of them to the social isolation of suburban life and to an existence of financial and emotional dependence upon men. Adrienne Rich has written most powerfully of:

> ...the invisible violence of the institution of motherhood, the guilt, the powerless responsibility for human lives, the judgements and condemnations, the fear of her own power, the guilt, the guilt, the guilt. So much of this heart of darkness is an undramatic, undramatized suffering: the woman who serves her family their food but cannot sit down with them, the women who cannot get out of bed in the morning, the woman polishing the same place on the table over and over, reading labels in the supermarket as if they were in a foreign language, looking into a drawer where there is a butcher knife.[4]

We have begun to ask whether children's development is indeed best served by sacrifice of the mother's rights. We have become interested in the development of children who have not been raised within a child-centred nuclear family. We have begun to debate whether or not children are a community responsibility and, if so, how this responsibility can best be exercised. During this century there has been growing acceptance of society's obligation to children: free, compulsory schooling is provided for all; laws relating to child abuse place the onus on professionals to report suspected cases; education and welfare agencies fund programmes which offer support for children who are disadvantaged by low socio-economic status, by race, by ethnic origin and by physical or mental handicap. A child's welfare is not held to be solely the responsibility of his or her parents. As a society we appear to accept that we all have responsibilities for children.

Indeed, community involvement in the nurture of children is a policy enthusiastically espoused by the helping professions. There is general agreement with the notion that children are best helped in their development through close co-operation between support agencies, parents and children. It is believed that parents, whatever the family's circumstances, should be supported in their parenting for the good of children. This policy is estimable in theory. It should remove from parents some of the burdens of responsibility for children and enable children to be helped in situations where the family is not able to act. We must be aware, however, that in some cases it may add rather than remove burdens on parents. For example, the development of community child-care centres and proposals for parental involvement in schools raise questions about the ways in which we can best support parents.

Community child-care centres were established in the belief that children in such centres are happiest when there is constant contact between the centre's staff and parents. In practice, this liaison is most often between staff and mothers, who are seen to have the major responsibility for children. Many mothers find it hard to live up to the staff's expectations. Do we know how the woman who is a member of the paid workforce, who may be obliged to manage house and to care for children outside the hours she is at work, copes with the demand to be closely involved in the life of the child at the centre? Are we only placing additional burdens of responsibility and guilt upon her for not fulfilling this responsibility adequately? Do we cut down even further her leisure time, her opportunity to be free of home, of work, of children, by actively promoting such policies? Are there other alternatives which could be explored?

Another no doubt praiseworthy move is to involve parents in their child's schooling. More and more schools are striving for parental involvement in the education of children. How is this demonstrated? Characteristically, schools have elective programmes and reading programmes in which they ask parents to participate during school hours. They have, as well, classroom visiting periods during the day in junior primary and primary schools when parents are invited to come to the school and spend time with children. Understandably, the children are very disappointed if one parent does not participate in some of these activities. But participation is almost impossible for parents in the paid workforce, and children of working mothers usually feel that it is their mothers and not their fathers who have failed them if a parent does not arrive at the school. All our social messages tell them that 'normal' mothers do not go out to work. 'Normal' mothers love their children enough to stay at home and are available to come to the school whenever they are invited.

Such programmes, then, which appear to support children and their families, if insensitively operated may contribute to the stress on families. In order to frame policies and develop programmes which support children and their families, professionals must be always aware of the gap that exists between people's expectations and the reality of having children; the redefinition of male and female roles which is taking place; and the diversity of family structures already apparent.

In times of change children and their families will be assisted by flexible organizations which ensure two things: first, a constant flow of information about the adequacy of services available, and secondly, some early warning system which alerts policymakers to the emergence of hitherto unmet needs. The early difficulties of developing women's shelters and children's shelters in Australia are a warning to all policymakers. Conservative views about the possible breakdown of the family initially influenced policymakers. The result was that for too long after the need had become apparent welfare organizations hesitated to provide support for women and children who wished to escape from oppression and violence.

Women and children who were already trapped by their family circumstances were refused the help they needed by welfare organizations which were supposed to have been established to aid them. People in the organizations were themselves operating within a value system which had traditionally condoned the oppression of women and children by men. As a result they were unable to recognize a need which was being expressed. It was articulated, however, by feminists who did not understand the structures of the bureaucracies which provided services and who found it difficult to be heard within them. The tardiness of this response and the conflict surrounding the policy changes should be a warning to all who are providing services to children and their families.

PART 3

Ethnic Children in Australia

J.J. Smolicz with *Roger Lean* and *Margaret Secombe*

In any discussion of children in Australia today, the lives and needs of those Australian children who belong to one of the many ethnic groups in our society must not be ignored. The term 'ethnic groups' (as it will be used in this chapter) refers to those people in our society who are of non-English speaking background and continue to preserve their culture in Australia. This does not mean that members of the same ethnic group are identical in their ways of thinking and acting. Social class, family and individual differences always exist. Nevertheless, membership of an ethnic group implies sharing patterns of living with other participants. The actions and attitudes of individual members are likely to bear a 'family' resemblance to one another. To some extent, at least, therefore, the way of life of ethnic-Australians differs from that of the Anglo-Australian majority. In some areas such as food and cookery, special celebrations, folk songs and dances, these cultural differences are generally recognized and accepted by the rest of the community. However, variations in other important areas of culture, such as patterns of friendship and family life, manners and ways of greeting, basic values and language usage, often go unrecognized. Sometimes a vague sense of not feeling at home with a person of another ethnic group is the only outward sign of substantial cultural differences.

In Australia, cultural pluralism occurred initially as the result of immigration. The future of cultural pluralism now depends on the extent to which the present adult generation passes on these ethnic cultures, and the future generations of children have the opportunity to reconstruct and act upon their cultural heritage. For this reason, attention has been focussed here on the roles of the home and the school in relation to the maintenance and development of ethnic cultures among children.

In the past it has been assumed by many teachers, educators

and others that any child born in Australia was automatically 'Australian', which was generally taken to mean not only 'Australian' by citizenship, but 'Anglo-Australian' by culture. The implication was that any child born and brought up in Australia would acquire the culture of the dominant Anglo-Australian majority alone. But there is no magical connection between cultural transmission and the mere act of birth in some territory. Nor does birth in some particular society require loss of the parental culture. In Australia it is possible to find fifth generation Jewish, fourth generation Chinese, and third generation Greek children who continue to preserve and use aspects of their ancestral heritage. It is important that we do not make unwarranted assumptions about the cultural uniformity of children born in Australia to ethnic-Australian parents, and expect them to have the same cultural patterns as their Anglo-Australian counterparts.

On the other hand, we must be as careful to ensure that members of ethnic groups in Australia are not thereby excluded from the right to be regarded as proper Australians. There are some patterns of culture in our society which are common to all Australians, no matter where they were born and what ethnic group they belong to. These shared values include support for such matters as parliamentary and others forms of democracy, economic opportunity for the individual, freedom of individuals to pursue their own private lives and acceptance of English as the common language of communication for all Australians. Thus, in the classroom, both ethnic- and Anglo-Australian children would expect to have equal opportunity to express their views and influence decisions, to have their school work evaluated on the same basis as that of other students, and to receive the same treatment and privileges as their peers.

Let us look now at some specific areas of culture where ethnic-Australian parents are succeeding in passing on to their children their own distinctive patterns of life. In this discussion, reference will be made to number of relevant studies, but examples will be drawn mainly from a recently completed interview survey of a hundred upper primary school children in five schools in Adelaide.

Differences in language

Probably the most striking difference between cultures lies in the field of language. Those who are skeptical of the reality of cultural variations cannot deny the barrier that exists between people who belong to different language groups. A Greek child who goes to school knowing only his native language cannot communicate verbally either with Anglo-Australian children, who are English monolinguals, or with his Italian classmate, who speaks only his mother tongue.

The extent to which languages other than English are used in Australian homes is often not fully appreciated, especially by teachers and educators. The Committee on the Teaching of Migrant Languages in Schools, after conducting the first Australia-wide survey on ethnic language maintenance and teaching, estimated that as many as 15 per cent of primary school children in Australia had a native tongue other than English. A survey of about 2 000 parents of Catholic school students in 1977 provided further support for this view. In that survey, 88 per cent of families in which both parents were Italian-Australian spoke Italian as the main language of the home. The corresponding proportions speaking their mother tongue as the main language of the home among Polish-, German- and Dutch-Australian families were 85, 70 and 65 per cent respectively.

Interviews with children conducted as part of the Primary School Study revealed that in most ethnic-Australian homes, parents spoke to each other and to their children in their native tongue. Generally, whenever ethnic-Australian children spoke with adults—whether they were parents, older relatives or family friends—they also used their mother tongue.

Many ethnic-Australian parents have succeeded in transmitting their native tongue to their children at the level of understanding and speaking. At two important points, however, the children's mastery of their mother language fell short of many parents' hopes and expectations. Although the language used between parents and children was in most cases the mother tongue, the children, almost without exception and in spite of the disapproval of their parents, used English among themselves once they started school. In addition, the children's ability to read and write in their ethnic language was often far below the level of their literacy in English. These two aspects will be discussed in more detail later in relation to school programmes.

Differences in patterns of family life

Ethnic groups have also been shown to differ in the patterns of family life they exhibit. Among the Anglo-Australian majority, the common pattern is the two-generational or nuclear family where the husband, wife and children live together as a separate unit. Grandparents and other relations often live some distance away and may not be seen very frequently. The ethos of the family is individualistic. Children are brought up to be independent as soon as possible. As adults they are expected to be self-reliant, and to take care of their own financial affairs, quite independently of other members of the family. Children are often encouraged to earn their own pocket money and have their own friends, and leave Mum and Dad free to pursue their separate interests. In addition, parents tend to be permissive in their approach to children; in some cases, this may result in an apparent lack of interest in their children's welfare and activities. As a general rule, Anglo-Australian parents believe that children should be treated as equals and friends, rather than be subordinate to parental authority.

In contrast, among most Southern and Eastern European ethnic groups as well as some Asian groups, the ethos of family life is more collectivist. Although most live outwardly as a two-generational unit, in much the same way as Anglo-Australians, contact with other members of the family in Australia is usually greater. Often grandparents and aunts and uncles live nearby, in the same street, around the corner, or in the same suburb. Visits between relations are frequent and always involve the whole family. For Mum and Dad to visit Auntie Maria, while the children stay at home by themselves (because the children would be bored or be a nuisance) is unthinkable.

The family is always thought of as a whole unit, with the welfare of one being a matter of concern for all. Children are expected to remain an integral part of the family until they marry. Finances and resources are shared among all members. In addition, many ethnic-Australian parents are very strict and protective in the upbringing of their children and insist on filial obedience. They are sometimes highly critical of the more permissive attitudes of Anglo-Australian parents and teachers.

One Polish girl involved in a memoir study (conducted by us in 1974) gave a typical, if somewhat idealized account of the pattern of family life found among many ethnic-Australian groups.

> Home life is Catholic, warm loving and caring. I've seen and felt a great family tie. I've realized that Europeans care about each other. I feel they worry together, laugh together and help one another as much as they can. They encourage their children to stay at home as long as possible to keep the tie. Life is too short to separate from and then forget parents. Now, at about my age, when a person begins to understand life more, is the time to show thanks and gratitude for everything they have done. Married Australian couples break away too quickly to become totally independent. So independent that they struggle and can't experience the warmth and support of a parent–grandparent relationship. Life is so wonderful, mysterious and unpredictable.

Each stage is really so fascinating—school, courting, marriage, parents and then a new generation's first steps and words. I've seen the joy my parents shared with their first grandson. To be able to speak to him in Polish because both parents were Polish was heartwarming.

The unquestioned nature of the extended family was also illustrated by children's answers to questions about family visiting patterns. At first many ethnic-Australian children said their families did not go visiting or have visitors often. When asked specifically about their relatives, however, it became clear that there was a regular visiting pattern to grandparents, uncles, aunts and cousins. Children who had said that they did not often go visiting, would say, in reply to a question about what they did after school and on weekends, that they played with their cousins down the street each afternoon, or that their family spent Saturday and Sunday afternoons with grandparents, uncles and aunts. And when the parents were involved in some activity, the children were usually included in the plans.

These patterns of home life have helped to ensure the maintenance of ethnic identity among children of non-English speaking origin. Three-quarters of these children identified themselves simply in terms of their parents' country of origin (such as Greek or Italian) or as being both ethnic and Australian (hence Greek and Australian, or Italian-Australian).

Religious differences

Australia's comparatively early acceptance of the principle of religious pluralism should not blind us to the great diversity of religious beliefs, customs and practices that ethnic groups have brought following the mass influx after the Second World War. The most important numerically has been the Greek Orthodox Church; however, the buildings of other branches of the Orthodox Church—from Russia, the Ukraine and Serbia, for example—are now distinctive and familiar landmarks too in most capital cities in Australia.

Despite the growing sense of unity among the Christian churches, important differences remain in doctrinal emphasis, patterns of worship and religious celebrations. Among the Orthodox churches, for example, the dramatic ritual to proclaim the Resurrection makes Easter a more memorable celebration than Christmas. Among Protestant Christians originating in north-western Europe, Christmas has always been the more popular celebration and has been retained, even when it has lost its religous significance; while Easter in Australia has become merely an excuse for a long weekend away from home.

The unquestioned nature of the extended family was also illustrated by children's answers to questions about family visiting patterns. At first many ethnic-Australian children said their families did not go visiting or have visitors often. When asked specifically about their relatives, however, it became clear that there was a regular visiting pattern to grandparents, uncles, aunts and cousins. Children who had said that they did not often go visiting, would say, in reply to a question about what they did after school and on weekends, that they played with their cousins down the street each afternoon, or that their family spent Saturday and Sunday afternoons with grandparents, uncles and aunts. And when the parents were involved in some activity, the children were usually included in the plans.

Within the Catholic Church, the various ethnic groups have distinctive traditions. Polish Catholicism, with its traditions of intense patriotism, devotion to the Virgin Mary (in Polish almost invariably referred to as the "Mother of God") and singing of sacred songs (to Polish words and music) is different from the Catholicism of the Southern Italians, many of whom like to continue to celebrate the Feast Days and Saints Days of their native region and village, with processions and community funfairs. The Italian Catholics share with the Poles the special veneration of the 'Madonna', while the Poles are also renowned for processions (such as the one for Corpus Christi), and for pilgrimages to the shrines of Our Lady, Mother of God. Both these groups differ from the ethos and the practice of the Australian Catholic Church, steeped in the Irish tradition, later moulded by Roman influences. The resultant religious patterns were marked by strict obedience of clerical authority, a stress on external observance of all ecclesiastical law, with piety confined to the private domain.

An appreciation of the different religious traditions now current in Australia is necessary in order to understand why Greek children in the Primary School Study described the way they celebrated Easter, rather than Christmas; why a Ukrainian-Australian child talked about having two Christmases—one with his Australian grandparents and the other, a fortnight later, with his Ukrainian Orthodox grandparents (celebrated according to the Julian calendar); and why Polish- and Italian-Australian children remembered the family celebrating name-days, but not birthdays.

The primary school interviews revealed that family and group celebrations, such as those for religious occasions and for birthdays and name-days, usually maintained the traditions of the family's country of origin. Observance of Easter among Greek families was a good example. They attended special church services, ate roast lamb on the spit, painted and cracked eggs, in the same way as has been done for generations; and, without exception, had a gathering of the whole family. Although not adhered to as strictly as religious occasions, name days, too, continued to be observed in the families of many children.

What sort of society?

Once we recognize the extent to which ethnic-Australian homes are maintaining cultural differences in Australian society, the question is what should be done about it. Should government policy generally, and our education systems in particular, aim to eliminate, modify, or encourage cultural diversity? To a large extent the answers we give to these questions depend on what sort of society we would like the Australian children of today to live in, as adults. There are four ideals that are commonly discussed as ultimate outcomes for a society like Australia, in which a dominant majority exists alongside other minority or ethnic cultures.

In the immediate post-war era the accepted ideal was what has been termed dominant monism or Anglo-conformism. According to this view all children, no matter what their ethnic origin, were expected to adopt the norms of the dominant culture and to give up their own cultural heritage. Schools were often consciously seen as the most effective instrument society had in achieving this aim. If this policy were to be implemented successfully here, Australian society would be characterized by cultural uniformity, based on the Anglo-Celtic heritage of the dominant British/Irish group.

An alternative to Anglo-conformism is hybrid monism or synthesis. The idea behind this is that the different cultures currently present in Australian society should be blended together into a mix containing elements of each in different proportions and combinations. It is not clear which elements of each culture would be retained or in what form; or who would decide these issues. What language, for example, would be used? It is difficult to envisage the evolution of some new kind of jargon, creole or patois; it seems likely, therefore, that in Australia this approach would result in children being brought up to communicate in English, and nothing but English, Hence, at least within the linguistic sphere, we would be back with Anglo-conformism. According to this ideal, Australia would also become a society with one culture. The children now growing up in Australia, or perhaps their children, would come to the point where they ignored their different cultural heritages and shared instead the newly evolved hybrid culture.

If the maintenance of ethnic cultures as discrete entities is regarded as preferable to cultural monism, two different types of pluralism are possible. There is a form of pluralism which would involve the separate existence of diverse cultures within the one society, while individuals remained largely within their own ethnic group. Thus even though society as a whole would be pluralistic, the children of the various groups would be familiar with only one culture in terms of their personal world. As they grew up, minority children would become involved in the culture of the dominant group for example, only insofar as it was absolutely necessary for economic and political coexistence.

The other form of pluralism involves what may be called multiculturalism, at both societal and personal levels. It calls not only for maintenance and development of ethnic cultures, but for individuals to acquire two or more of these cultures. This is the solution of dualism. An ethnic group would maintain its culture not simply for the benefit of its own members, but also in order to share its culture with other Australians. This would result in bicultural individuals who would feel at home in two cultural groups. This sort of biculturalism would be distinct from the synthesis mentioned earlier, in that the different cultures would coexist as separate strands within the individual, and be used in different situations, depending on the cultural context.

The most obvious example of this is the balanced bilingual person, who has a mastery of two languages at both the oral and literary level. He or she thereby has access to the culture of two ethnic groups, can interact easily with members of both and use whichever language seems appropriate. Such individuals already exist among Australian youth, although our research (e.g. on tertiary students of Polish background in South Australia) has shown that they are still only a minority. This situation could alter under the impact of new government policies and changing attitudes of both parents and teachers.

Parental attitudes and official policies

If we are to understand Australian children of ethnic background, it is important to know which of the above outcomes is generally accepted in society and reflected in government and educational policy. The survey of Catholic school parents in 1977 revealed wide ranging attitudes among parents varying from strict Anglo-conformism through to multiculturalism. A majority of the respondents from all ethnic backgrounds supported multiculturalism and only a small minority expressed undisguised disapproval of diversity. There was no support for the separatist solution.

Until the early 1970s state and federal governments in Australia adopted an essentially Anglo-conformist policy. Over recent years, however, their stance has gradually evolved to the point where now they claim to embrace the ideal of multiculturalism. This is reflected in a statement made in 1978 by the Prime Minister:

> The Government accepts that it is now essential to give significant further encouragement to develop a multicultural attitude in Australian society. It will foster the retention of the cultural heritage of different ethnic groups and promote intercultural understanding.

Although the climate for multiculturalism is now more favourable, the need for Australian schools to contribute to ethnic cultural maintenance and development is still not fully understood. There are two factors which are crucial for the maintenance of culture. Individuals must firstly have access to the culture concerned. Thus, for example, a child cannot develop literacy in a given language unless the teaching and the written material are available to him. Access alone, however, is insufficient. It must be accompanied by a willingness to make use of the opportunities available. A child does not develop literacy simply because the lessons and material are presented to him. He must also want to become literate. In this way it is possible to take account both of the older generation's transmission of the culture, and of the younger generation's evaluation and use of this heritage.

The home and the school have complementary roles to play with respect to these two factors in the maintenance of culture. Both parents and teachers can have a significant influence over the *attitudes* that children have toward the cultural patterns they are exposed to. The home and the school share different duties when it comes to providing *access* to the various aspects of cultures. Although very few aspects of cultural transmission could be said to be exclusively the home's or the school's responsibility, there are some facets of culture in which the home is primarily concerned and others in which school plays the major part.

Education for multicultural society in five schools

Some idea of the nature and extent of the contribution that schools are making toward the maintenance of ethnic cultures and hence the development of a multicultural Australia can be gained from a study of the five primary schools in which the interviews mentioned earlier were conducted. The five schools had two common features. Firstly, although there were variations in the ethnic composition of each school, the proportion of ethnic-Australian children in each was much greater than is found in the Australian population generally. In three schools at least half the students came from one particular ethnic group (either Greek or Italian). In the other two schools, the Greek and Italian groups were equal in size; taken together, they represented a half of one school's population and a third of the other. The parents in all five schools were predominantly working class in background, with fathers employed mainly as semi- or unskilled labourers.

The second common feature lay in the fact that each of the five schools was a member of the South Australian Education Department's Ten Schools Project. This project, which was initially intended for ten schools but now involves more than thirty, aims to provide guidance and assistance, as well as a common forum, on matters relating to education for a multicultural society. Inclusion in the project is open to all primary schools in South Australia, but occurs only if a school expressly asks to participate. That these schools are members of the project indicates that they are aware of, and to some extent concerned about, the multicultural composition of their school population.

The five schools differed in the programmes they provided for their ethnic-Australian students, and the extent of their contact with local ethnic communities. One of the five schools had so far provided no special courses in ethnic languages and cultures for its Greek- and Italian-Australian students, although it was planning to. Some contact had been established with the surrounding ethnic communities through the provision of English classes for mothers. In addition, the local Greek community held classes after school on several afternoons each week on the school premises. At a second school, weekly multicultural lessons in Greek and Italian had just been introduced and appeared to be attracting a reasonable level of interest and participation from children of all backgrounds. This school provided courses in English for mothers and gave support to the local Greek Saturday school.

A third school had been notable as being one of the first to make provision for its ethnic-Australian students. In addition to introducing special English classes for children who had difficulty in mastering the written forms of English, it had experimented over a number of years with general exposure courses in Greek and Italian language and culture, given once or twice a week to all levels of the primary school. At the upper primary level, however, it had been thought advisable to eliminate any linguistic component, which the teachers claimed the children had found too difficult, and concentrate instead on courses in ethnic cultures, which the children appeared to enjoy. The school had also developed a tradition of holding special days and festivals where each ethnic group was encouraged to participate and share its folklore with students from other groups and with the surrounding community.

A fourth school had established an Italian-English bilingual education programme in its junior primary school and in previous years had taught Italian as a regular school subject to all grade 4, 5 and 6 students on a twice-weekly basis. This had been phased out in grade 7 because of difficulties in staffing and organization.

Only one of the five schools had a fully-fledged ethnic language programme which provided Greek, Italian and Serbo-Croatian students throughout the school with four lessons a week in their mother tongue, and gave Anglo-Australian students the chance to study one of these. This school had also gone out of its way to maintain close links with surrounding ethnic communities.

Ethnic-Australian children's acquisition of English

When a child's mother tongue is a language other than English, he is likely to begin school at five or six years of age with a reasonably extensive oral grounding in his native language (equivalent to that which Anglo-Australian children of the same age have in English), but with a much more limited experience of English. In some cases such children know little or no English at all. Among the children in the primary school survey, 14 per cent of the ethnic-Australian children said they could not speak English when they started school and another 41 per cent knew only a little.

It is remarkable that most of the children interviewed considered they had learned to understand and speak English fairly quickly, even when they were given no special help. The continual exposure to an English speaking environment for about seven hours every day, as well as one or two hours in front of English television programmes, was sufficient to ensure that most children had no difficulty communicating orally in English. The success of the school in oral acquisition of English is seen most clearly in the fact that once they started school the children almost without exception spoke English to their brothers, sisters, cousins and other children of ethnic background. All the efforts of parents to maintain the home as a domain where the mother tongue only was spoken failed to counter the "press for English" that came from the school.

Difficulties with the acquisition of oral English occur most frequently with the students of post primary school age who have come with their families as immigrants to Australia. By that stage they have lost the young child's facility for picking up a language orally and many never learn to speak English without some trace of an accent. In the past, the schools did nothing to help these older children. It was assumed that general immersion in the English speaking environment of the school would enable them to gain an oral and written mastery of English, as well as provide them with the opportunity to continue their intellectual development through lessons taught in the very language they were supposed to be acquiring. Under these conditions, only the brightest and most determined children succeeded in gaining a mastery of English at more than an oral level, and at a standard that would enable them to pursue further secondary and perhaps tertiary studies.

It was not until 1971 that the Commonwealth government announced an education programme which for the first time acknowledged the existence of ethnic children in Australian schools. Under the Child Migrant Education Programme funds were made available to ensure that ethnic-Australian children gained a proper mastery of the written forms of English.

The Schools Commission has now accepted the findings of several recent studies which suggest that the literacy level in English of children of ethnic background born in Australia is in most instances comparable with that of their Anglo-Australian peers. This is not to deny that there is a considerable minority of ethnic-Australian children who, the Schools Commission believes, need additional help to master the written forms of English. The difficulties they face, however, are regarded as basically similar to those experienced by a comparable proportion of Anglo-Australian children. The Schools Commission argues therefore that what is needed is "sustained support in the development of English language competence across the whole curriculum" for students of all backgrounds.

The Schools Commission recommendation, however, takes little account of the theory propounded by American bilingual educators that children with a mother tongue other than English come to school ready to read and write in their own ethnic language, but not in English. They argue that there is a definite sequence by which young children best learn a language. It is necessary to listen to and understand what is being said before it is possible to speak the language. Not until there is some degree of oral mastery is it possible to read the written forms of the language and later write them. In Australian schools ethnic-Australian children have been expected to learn to read and write English in the same way and at much the same pace as their Anglo-Australian contemporaries with five years' oral experience in English.

Experience in Canada and the United States suggests that perhaps the best way of ensuring that ethnic-Australian children gain a thorough mastery of English is to allow them to gain literacy in their mother tongue first. While children are learning to read and write in the language in which they have an appropriate oral background, they can be given oral experience in English as a prelude to learning to read and write in English. The principles underlying such a bilingual programme are that the acquisition of literacy in a second language is easier once literacy has been achieved in the first, and that literacy can only be successfully developed on the basis of oral experience in a language. The end result of such a programme is a balanced bilingual child, competent in two languages.

If this theory is accepted, then the worst possible situation is that which prevails in most Australian schools, where a child with an ethnic mother tongue is expected to read and write English before he has any oral background in that language, while being denied the chance to gain literacy in his home language. Such a practice ensures that many ethnic-Australian children are fully literate neither in English nor in their mother tongue. Although it would be unrealistic to expect such a bilingual programme to be developed for all Australian languages other than English, it is certainly a possibility in schools which have a high proportion of one or two ethnic groups.

Children's attitudes, cultural diversity and social interaction

No matter what their cultural background, the children interviewed revealed similar attitudes on several important issues. In the first place their comments reflected a consistently positive attitude to other cultures and cultural pluralism generally. When asked whether people of non-English speaking origin should keep up their own language and ways of life in Australia, 84 per cent supported the idea, while only 8 per cent opposed it. Most of the children also liked the idea of studying ethnic languages and cultures at school. What criticisms were made did not oppose the principle of having ethnic language and culture lessons, but referred to their organization (too few a week), their content (too easy and basic, not enough reading and writing), or to their dislike of a particular teacher. These sorts of comments were made most often by students who also attended ethnic language classes outside normal school hours.

Friendship patterns in the schools suggested that most children paid no attention to a child's ethnicity when making friends. Only 16 per cent of the children named a circle of friends that was exclusively of their own ethnic group. In most cases friends were drawn from a number of different ethnic backgrounds, although those of the child's own ethnicity might predominate. Discussion revealed that most of the children felt that their ethnicity did not constitute a barrier to social interaction. Only a few mentioned name-calling, teasing or a sense of feeling excluded by those of a different ethnic background. Often the child being interviewed was not sure whether his friends were Greek-Australian or Italian-Australian or something else.

In the eyes of the children, teachers were even less likely than their classmates to differentiate between children of different ethnic backgrounds. Less than 40 per cent of the ethnic-Australian children believed that the teachers thought of them in terms of their ethnic origin. The remainder of the children indicated that the teachers either considered them to be simply Australian (20 per cent) or said the teachers didn't know, or at least didn't take ethnicity into account (over 40 per cent).

Many of the ethnic-Australian children seemed pleased at this. Having pointed out that teachers or students thought of them as being the same as everyone else they would add, "They don't treat me badly, or call me names." Rather than being upset at having their culture disregarded they seemed thankful for the lack of discrimination. This attitude appeared to be based upon their earlier experiences and, if they had been ill-treated in the past on account of their ethnic origin, they were pleased that this no longer occurred.

The significance of these attitudes and patterns of friendship needs to be considered carefully. In some instances, at least, it seemed that the lack of barriers to social interaction, was achieved not so much by raising the children's understanding and acceptance of other cultures, but rather by sweeping cultural differences aside through refusing to acknowledge them.

It should be noted that "sameness of treatment" could refer to two different things. On the one hand it could mean absence of negative sentiments by the majority towards those of ethnic background. This is the interpretation that the children themselves appeared to emphasize. Indeed, there is a sense in which there would be good reason for dismay if all Australian children were not treated the same, irrespective of their ethnic origin. If children were not given the same opportunity to learn, to express themselves, and succeed in occupational and social life, schools would be going against values upheld by Australians of all backgrounds.

On the other hand, complete equality of expectations in language learning and attitudes, for example, could obscure the fact that, for some students, a particular subject may be their mother tongue, and the culture concerned may not be 'foreign' but represent part of their everyday experience. It is this type of differentiation that could be accepted as appropriate to the school situation. As has been recognized in many other spheres of educational policy, equality of opportunity is not achieved through insisting on uniformity.

According to the terms of our discussion a multicultural society should be one where all children have an opportunity to maintain and develop both their own and another culture. Teachers would then recognize and welcome the fact that children of various backgrounds bring different experiences and expectations into the classroom. The school would also seek to provide a variety of programmes that would encourage and maintain a plurality of interacting cultures in Australia. In this regard the place of ethnic languages in schools is a critical issue. The policy of a school in relation to the teaching of ethnic languages is often the clearest indication of the extent to which the teachers, administrators and parents have accepted the basic principles of multiculturalism.

Ethnic languages and Australian schools

Despite their apparent success in developing positive attitudes to cultural diversity and encouraging interaction between children of different ethnic backgrounds, only one of the five schools studied made provision for upper primary students to study ethnic languages as a regular school subject, requiring a comparable degree of time and effort as other subjects in the curriculum, like reading and writing English, Maths, Science and Social Studies. There was only one school, therefore, where ethnic children at the upper primary school level could learn to read and write in their native tongue, and Anglo-Australians had the opportunity to become literate in another Australian language. Even this programme had only recently been introduced and its effects on the primary school children interviewed were as yet minimal.

The interviews revealed that the knowledge and mastery of ethnic languages among Australian children is well below what they have already achieved in English. In the case of Anglo-Australian students who had the opportunity to learn another language, none in any of the schools had got further than learning to speak a few words. In contrast, a good many of the ethnic-Australian children claimed to be able to read and write their mother tongue, to some extent at least. Further questioning revealed that this usually involved only the reading and writing required for lessons in their ethnic language and correspondence with other family members in the homeland.

Moreover, it was quite clear that the Australian school could claim no credit for what degree of literacy did exist among its ethnic-Australian students. By far the majority of students who were literate in their mother tongue were Greek-Australian children who regularly attended 4–5 hours of Greek classes a week, outside the normal school programme. In two schools almost every child of Greek origin attended these classes and most had done so for years. The fact that ethnic schools and not the Australian school system were responsible for teaching these children to read and write their native language was shown when figures on ethnic school attendance were correlated with ability to read and write the mother tongue.

If multiculturalism means giving all Australian children the opportunity to maintain or acquire an ethnic culture as well as the Anglo one, it should be recognized that at present the school system is failing to transmit ethnic languages and cultures. There are inefficiencies and weaknesses in the Australian education system which allows some children from all backgrounds to become adults without mastering basic English skills. With respect to ethnic languages and cultures the problem is more fundamental. Children acquire and develop Anglo-Australian culture, especially its literary aspects, because of the education system. The few who fail to develop basic skills in this area do so in spite of the efforts of the educators. With ethnic languages and cultures the opposite situation applies. Children fail to acquire and develop ethnic cultures at the literary level because there is still virtually no provision for them in Australian schools. Those Australian children who have become competent biculturals, by gaining a mastery of an ethnic language and culture, have done so in spite of the past indifference of our education system.

In the last few years an increasing number of those in charge of educational policy have come to accept the need to teach ethnic languages and cultures in Australian schools. The 1976 Report of the Migrant Languages Committee was the first formal sign in this direction. The report claimed that Australia was now "a cultural mosaic", and becoming "increasingly aware of its multicultural nature". It went on to argue that "the social changes resulting from migration (and particularly) the concentrations of certain language groups in schools have implications for school programmes". Children in Australian schools should have the chance "to study their own language and the language of their neighbours if they so desire". Hence it recommended that educational authorities "should create widespread opportunities for children to study migrant languages and cultures in schools".

This approach was also advocated in the report submitted by the Schools Commission Committee on Multicultural Education in 1979. The report is the most progressive and advanced statement that has yet appeared on the need to respect and preserve the many cultures that make up Australian society. The committee stated unequivocally that "in relation to ethnic groups, language has the initial function of preserving ethnicity. It is felt that a policy of cultural interaction or cultural pluralism will only be successful if the society as a whole accepts that there is a need to preserve and develop the ethnic languages in daily use in the community." To stress this last point, the report introduces the term "Australian languages other than English" in order to give the ethnic languages spoken in Australia "the status ... dignity and worth" of being recognized as an integral part of Australian cultural life, and an accepted component of the curriculum of Australian schools. The committee concluded that, "Steps will need to be taken to provide an opportunity for students coming from non-English speaking backgrounds, to study their mother tongue in schools." At the same time, the committee insisted that all Australian students participate in some form of education for a multicultural society. In accordance with its terms of reference, the committee then recommended an allocation of financial resources to achieve these aims.

Our study of children in five schools leaves no doubt that unless the policies advocated in these reports become a reality, Australian languages other than English will fall into disuse. Access to anything but the folkloric aspects of the culture will be cut off through the inability of ethnic-Australians to read and write about such things as literature, history, geography, art, music, religion and technology in their own language. At present ethnic cultures are not being transmitted to the next generation(s) in Australia in their 'authentic' and integral form, but in their oral, folkloric and mainly truncated versions.

Older ethnic-Australians are still retaining their cultures but live on the edge of Australian society, often preoccupied by their search for economic stability and social acceptance. Their Australian-educated children, on the other hand, are fast losing many vital parts of their ethnic heritage, particularly in relation to language, which lies at the core of many cultures. The loss of ethnicity is not complete but represents, rather, its attentuation. This cultural dilution shows itself in two main ways. Almost always there is a loss of literacy in the language concerned and an absence of intellectual vitality that is necessary for cultural maintenance and development. In fact the literacy of the second generation children is usually limited to occasional letter writing. Young ethnic-Australians, and this includes even fluent speakers, use their mother tongue only in conversation with their elders and resort to English in communication with their ethnic peers. These young people will be unable to pass on to their own children and to Australians from other groups any significant aspects of their native cultures. The culture of our country will remain essentially uniform and any chance of interaction or synthesis will be lost.

It can be argued, therefore, that we still lack in Australia the basic conditions required for a multicultural society. There is no distinct line of transmission of ethnic cultures which would enable young ethnic-Australians to make use of the full range of their ethnic cultural heritage for their present life in Australia and transmit it to their children. This is the consequence of the past failure of Australian schools to help teach ethnic languages and cultures and proves that in our type of society even a strongly ethnic home is not in itself sufficient to ensure the transmission of an ethnic literary heritage.

Education for a multicultural Australia

If Australia is to become established as a multicultural society certain social and cultural requirements must be satisfied:

(i) Australians of all backgrounds must accept and support the idea of Australia as a multicultural society
(ii) Ethnic-Australian groups must maintain their cultures and languages
(iii) Anglo-Australians need to acquire aspects of ethnic-Australian cultures and languages
(iv) Ethnic-Australians must acquire English and other elements of Anglo-Australian culture
(v) Anglo- and ethnic-Australians need to interact socially and culturally.

Australian schools have not yet accepted their responsibilities with respect to these requirements and for that reason there is a danger that the opportunity for Australia to become a multicultural society will be lost.

Some argue that if ethnic-Australians place so much importance on a certain aspect of their culture, then there is no need to provide formal instruction at school in it, since ethnic-Australian children will be motivated to learn it for themselves at home. This argument has two flaws. Firstly, multiculturalism is not only for ethnic-Australians. To confine the maintenance and development of ethnic cultures only to ethnic-Australians is to encourage pluralism of the separatist type. Secondly, even amongst the ethnic-Australian population the transmission of their culture cannot be regarded solely as the responsibility of the home. The argument that if it is important enough then the parents should ensure that children learn it, does not hold as the official educational policy of schools in Australia in respect to Anglo-Australian culture. Rather, the reasoning is that those aspects of our culture which are most important and most highly valued are given most prominence in the school. No one argues that there is no need for children to learn to read, write and calculate in the schools since these tasks are so important that they can be learnt at home.

Just as few Anglo-Australian families have the ability, time or resources to teach their children to read and write in English, so, too, ethnic-Australians are not in a position to develop the literacy of their children. This applies to areas beyond initial literacy and includes other cultural values and perspectives ranging from literature, history and geography to art, craft and music.

In order to complement the home effectively, courses in ethnic languages and cultures should be introduced in the early primary years, when home retention of the mother tongue is still high. School programme can then develop literacy in the ethnic tongue, in the same way as schools currently do for English speaking children. Without reinforcement at this early stage, ethnic language usage deteriorates sharply. For Anglo-Australian children, too, the acquisition of an ethnic language, first at the level of oral experience, with the later addition of literacy skills, is easier at an early age.

In conclusion, multiculturalism will never be achieved in Australia unless ethnic cultures are maintained and developed in their entirety within society. Attitudes are not enough; these must be given the opportunity to be translated into action. Similarly, smatterings of folkloric elements of the cultures cannot lead to multiculturalism. The establishment of a multicultural society depends on the widespread and comprehensive maintenance and acquisition of ethnic cultures. To know a few words of an ethnic language, to eat some ethnic food, or to be able to do an occasional ethnic dance represents only the first halting steps toward a multicultural Australia. Acquisition of this sort of knowledge may help to develop positive attitudes to diversity in residual areas of culture. The danger is that the schools' failure to teach ethnic cultures at a literary and intellectual level to the present generation of ethnic-Australian children will limit the transmission of the full range of ethnic cultural heritage to the next generation. The development of Australia as a multicultural society would then be stifled in its embryonic stage.

Only if Australian schools accepts responsibility for teaching ethnic languages and cultures to students of all ethnic backgrounds is there likely to emerge a growing number of bilingual, bicultural individuals. Such individuals not only have the chance to broaden their own knowledge of people and deepen their understanding of life, but provide for the community as a whole living bridges between the different ethnic groups and thus promote a creative interchange of cultures in a plural society.

Aboriginal Children

Anne-Katrin Eckermann

This chapter explores Aboriginal children's needs on the basis of a framework employed by Erikson, Maslow and White.[1] Case study evidence is presented from an Aboriginal group in south-west Queensland where research was carried out between 1970 and 1976.[2] Aboriginal children's needs, how these are met within the family and how they may be frustrated by direct or indirect 'outside' forces beyond the family's control, are examined. The evidence indicates that Aboriginal children in this area grow up in two worlds: one, the warm, supportive, 'inside' world of their own family and community, the other, the often condemnatory and hostile world of 'outside', non-Aboriginal family, community and state. Analysis of the 'outside' world indicates that neither the non-Aboriginal community, nor the state and its policies, provide a positive environment for Aboriginal-Australian children.

Generally children's needs may be categorized into two broad areas: basic physiological needs for food, shelter and security; and psychological needs for identity and competence. It is beyond the scope of this chapter to carry out a detailed analysis of Aboriginal children's needs, but some aspects of the psychoanalytic tradition, as interpreted by Erikson, White and Maslow may help us to recognize the pressures which shape, develop and frequently cripple young Aboriginal-Australians. Consequently, I shall first examine briefly their needs in relation to Maslow's "five needs systems," Erikson's "eight ages of man" and White's "sense of competence", paying special attention to children's needs for a sense of trust, initiative, industry and identity.

No single chapter can adequately describe all Aboriginal groups in Australia today. The scope is too broad. To overcome problems associated with diversity we frequently distinguish between those Aboriginal people who live in the north of Australia (and follow a substantively traditional life style), those who live in cities, and those who live in country areas. We justify these distinctions on the grounds that environment interacts with life styles, values and traditions to create unique group characteristics. One chapter could not address itself to the needs of Aboriginal children in all three environments. To avoid overgeneralization, I propose to present original field data collected among Aboriginal people in Rural Town, south-west Queensland, between 1970 and 1976, and show how these children's needs are met within the family and community network and how easily their needs may be frustrated by the larger non-Aboriginal society.

Our case-study demonstrates that Aboriginal children's needs must be met in the Aboriginal as well as the non-Aboriginal community which dominates their environment. Within this framework the non-Aboriginal state remains a powerful influence. Consequently, we will examine some government policies affecting Aboriginals today. I believe such policies have done little to meet Aboriginal children's needs for a sense of trust, initiative, industry or identity. Yet changes are in the wind; not because of drastic innovations in government philosophy, but because Aboriginal people themselves have taken initiatives.

Children's needs

Psychologists generally agree that a child's needs are closely related to his or her development and growth. Maslow argues for higher and lower order needs. Although this order is not specifically linked to a child's physical maturation, Maslow suggests that the needs system is arranged in a hierarchical form and that progression through this hierarchy will occur only when the needs of each individual system are met. Consequently, physiological needs for food, shelter, clothing and physical comfort are basic, lower level needs, as are safety and order needs which focus on issues of security, orderliness, harm-avoidance, predictability, protective rules and regulations. Unless these lower needs are met, the child will be unable to fulfil such higher needs as social and belonging needs, ego needs or self-actualization needs. These in turn focus on a desire for meaningful relationships, for recognition and individual status, for personal growth, achievement and satisfaction.

While Erikson does not necessarily advocate a hierarchy of needs, he stresses that developmental phases and the learning, maturation and need fulfilment associated with each, progress from one to another, are continuous, and merge into one another. Thus the child builds from a sense of trust and a sense of autonomy, progresses to a sense of initiative and then to a sense of industry, builds a sense of identity and develops a sense of intimacy, a parental sense and a sense of integrity in that order, under optimal conditions. Erikson also cautions that achievements in any phase may be threatened by later experiences, and White agrees with this. White's emphasis centres around the sense of competence. He argues that competence, the need to establish and maintain effective control over the socio-cultural-economic environment, permeates all other aspects of development and underpins all needs systems.

Considering these varying, yet overlapping approaches to children's needs we can identify the following which must be satisfied if the child is to develop a strong, healthy, independent adult personality:

1. Biological needs for food, shelter and comfort
2. Trust needs, for assurance that the environment will satisfy biological needs, that there is order and security
3. Needs for autonomy, industry and initiative which ensure feelings of competence, of being able to manipulate the environment within a predictable and protective framework
4. Needs of knowing who one is (identity), of having meaningful relationships with intimate others who belong to a group with which one identifies and in which one is acknowledged as a competent member
5. Needs of extending oneself beyond one's own internal satisfaction, for individual growth and satisfaction by competent manipulation of the environment and acceptance of one's own strengths and weaknesses as well as those of significant others with whom one shares the environment.

Our discussion will focus on Aboriginal-Australian children's needs within the five areas outlined above. The three writers emphasize that it would be wrong to dismiss learning, exploration and manipulation which take place for their own sake rather than for need-fulfilment. They also maintain that it would be just as wrong to minimize the influence of environment or significant others in the child's striving to satisfy needs and develop new needs. Thus Maier, discussing Erikson's framework, says that "the physical, social and ideational environmental influences serve as partners to the biological and psychological innate processes which shape the individual's personality development.... Environmental forces both limit and free the individual."[3] Consequently this discussion must consider Aboriginal children's needs within their environmental context, using the term 'environment' in its broadest possible sense, including social, cultural, physical and economic aspects.

Aboriginal-Australians' environment

Aboriginal children tend to grow up in two quite often separate and frequently hostile worlds. One is the familiar and warm world of the Aboriginal family and community; the other the equally familiar but often condemnatory and inimical world of the non-Aboriginal town and region. Strong, pervading historical patterns have been responsible for creating and maintaining this division.

We all know that contact between Aboriginals and settlers during the early nineteenth century was marked by armed conflict, extermination and dispossession.[4] Australian history was characterized by violent and traumatic culture clash which resulted in wholesale genocide, dispersal of Aboriginal groups, waning of traditional Aboriginal political structures, demoralization of the custodians of Aboriginal law and degradation of the Aboriginal people. Between 1870 and 1890 depopulation had reached such a degree that the Aboriginal's eventual extinction was generally accepted and expected.

In order to salve the public and private conscience, and to remove Aboriginal groups from land which settlers wanted, governments of the day pursued a policy of resettlement and protection, of 'smoothing the dying pillow'. Aboriginal people were encouraged or forcibly removed to mission stations and government settlements, rations were handed out and the people's lives were ordered and controlled by non-Aboriginal staff. Culture clash, characterized by disorientation and social disintegration, was thus followed by institutionalization. Acts were passed to ensure Aboriginal protection; in the process they also ensured that Aboriginal people were deprived of civil rights and became legally minors, totally dependent on government and mission organizations and goodwill. Such institutions bore (and to some extent perpetuate today) the characteristics which Goffman[5] associates with asylums.

Individuals exposed to this experience are likely to suffer gross environmental stress,[6] with which is associated such symptoms as chronic anxiety, fatigue and indifference, personality change, unfavourable concepts of self, the group and the world, hostility and aggression expressed passively against authority. These pressures are unlikely to fulfil people's needs of autonomy, initiative, industry and identity. Many Aboriginal parents, responsible for socializing children today, have been subjected to such stressful situations. Consequently, although government policy has changed from protection to assimilation, to integration, and is now focusing on self-determination, the history of contact has left its mark on Aboriginal people. It has also had profound effect on how Aboriginal and non-Aboriginal people relate to one another and the structure of the 'outside' world in which the Aboriginal child has to satisfy some of his or her needs.

A case study of duality

To stress the duality of Aboriginal children's environment let us take a brief look at Rural Town, south-west Queensland. In Rural

Town the Aboriginal minority comprises approximately 15 per cent of the town's population. Until the mid-1960s Aboriginal people tended to live on the *Yumba*,[7] a fringe settlement separated from Rural Town by the river. (It was bulldozed down in 1967.) Here families set up a shanty town of corrugated iron shacks and tents around half-a-dozen two-room cottages built by shire authorities during the 1930s on a clearly demarcated Aboriginal Reserve. Aboriginal people were strictly segregated from life in the town. They worshipped at the 'dark church'; they went to school (but only to fourth grade) in the 'dark school'; in the cinema they were permitted to occupy only the front stalls; except for casual sexual liaison, they were sought out only for employment.[8] Even within this restrictive framework, Aboriginals consistently occupied inferior status. In work situations, for example, pastoral employers frequently allocated substandard accommodation, and some graded Aboriginal employees according to skin colour. As one Aboriginal employee explained: "The real black ones'd have to camp on the woodheap, the brown ones in the laundry and the lighter ones near the kitchen."

This segregation began to break down during the late 1940s when the first Aboriginal children started to attend the 'white' school, although they were still segregated from white children in the classroom. Aboriginal people experienced extreme tensions and rejection in this situation, which intensified when they were resettled throughout the town's precinct by government action during the 1960s. The following statement is included as an example of the minority's reception and reaction:

> When the dark people lived across the river, the whites wanted nothing to do with the blacks and the blacks had nothing to do with the whites except to cross the river to shop or go to the pictures. We didn't know what town was then. Then they brought the Aborigines across the river and said that they had to live in town; but here we're only tolerated. Neighbours go out of their way not to meet us or talk to us. No one offers a helping hand. I reckon white people are pretty cruel, even to their own kind, and they have no love lost for dark people. It wouldn't be so bad if the white people welcomed the blacks, but they just tolerate us, that's all. . . .

Today Aboriginal people in Rural Town continue to form a 'closed' community. There are no obvious barriers to Aboriginal participation in general social functions or voluntary associations but they are noticeably absent from all except those associated with the football club and rodeo. Why do Aboringinal people fail to become involved? Aboriginal people fully understand the invisible barrier which separates them from the majority and consequently they try to avoid those situations which might expose them to slight and rejection. Once they suspect that they are not welcome, they rarely try to break down the barriers of segregation.

The same tensions and conflicts are carried over into all other aspects of life. Thus only two members of the Aboriginal community have ever found employment in Rural Town's retail businesses. Aboriginal girls are not employed in cafes or shops and their parents attribute this to discrimination on the basis of 'colour'.

> She applied for that job at the bakery. She was the first one there in the morning and the bloke told her he'd think about it and let her know in two–three weeks. I told her then to forget it, if he'd wanted her, he'd have taken her straight on. It's terrible for the kids 'cause they get too frightened to ask then. . . .

Similar invisible and difficult-to-combat criteria are applied when Aboriginals seek to rent accommodation. They are usually interrogated about their ability to pay rent, the number of people to occupy the house and their employment history. No such criteria are applied when non-Aboriginals wish to rent.

Generally Aboriginal people acquiesce to non-Aboriginal authority and domination, whether this be public authority and domination, whether this be public authority or informal, historically established *de jure* white domination. However, such acquiescence is deeply resented. So far the Aboriginal community has not been able to change its subordinate patterns of interaction with the majority. This 'outward' acceptance of domination is probably the only way the community has been able to adapt and survive, because it is totally dependent on the majority for employment and services.

Further, the Aboriginal group in Rural Town has never experienced the effects of various national Aboriginal movements. Consequently, even though some apparently major changes have taken place in Rural Town during the last fifty years, such as settlement in town, equal choice of seats in the picture theatre, access to stores and services, and equal pay (except where private contracts are negotiated by private employers), interaction between black and white has changed very little. This is demonstrated in European perceptions of Aborigines.

European attitudes towards Aboriginals

Although we did not directly investigate racial attitudes in Rural Town, we did conduct a cross-cultural, value-orientation survey (1970–72) and during the second period of fieldwork (1974–76) collected data on intergroup relations through participant-observation and interviewing.

The value-orientation survey[9] employed the Kluckhohn-Strodtbeck Schedule with one modification. It asked both Aboriginal and non-Aboriginal respondents to say how each thought the other would respond to all items. An interesting pattern emerged. Aboriginal people generally predicted non-Aboriginal responses correctly. Non-Aboriginals, on the other hand, consistently perceived Aboriginal responses incorrectly. Thus members of the majority believed Aboriginals in Rural Town to be predominantly fatalistic, to prefer living in the past and consequently to be incapable of planning for the future, and certainly to require supervision at work by non-Aboriginals. Further, non-Aboriginal respondents perceived themselves as being different from Aboriginals, and consistently under-estimated consensus with them while over-estimating consensus with their own group. Obviously they did not wish to identify with their perception of 'Aboriginals'. Ethnographic data support this pattern.

On the basis of this evidence, it is possible to isolate a number of opinions which are shared by some members of the Rural Town majority. These include the following: Aboriginals do not like work, they are more easily and more frequently addicted to alcohol, they cannot save money and they will always exploit Social Services if they are allowed to get away with it. Such stereotypes are not unique to Rural Town. Lippmann[10] reports that 24 per cent of her non-Aboriginal sample in New South Wales and Victoria considered Aboriginals generally "dirty", 15 per cent believed them "drunken", while 14 per cent thought them "irresponsible" (including lazy, unreliable and thriftless) and 10 per cent considered them "inferior" to whites. Taft recorded similar results from a Western Australian survey. In Rural Town majority members share many of the stereotype ideas prevalent about Aboriginals in different parts of Australia. Similarly, like white people cited by other writers, those in Rural Town consciously preserve a clear social distance between themselves and the black minority. For most of them Aboriginals simply do not exist—they are not part of their social, physical or emotional life and Aboriginal people are aware of this.

This, then is a brief outline of the 'outer world' in which Aboriginal-Australian children grew up in Rural Town. There is other evidence that many Aboriginal children are coping with a similar and frequently more severe 'outside' world. Gilbert's and Perkins' writings,[12] and Kath Walker's poetry, confirm that Aboriginal people themselves often consider white society a hostile world which can hurt and destroy. We would be foolish to underestimate its effects on Aboriginal children's needs, their development, fulfilment and frustration.

While the 'outside' world can harm Aboriginal children, their own family and community are not always able to ensure security and protection.

The Aboriginal child, family and community

We are born in poverty, live in poverty and die in poverty.[13]

Aboriginal people's own perception of their inability to survive economically in Australian society, is well supported by the Poverty Reports.[14] The National Population Inquiry provides evidence that Aboriginal groups "have the highest growth rate, the highest death rate, the worst health and housing, and the lowest education, occupational, economic, social and legal status of any identifiable section of the Australian population".[15] These pressures have led to a breakdown of the Aboriginal family and the displacement of the Aboriginal male as provider, father, model and protector for the Aboriginal-Australian child. Much of this present situation is a direct aftermath of the history of contact and its heritage of prejudice, discrimination, regimentation, institutionalization, limited educational achievement and low skill training. Rural Town Aboriginal people have not escaped their heritage.

A case study in poverty

Economics

The detailed economic patterns of Rural Town are given elsewhere.[16] For the purpose of this discussion, the following facts are important because they describe the social and physical environment in which the Aboriginal child grows up. Aboriginal men and women are located at the bottom of the employment ladder; all work is either unskilled or semi-skilled. Employment opportunities fluctuate with the weather (the sawmill, council and pastoral properties put men off when it rains); whether seasons are favourable or not; marketability of produce; whether properties choose to diversify and mechanize and consequently need fewer men. Men and women start employment in their mid-teens, men between the age of 14 and 16, women between the ages of 15 and 17. Almost all work is acquired through informal channels—relatives' recommendations, inquiries at the local agent or hotel, employers driving to houses and personally recruiting. Almost all work for those aged under 30 years is seasonal and casual. Progressively, work opportunities have decreased, casual employment has increased and this is clearly reflected in employment histories: men aged 50 and over have retained one job for a mean maximum of 14 years; men aged 30–49 have retained one job for a mean maximum of $4\frac{1}{2}$ years; men aged under 30 retained one job for a mean maximum of $1\frac{1}{2}$ years. Unemployment varies with the availability of casual and seasonal work but exceeds the Australian average.

These factors demonstrate that forces beyond the Aboriginal family or community's control create and maintain economic depression. Aboriginal people are not unwilling to work. In fact, work in itself is considered commendable in the community. Less importance is attributed to the type of work performed than to the fact that it is steady employment which brings in regular money. A man's reputation as a man, father, person of importance, is dependent on his capacity to support his family. But unemployment, underemployment and low-skill, low-status employment are a fact of life among Aboriginal people in Rural Town. Economic depression, living on or close to the poverty line, is the reality.

Housing

At the first survey (1970–72), 90 per cent of Aboriginal housing was found to be totally inadequate, and fit only for demolition. During the second period of fieldwork (1974–76), some 40 per cent of Aboriginal housing fell into this category. The situation had been partially relieved by the Department of Aboriginal and Island Advancement which has extended its housing programme. Today only 10 per cent of Aboriginal accommodation can be described as substandard. When Aboriginal families have rented accommodation from European landlords in Rural Town, they have been let only rather substandard houses. These have tended to deteriorate further because the Aboriginal household has had neither the financial resources nor the responsibility to carry out necessary repairs.

When accommodation is run-down and landlords feel no responsibility towards tenants, apathy and resentment soon sets in. As one man complained:

> We pay rent on this place. At one stage we thought of buying it, but we couldn't raise the $1 000 he was asking. He's still trying to sell the place and won't do anything to it while he's waiting—won't do any repairs, won't do anything against the white ants, won't put in new lino, won't even have the extra power point put in the lounge we asked for. Now I won't do anything either—there's plenty of small things I could do but while ever he won't keep it up, I won't either. . . .

Apathy and resentment are generated also by insecurity of tenure. Landlords usually want to sell these premises. If all the vacant homes in Rural Town were made available, there would be no housing problems in the Aboriginal community and no need for the Department of Aboriginal and Island Advancement to spend money on Aboriginal housing programmes.

Similarly, because landlords' prime consideration is selling their premises, families live under constant threat of eviction, should a buyer be found. Further, economic insecurity makes it extremely hard for Aboriginal people to maintain regular rent payments. Fear of eviction and associated anxieties are thus another fact of life for many Aboriginal families in Rural Town. As one woman explained:

> Sometimes I can't sleep at night. What if he gets put off tomorrow, we'll have to be out of here, packed up and out of here in two days. What's going to happen to us then.... Where are the kids going to sleep—how're we going to keep the payments up on the furniture....

Yet even in inadequate accommodation, people store up treasures such as linen or lace tablecloths, fine glasses and delicate china, for the time when they hope to move into better houses or perhaps even their own homes. Families who have been fortunate enough to acquire or rent 'a decent place' exert great effort to improve the house. Money is readily and consistently invested in new furniture, lino and appliances to make the family as comfortable as possible. However even in 'a decent place' over-crowding strains family resources and accommodation facilities. During 1974–76, for example, accommodation pressure among the permanent Aboriginal population in Rural Town was great: an average 8.2 individuals shared the same dwelling. Many other writers have reported similarly for other parts of Australia.[17]

When these statistics are compared with the Australian average, Rowley[18] suggests that:

> Aboriginal families have on average almost twice as many person per dwelling, and almost three times the number of persons per room, as other Australians, irrespective of size and construction of dwelling and rooms....

The average of 8.2 individuals per Aboriginal household in Rural Town, then, corresponds with some of the highest accommodation pressures recorded by other writers: particularly as the Rural Town average represents only permanent residents. When impermanent residents, visiting the area to find work or maintain social contacts, are included in the statistics, the mean number of persons per household rises to 9.2 and even 9.8 on occasions.

It would be a mistake to interpret these patterns as evidence that Aboriginals indiscriminately open their doors to whoever wants to share their house. In reality, people are offered hospitality according to strict rules. A visitor must "pay his or her way" either by monetary contributions or by services for the good of the whole household. People who share a house are generally related. However, even close relatives are pressured to leave and find a place of their own, or actively expelled from the household if they need accommodation for longer than a month. Exceptions are women and children left in the care of relatives while men follow up seasonal work.

Extended families frequently share accommodation because some household factions such as the aged, unmarried or deserted mothers, find it hard to maintain an economically viable, independent unit. Like the people of Adelaide,[19] they find stability and support by pooling resources. The Aboriginal-Australian child thus frequently grows up in overcrowded, substandard housing where pressures on facilities are great. This creates an 'inside' world for the Aboriginal child over which few parents have any control. Powerlessness of this kind restricts both Aboriginal children's need developments and their parents' ability to assist in need satisfaction. Thus inadequate and substandard housing, un- and underemployment, poverty and economic depression can prevent satisfaction of basic physiological needs for food, shelter, clothing and physical comfort. The associated anxiety, lack of economic security, prejudice and discrimination may seriously undermine the child's striving to fulfil needs for security and order, for initiative, industry and identity. Aboriginal parents show awareness of some of these dangers and compensate for them in their child-rearing practices.

Socialization and Aboriginal children's needs

The following account is based on intensive interviews with 27 mothers in the Rural Town Aboriginal community.[23]

Analysis of the mothers' perception of the socialization process suggests the following major factors in Aboriginal child rearing in Rural Town:

(i) The aims of socialization are to encourage the child to be a 'good person', able to mix with everyone, obedient, polite, conforming, quiet, respectable and respecting

(ii) In the process of learning their parents' expectations, children pass through at least three successive stages, from complete indulgence, through learning how to behave, to demonstrating that they have internalized these expectations. Each of these phases is progressively marked by stress on independence, 'standing on their own feet', responsibility and 'knowing their place'

(iii) Mothers play a dominant role in the process because fathers are frequently absent, because child rearing is considered "women's work", and because fathers are "too soft" to demand conformity. Mother's authority is obviously supported by close, affectionate relationships between her and her children, but is also based on her power to chastize or to withhold privileges

(iv) The desirable adult person is one who demonstrates responsibility, independence, good manners and respect.

At no time do mothers underestimate their children's basic physiological needs. They perceive one of their major duties as "looking after children in terms of food, clean clothes, washing and ironing, looking after the home and caring for their children's health". Given their economic situation this is difficult task, often associated with much family hardship. But, while they consider satisfying children's physiological needs important, they believe it as important to give children love and attention; to teach them good manners (that is, to have respect for adults, to be polite and quiet); to insist on discipline (to ensure that they do as they are told, are not cheeky or swear); and to be self-reliant and demonstrate commonsense.

If we return to our five areas of basic needs we can relate these to mother's expectations and practices, as well as to their perception of children's expectations during the child-rearing process. Table I suggests that mothers attempt to meet children's needs for competence, industry and identity by emphasis on self-reliance and independence, by guidance and discipline and, most importantly, by acceptance and support for the child within the 'inside' world. They believe that children mostly need and expect love, kindness and comfort. Getting advice, knowing Mum will always be there, interested in them, ready to listen and prepared to help, protect and even fight for them, form the next major group of children's needs and expectations as seen by these mothers.

Mothers attempt to satisfy children's needs by focusing on affiliative channels. They encourage children to be 'people-oriented', to draw satisfaction from competent interaction with significant others, to develop ego strengths by meeting such 'people' obligations as respect, kindness and generosity. The end-product, 'self-actualization' in Maslow's framework, is consequently a good person, as this concept is defined by the Aboriginal group. 'Good people' within this cultural group are thought to possess the following characteristics: they mix, don't 'big-note' themselves (make themselves feel big at the expense of others), they aren't 'stand-

Table 1: Children's needs related to mothers' expectations and practices

Area of Need Satisfaction	Mothers' Expectations	Mothers' Practices	Children's Expectations as Perceived by Mothers
Basic biological needs		Complete indulgence, much physical contact, protection, physical care	Satisfaction of bodily needs, love and attention
Trust needs	Child to take notice, to share, to give love	Some direction, some discipline, reliance on good manners and respect, protection	Love, attention, direction
Needs for autonomy, industry initiative and competence	Child to begin taking on small tasks and responsibilities	Advice, stress on acceptable behaviour and discipline, protection	Love, attention, direction, responsibility
Identity and social needs	Self-sufficiency, independence	Giving advice and guidance, joining in activities, encouraging ventures, protection	Love, attention, acceptance, responsibility
Needs for self-extension, competence and acceptance	Self-sufficiency, independence, generosity discipline, respect	Support, giving advice, listening to plans	Love, acceptance, support, responsibility

offish' or snobbish. They are warm in interpersonal relations, have a sense of humour, can laugh at themselves, don't condemn or find continual fault. They are generous and share; they show kindness and respect to others.

These qualities strengthen and maintain the Aboriginal child's 'inside' world. The values of kindness, respect and responsibility give clear guides to the Aboriginal-Australian child in relation to his or her biological, trust, accomplishment, industry and identity needs. The child grows up in a world where personal worth is measured against fulfilment of obligations to other people. Economic uncertainities and anxieties may be cushioned by a system of reciprocal rights, duties and obligations where one good turn begets another. Reciprocity is not indiscriminate sharing or 'bludging', it is a well-recognized process in the Aboriginal community which acknowledges people's responsibilities to one another and strengthens the group which lives under almost constant economic and social threat from the outside.

The influence of the 'outside' world

The nature of this threat is clearly revealed in children's identity. While it is undoubtedly true that Aboriginal people consider dark people 'good people', their sense of worth is jeopardized by non-Aboriginal perception of Aboriginals and by the economic climate. A man's *areté*, his sense of competence, his ego, are dependent on fulfilling the qualities his group demands. Loss of *areté*, as Goldschmidt argues has grave consequences for:

> . . . no individual can be healthy and reasonably happy if he cannot find within himself those qualities which he knows are the measure of a man—as that is defined in terms of the society in which he lives. . . .[21]

In this Aboriginal community a man's worth is closely tied to his ability to work and earn money. When economic changes lead to under- or unemployment, his reputation is threatened, particularly if he is still in his teens and has not yet been able to establish a 'good reputation' as a conscientious, responsible worker. Older men may refer back to the time when they were fully employed and productive, younger men often don't have that opportunity. Consequently their own community quickly condemns them as 'no-hopers'. Their sense of competence, which White[22] argues can be strengthened or crippled most dramatically in the work situation, is under threat. Boys, who from the age of 12 onwards, aspire to be men, must doubt their own competence when the models to whom they look for guidance meet frequent and constant set-backs. So the negative economic situation has repercussions, not only in terms of the family's physical needs, but also in terms of children's developmental needs. If the community's value system did stress a life of leisure or at least inactivity, then economic depression might not affect psychological needs. The importance of work, industry and accomplishment have however been clearly inculcated into the value system of the Rural Town Aboriginal people.

Economic depression also highlights those features which non-Aborigines in Rural Town consider most reprehensible in the minority—living on social services, unemployment, drinking, sharing (misunderstood though these features may be), and intensifies established patterns of prejudice and discrimination. The effects are far-reaching but their negative impact is seen most clearly in Aboriginal people's ambiguous feelings towards themselves, their colour and their traditions. Identity is both positive and negative: postive within the security of the Aboriginal minority but largely negative when confronted with the outside world. 'Colour' plays an important part in this negative perception. As Simpson and Yinger point out:

> The evaluation of one's own colour is affected both by what he is taught in his own group and by the attitude of the dominant group. White people ... have generally and consistently shown a preference for the lighter shades of brown. ...[23]

In Rural Town 'colour' is not a valued attribute. Non-Aboriginals make derogatory remarks about colour, use colour as a basis for insult and as justification for assigning inferiority to the minority. This has had obvious repercussions among Aboriginal people.

> When I was a kid I always wanted to be white, I hated being black and if anyone ever called me black I cried and cried. I used to scrub myself and scrub myself until I found out it didn't do any good. But now I don't feel 'shamed of my colour anymore. Since I've been living with these white people I found out that they look like butter wouldn't melt in their mouths when they're all in town, but when you see them and hear them in their own backyards they got the foulest language. ...

A great deal of tension is associated with Aboriginal people's own perception of 'colour' and this finds ready expression in child-rearing practices, in their distinction between 'black' and 'dark', and in their own use of 'colour' as a basis of insult and slight. Aboriginal people in Rural Town do not like to be called 'black', particularly by the majority. They see themselves as 'dark' people. Being called 'black', is a serious slight. Paradoxically the insult 'black' is also used extensively in child-rearing practices by parents to chastize children, to shame them. This has its effect on the children's own perception of 'colour'. As Cooley[24] points out, we have a "looking-glass self", compounded of others' reactions to us, our interpretation of those reactions, and a response to the interpretation. Young Aboriginal children, on the basis of others' reaction, acquire a negative attitude towards colour at an early age.

Paradoxically 'black' is also used as a form of affection or in humourous comments. Significantly, this occurs only among intimate friends. "You want to smile when you say that, mate" is a common response. The operant factors here are the tone of voice and the situation in which the remark is made. If the tone is joking and friendly and the situation intimate, reference to 'black' serves as a claim of membership. If the tone is sneering and the situation tense, the same remark may lead to bitter fighting.

Some individuals have tried to cope with their ambivalence towards colour by denying it—by 'passing' and disputing any ties with the Aboriginal minority. Thus most Aboriginals in Rural Town know, or are related to, someone who has 'gone white'. People who try to 'pass' are treated with contempt. Thus, although 'passing' is not a method of 'coping' within the Aboriginal group in Rural Town itself, it does provide a means of escape from 'colour' for people who leave or who migrate into Rural Town. Such an 'escape' is fraught with danger—fear of discovery, fear of ridicule by those who know. The fact that some people are 'passing' as their only solution to inferior status and prejudice is indicative of the extreme tensions associated with minority group membership. The fact that similar patterns have been reported by other writers for the last 20 years or more, demonstrates that despite changes in government policies, educational programmes or supposed majority attitudes, very little has changed at the grass-roots level and identity problems remain for many Aboriginal children.

All members of this minority must somehow come to terms with their Aboriginality, and the whole climate of minority–majority interaction is marked by anxiety and self-consciousness. The most common way of dealing with this situation in Rural Town is to become excessively critical of one's own group. Aboriginal people have internalized many white stereotypes and are the most devasting critics of their own people.

> Some of them dark people here make you feel ashamed of your colour, never working, always drunk, and some are real stirrers, expect the Government to do everything for them while they sit back and do nothing. . . .
>
> I learned early on that I had to be just as good or better than the

whites or I'd always only be a boong.

Them other darkies here, well a whole lot of them drink too much and don't worry too much about keeping a house clean. If I ever owned a house and thought of renting it I'd never rent it to a darkie, they'd just let everything go to ruin.

Psychologists tell us that this type of reaction is common among minority groups subjected to prejudice and discrimination. It is a destructive reaction, intensifying intra-group hostility and weakening group solidarity. Exposed to such internal and external threats it is difficult for the Aboriginal child to satisfy such higher order needs as initiative, industry and identity. A belief in oneself as a 'good person' is not an effective counterbalance.

The preceding discussion has indicated the often negative interaction between Aboriginal children's 'inside' and 'outside' worlds. However, the influence of the state, a vital aspect of this 'outside' world, closely allied to the attitudes and actions of the non-Aboriginal family and community, is also important and needs to be considered.

The influence of government

Between 1972, when government policy changed to one of 'self-determination' in relation to Aboriginal affairs, and 1978, when government formally acknowledged the multicultural nature of Australian society, a spate of innovative programmes have been initiated on both Commonwealth and State levels. This shift in government policy has included such educational developments as the Aboriginal Secondary Grant Scheme, Aboriginal Studies programmes and kits, bilingual education, the use of teachers' aides, environmental-based learning programmes, pre-service and in-service teacher training courses, school–community liaison, parent-aid programmes, out-station education and black community schools.

Recognition that the law consistently discriminates against Aboriginal people, either by omission or commission, has led to the establishment of Aboriginal Legal Aid offices in all states. Northern Territory courts consult traditional Aboriginal law and its custodians under special circumstances. Western Australia is experimenting with Aboriginal Magistrates in its more remote, traditionally oriented areas. New South Wales has repealed the Summary Offences Act and this may help to keep Aboriginals out of jail for civil and misconduct offences. The Northern Territory is experimenting with Aboriginal Police Aides to take on the duties of law enforcement on remote settlements. The Racial Discrimination Act now makes it illegal to exclude Aboriginal people from majority ventures and the Commissioner for Community Relations prosecutes instances of discrimination. Probably the greatest and most far-reaching concession made by government has been its recognition (limited and provisional though this may be) of Aboriginal land rights.

Social Services have attempted to meet more adequately the needs of Aboriginals. For example, although Aboriginal orphans and children in need of care continue to be placed in non-Aboriginal homes, social welfare departments in the 1970s have been more ready to appoint Aboriginal foster parents or house parents for these children. Departments of Aboriginal Affairs support the work of liaison and community workers on settlements and provisions are made for adult education. Aboriginal councils and co-operatives are encouraged to undertake 'self-help' programmes in housing, employment and health.

Because general health agencies have not provided satisfactory service to Aboriginals, because Aboriginal infant mortality is the highest in the world, because Aboriginal people continue to suffer disproportionately high rates of diseases such as tuberculosis, rheumatoid arthritis, rheumatic fever, trachoma, diabetes and even leprosy (to mention a few), governments have supported Aboriginal Medical Services in all states. Departments of Labour and Industry as well as the Commonwealth Employment Service have been active in developing vocational training and employment schemes aimed at alleviating unemployment and the low level of vocational skills in Aboriginal communities. In the political arena the Federal government has attempted to recognize Aboriginal viewpoints through the formation of the National Aboriginal Congress, an elected body of Aboriginal representatives set up to advise the Minister for Aboriginal Affairs.

Considering this brief outline of governmental response to Aboriginal needs, it would appear that it's influence on the Aboriginal child's 'inside' world must be positive and extensive. In fact, some non-Aborigines have complained vigorously that the sorts of 'privileges' and support granted to Aboriginal people by the state far exceed reasonable limits. We strongly believe that this 'white back-lash', as it is often called, arises because:

(a) attitudes towards Aboriginal people by the majority have changed little over the last century
(b) economic depression has set one vulnerable group (the 'poor white') against another (the 'poor black')
(c) government expenditure on Aboriginal projects only appears huge

(d) the way in which government has dealt with Aboriginal self-management, has meant that some projects have failed while large sums of money appear to have been wasted on others

(e) there is no consistent media coverage of programmes which have worked and practically none of Aboriginal initiated and managed projects.

Let us take each of these points in turn. Evidence from the preceding discussion supports assertions that, in general, Australian society retains its negative perceptions of the Aboriginal minority. Economic depression and competition for basic goods and services strengthens such negative attitudes. Thus those sections of the community most affected by fluctuations in the economic climate today—the poor, the unemployed, the deserted and homeless, and those with limited marketable skills—are not only competing against the system for survival, but also against each other for progressively shrinking opportunities. Within such competition, the minority out-group which appears to receive positive discrimination by the state, readily becomes the scapegoat, the focus of envy and resentment.

Relatively large sums of money have been spent on Aboriginal projects, but we are not often made aware that most of these funds are spent employing non-Aboriginal advisors, managers and planners. Basically governments do not consider Aboriginal people "ready", "capable" or "trustworthy" to select programmes, allocate resources and manage facilities. This means that in some measure governments are responsible for many Aboriginal 'failures' because they generally neglect to gauge Aboriginal wants or needs before programmes are selected.

Consider housing schemes. Aboriginal accommodation is characteristically substandard and overcrowded; government has recognized its obligation to alleviate this situation. But how much money has been spent consulting administrators, architects and town planners and how much money or time have been allocated to consulting Aboriginal people and identifying their needs and wants? Even minimal time is rarely invested in the latter. Consequently many resettlement schemes have failed. Yet, when Aboriginal co-operatives have approached governments for funds to allocate and manage their own housing policies these have been more successful. Every year, however, such co-operatives are threatened with monetary cut-backs. Aboriginal Legal Aid and Medical Services, two nationally successful organizations, instigated at the request of Aboriginal communities and indeed after much Aboriginal political pressure, also face continual cut-backs and erosion of funds.

Over the last 200 years a vast network of administrative and bureaucratic machinery has grown up around Aboriginal Affairs.

It's size has increased dramatically during the last 20 years. Indeed it may be argued that some northern parts of Australia derive a good part of their economic viability from the 'Aboriginal industry' i.e. non-Aboriginal administrative, clerical, liaison, and education staff. The sheer size of this machinery precludes Aboriginal self-management for two reasons: firstly, although non-Aboriginal staff profess to be "working themselves out of a job", few see this as an immediate possibility or desirability; and secondly, the bureaucracy expects fairly rigid rules of procedures which few Aboriginal groups would use in day-to-day activities. The bureaucracy perceives one of its roles as that of supervising correct administration. As a result little is done to train members of Aboriginal organizations in procedure, to work out new rules and regulations to accommodate Aboriginal groups or to promote Aboriginal people within the bureaucracy to sufficiently high levels so that they may influence the system.

There is ample evidence that although the state has expressed concern for Aboriginal groups and their socio-economic situations, there has been little co-ordinated planning. Education is a good example. At present it is seen as *the* avenue by which Aboriginal groups may gain recognition and acceptance in the wider society, and many programmes have grown out of this approach. All have some merit because they could increase the Aboriginal child's life chances in the system. Yet, although such innovations exist in principle, few schools have taken a co-ordinated approach to Aboriginal education, few teachers have really examined their value positions and no education department has really come to grips with the vital question: Education for what? Given that education is one influential way of socializing children, what are we educating children for? How do we perceive our future society; with what kinds of social, economic and political situations will children have to cope? Because we have failed to address ourselves to these issues in education, programmes in Aboriginal education have been dissipated.

'Aboriginal education' has become a panacea for the minority's social, economic and political depression. Not only has the majority convinced itself of this (indeed has believed it since the time of Governor Macquarie's school), it has also persuaded the minority that with 'education' their world would improve. But education is only one aspect; it will remain ineffectual as long as there is no corresponding planning in politics, economics, welfare, and health, and as long as these approaches remain haphazard and unco-ordinated.

Perhaps this analysis of the state's role in Aboriginal children's lives is too negative; nevertheless it is important to recognize that neither the Aboriginal child, nor the Aboriginal family and community, nor society at large is really getting their money's worth out of the state's policies and expenditures. Where real gains have been achieved, they have most frequently been associated with programmes and innovations initiated, developed and managed by Aboriginal people themselves.

The role of Aboriginal decision making

Wherever Aboriginal people have been given a chance to declare their needs and preferences, they have done so, though mechanisms of decision-making have often varied from those employed by the larger society.

An obvious example is the National Aboriginal Education Commission, established after the Schools Commission consulted with various Aboriginal groups and organizations. The National Aboriginal Education Commission is endeavouring to develop policy which will ensure its participation in all matters related to Aboriginal education. All policy and decision-making processes are dominated by Aborigines, although funds are supplied by government.

We can point to numerous other 'Aboriginal successes': the Black Community School in Townsville, the Aboriginal School at Strelli (Western Australia), the Aboriginal Counselling and Medical Centre in Townsville, the Black Theatre and Dance groups in Sydney, the Aboriginal Culture and Training Centre in Sydney, the Tangatjira Aboriginal Council in Alice Springs, Kalano and Yulngu Associations in Katherine, to mention a few. Add to these the various housing, health and legal aid organizations which have sprung up in all cities and major country centres.

These organizations, operated and dominated by Aboriginals for Aboriginals, more than any other may encourage Aboriginal children to develop positive, strong identity, a sense of industry and competence.

A Faint Ray . . .

Jim Giles

Ethnic children

In responding to Dr Smolicz's paper, with which I find myself very much in agreement at an intuitive level, I want to tease out some major ideas which are either implicit in or absent from the discussion.

The first of these is the concept of diversity. It is assumed that, at a national level, diversity is intrinsically a good thing, that it is better for Australia to be culturally diverse than culturally homogeneous. The first distinction to be made here is between those differences related to income and power, and those related to language, heritage, literature, religion, customs and traditions and so forth. I do not wish to advance the idea that it is desirable to have an Australia in which socio-economic difference is encouraged. But it is demonstrably a good thing to encourage cultural difference as distinct from class or income differences. Different modes of speech, of worship, of relationships, of social organization and, at a lower level, of food, song, and dance are desirable for several reasons. The first reason relates to a theory of adaptation. In a rapidly changing world, in the silicon chip revolution, a nation is more likely to survive if it has developed a wide variety of life styles. The analogy, of course, is geological and biological.

The second reason for the encouragement of cultural diversity is aesthetic and psychological. It is difficult to explain why difference or diversity is aethetically desirable: it is the difference between a patchwork quilt and a monochrome sheet; between a mosaic of fields and forest seen from an aircraft and an asphalt car park in a supermarket. Psychologically, there is a reassurance and a kind of liberty in a society which offers a wide range of options, and which avoids hard and fast judgements on what is 'correct'.

The third reason is political and social. We are, inevitably and irrevocably, part of the global village. Rapid transit, lower air fares, satellite communication have dragged Australia from isolation into the world and it is quite apparent that the global village is multilingual and multi-valued. It is reassuring to find that our own country in fact reflects that diversity. Furthermore, it is clear from statements such as the Declaration of Human Rights that people may expect to inherit their cultural birthrights. Conformity and uniformity are inimical to human rights.

While the concept of cultural difference and diversity may be strongly defended as a desirable national goal, there is a concomitant fear that diversity may mean fragmentation, lack of cohesion, hostility and inter-group rivalry for political and economic power. If difference and diversity are to be accepted widely in the community as desirable ends, then there must be, in my view, some kind of guarantee that national cohesion will be maintained. That is, there will need to be a national identity, or at least an Australian identity, within which cultural difference and diversity may flourish.

Acceptance of difference is likely to be wider if it can be demonstrated that such an acceptance will not result in fragmentation or loss of national cohesion. It will therefore be useful to emphasize an Australian identity based on a legal description of rights and responsibilities of citizenship, some shared values and beliefs, the use of English as the official language, pride in the country itself and the development of national myths emerging from our diversity. Such a description could well enter schools and replace that ceremony which in South Australia used to be called "saluting the flag".

Smolicz's hope, and it is one I share, is that within an Australian identity there will not only be an acceptance and encouragement of diversity, but a biculturalism whereby a significant number of individuals are able to feel at home in two or three cultures. This remains the matter of transmission of culture, but particularly the sharing of different cultures. The possibility of this is the major plank of multiculturalism.

The possibility of becoming a genuine bicultural person is more open, it seems to me, to a member of one of Australia's ethnic communities than it is to an Anglo-Australian. Many people are equally at home in two worlds, moving naturally and easily from an Anglo-Australian work situation, for instance, to an ethnic social and family setting. The same bicultural competence is given point when people describe how they feel Italian in Australia, but Australian in Italy. Whether the same capacity to move surely and gracefully in two cultural settings is within Anglo-Australians is doubtful. Given Smolicz's view that access and willingness are two determinants of the maintenance of a culture, both are limited at the moment. There is a catch 22 in this: the likelihood of Anglo-Australians becoming bicultural depends upon the wide availability of programmes and an attitude of willingness, whereas the provision of those programmes and the funding of the necessary arrangements depend upon acceptance of the value of biculturalism. Nevertheless, there are signs. The interest by a large number of Anglo teachers in learning community languages, the re-description of the rationale for offering languages in schools, and a burgeoning interest in aspects of culture other than food, song and dance, seem to offer hope.

Biculturalism is best achieved through bi-lingualism, and I should like therefore to look at language teaching. First of all, the teaching of English as a second language has not been handled well in this country. Smolicz points to the rapid acquisition of the language by non-Anglos, and there is some evidence that playground interaction produces as much facility as does special English classes. But Smolicz also suggests, and approves of the Schools Commission's view on the matter, that after the stage of initial acquisition of English, children's difficulties are of the same kind as those experienced by Anglo-Australian children, and that what is needed is "sustained support in the development of English language competence for students of all backgrounds". I am not sure about this: there is detailed evidence, based on a careful linguistic analysis, that the lack of English competence in non-Anglo children is of a significantly different kind from that in Anglo children. This is especially true in writing and reading. The difficulty is to devise programmes which at the same time deal with general principles from which further language items may be generated and with the idiosyncratic difficulties of particular individuals.

The whole 'English as a second language programme' in Australia needs to be critically examined. For this reason, it is heartening to see that the Schools Commission is moving in the area, and gathering data. Whatever does come out of that survey, must take into account the new views of language teaching emerging from the Council of Europe, van Eck's work and programmes such as "Threshhold English".

When we come to the teaching of Australian languages other than English, we meet a similar problem. In the main, language teaching in Australia is confined to secondary schools, does not stress communicative competence, is limited to academic stream students (with a substantial falling away of numbers) and is pre-occupied with grammar and translation. Furthermore, there is little attempt to take advantage of the living linguistic community outside the school.

To change this situation will not be easy. Under Schools Commission funding, curriculum for primary school language teaching is beginning to be developed, based on a functional-notional approach and emphasizing communicative competence. Victoria and South Australia are co-operating in the developing of Greek for the primary school. A start has been made on an Italian curriculum for the primary school. The relationship of mother tongue development to learning a second language has been explored. But apart from matters of curriculum development, methodology and organization, there is the enormous question of teacher recruitment and training in a time of falling enrolments and reduced expenditure on education. The future of multiculturalism in schools is dependent upon attitude changes, and programme development but these in turn hang on funding. It is eventually a resource question.

Aboriginal children

The history of the white man's relationship with the Aboriginal people in Australia is encapsulated in the description of Rural Town and its fringe shanty settlement. In the Rural Towns of this continent, Dr Eckermann shows us a group of people who are discriminated against, subject to prejudice, at the bottom of the socio-economic heap. This is one of the worlds they and their children find themselves in. It is not a world designed to meet the needs of children.

The other world is warm and accepting. In particular, it is a world in which mothers bring their children up and try to mould them as good persons. When we examine the concept of the 'good person' we find that he or she is someone whose personal worth is measured in the degree to which he or she discharges obligations to others in a spirit of good will. That concept stands uneasily alongside Rural Towns's concepts of the good person. Where are the competitive drive, the individualistic urge, the obligations to self and self-interests? Nonetheless it is a notion of the good person into which Aboriginal mothers try to mould their children.

The process of socialization into these values is managed by the extended family. Dr Eckermann does not tell us about the competing values of television, the school, teachers and white classmates. One would have thought they were considerable. However, even though there is a clearly established process of socialization by Aboriginal mothers, and the possibility of meeting the child's needs in spite of the hostile second world, there are yet further countervailing influences. For instance, there is ambivalence among the Aboriginal people about their colour. It is not a valued attribute. And these feelings are passed on to children in all sorts of subtle ways. This ambivalence, this sense of confused hurt, is dealt with by the Aboriginal people by excessive criticism of their own people, and ironically, a criticism which is conducted in terms of white stereotypes. Furthermore, the sense of identity which enables the confident socialization of the young is absent in the Aboriginal male. He has lost his sense of competence, his ability to handle the environment. He is powerless, because of his economic and social inadequacy in Rural Town.

Thus, what at first sight might have been a realization of a second and caring world becomes, under these dual circumstances of intense self-criticism and loss of self-esteem, a less than adequate thing. The enjoyment of the second world is limited, one feels, to a brief but happy period between conception and attendance at school.

It is then that Dr Eckermann introduces us to Government, and the Bureaucracies. She demonstrates how, after the acceptance in 1972 of self-determination as a policy, governments and bureaucracies produced a spate of innovations, in education, legal aid, land rights, social services, medical assistance, community liaison, employment services and consultation. These were to be the means by which the Aboriginal people could break out from the prison of Rural Town and its replicas around Australia.

Unfortunately, says Dr Eckermann, it was not as simple as that. In the first place there has been a lack of co-ordination in the various efforts of government with a resultant confusion and overlap, even contradiction, in the objectives of the various endeavours. The world of white Rural Town can only be made more of a place in which Aboriginal children's needs can be met, if at a local level there is an integrated and co-ordinated effort by agencies concerned with education, welfare, health and employment. But efforts are conducted from afar, from Canberra and the capitals, and so much of the money goes into the establishment of bureaucratic systems and the salaries of planners. Fundamentally, Dr Eckermann suggests, agencies do not trust the Aboriginal people to manage their own affairs.

Then again there has been a considerable white backlash, ostensibly based on an argument which queries the relative levels of government support of Aboriginals, unemployed young whites, destitute and poor whites. When there are limited funds and several competing claims, the Aboriginal recipient rapidly becomes the scapegoat, the focus of discontent. Never mind that the real level of funding is only a minor improvement, and that much of it goes into the establishment of systems. And although Dr Eckermann does not specifically say so, we may be certain that some of the backlash springs from fear. The welfare programmes may all suffer from inadequacies of one kind or another, but they are an outward and visible expression of a changed attitude at least at an official level. Additional money, equal pay, drinking rights all add up to an Aboriginal person who is rather more difficult to keep in his place.

Tantalisingly, Dr Eckermann shows us a glimpse of a possible way through. It is apparent that whenever Aboriginal people have been given a chance to say what they meant, and how their preferences and needs might best be met, they have done so, and the subsequent action has resulted in success and an improvement in circumstances. Disconcertingly for bureaucrats and local governments, the decision-making processes employed by Aboriginal people have not been those of committees, minutes, agenda and working papers. Slowly, and gently, it would seem, the people work towards a consensus about a particular course of action, not as a working party producing a service of recommendations, but as an almost organic group involving through frequent discussion the wider Aboriginal community.

That is, where there is bureaucratic trust in the Aboriginal people, where there is a willingness by the white community to recognize the legitimacy of Aboriginal means of working, there is likely to be success. Of course, the matter is more complex than that. Bureaucratic notions of accountability, of cash flows, of good housekeeping, and indeed productivity must be modified. There is in all this a paradox with which Dr Eckermann is reluctant to come to grips. If self-determination by Aboriginals is to be more than a platitude then it must be exemplified in Aboriginals' terms. The criteria of success must be Aboriginal criteria; the processes of decision-making must be Aboriginal. But these criteria, these processes, do not emerge from western notions of efficiency, accountability and productivity upon which a guarantee of continued funding by governments depends. The whole business requires an act of faith and a degree of trust which in my view governments and bureaucracies are incapable of.

Thus Aboriginal affairs are likely to continue in an atmosphere of modified paternalism with occasional brilliant exceptions. In this context it is interesting to note that the Labor Government's plans for unrestricted land rights for the Pitjantjatjara people in South Australia, including total control over entry and mineral rights, are likely to be modified by the newly elected Liberal government by the deletion of mineral rights from the legislation.

While Dr Eckermann's comments upon Rural Town in south-west Queensland appear to be capable of general application, it is important to recognize that policies of governments and agencies should be modified by local circumstances. Aboriginal people are not all the same: they exhibit a wide variety of languages (where those are retained) and cultural traditions. Their relationships to white communities vary from place to place. Therefore, it is important to separate the general observation made by Dr Eckermann from the particular details, especially those of an anecdotal kind based on her field research. If as a majority society we are to develop that necessary trust in the Aboriginal people's capacity for self-determination, it will be likely to develop in relation to particular local endeavours in a climate of understanding free from stereotypes. That is, I am of the view that Aboriginal self-esteem and confidence, without which children's needs will not be met, is likely to develop in small, particular, and local situations under the aegis of broader national policies.

Dr Eckermann tells us that the lack of esteem of the Aboriginal fathers is visited upon their children, that Aboriginal children will not grow up to be autonomous and competent adults unless their people achieve that same autonomy and competence. Child and community are irrevocably bound together, and no amount of effort by church or school or youth clubs will improve the chances of children's needs being met unless Aboriginal needs are met. That is an important insight.

PART 4

Children and Values

Graeme W. Speedy

This chapter is not concerned with the whole range of values as they affect children, but with moral and religious values. Since 1945 many changes in society have brought into question traditional values, particularly moral and religious values. Increasing diversity, challenges to authority, and relativism are three important characteristics of our society today which influence morality and religion.

Any comment about morality and moral standards in Australia is likely to be impressionistic and partisan. There are those who consider that there is a decline in moral standards particularly in personal morality. Others see the same phenomena as an increase in personal choice and morally preferable. Others, again, percieve the behaviour of large corporations and the widening gap between rich and poor in this country and elsewhere as much greater problems of morality than the interpersonal moral issues. There are yet others who do not express any moral concern about personal or social issues but whose philosophy of life appears to be "live and let live". What can be said is that there are wide differences of opinion in Australia concerning what constitutes moral and immoral behaviour at the personal and social level.

Diversity is evident also in religion. More varieties of religions are practised in Australia today than before the Second World War. European migration brought large numbers of migrants from Orthodox and Reformed Churches. Religions such as Mohammedanism, Hinduism and Buddhism now have significant practising groups in Australia. Many people, particularly young people, have become dissatisfied with traditional forms of Western Christianity and are showing interest either in Eastern religions or in cults which are offshoots of Christianity. There is a decline in church-going, but this does not necessarily represent a decline of interest in religion.

Hierarchical patterns of authority are under question. The rights of individuals and the emphasis on personal choice together with moves towards participatory democracy in institutions and in industry has challenged longstanding authority structures. In morality and religion there are challenges to the authority of tradition and institutions.

A concomitant of all of this is a somewhat undefined but pervasive relativism which, in its most naive form, assumes that any belief, opinion or behaviour is as valid as any other. In this context the development of moral and religious values in children is fraught with problems. On the one hand, it seems that the demise of traditional patterns of authority and the broad spectrum of moral and religious beliefs and behaviours in our society render the development of moral and religious values problematic. On the other hand, the present fluid situation may be taken as presenting both a challenge to think more deeply about moral and religious issues and an opportunity to develop a more autonomous approach without issues being predetermined by authority structures.

Values

Many definitions of 'value' have been proposed, and there is no clear consensus. In recent years the work of Milton Rokeach in the area of values has been influential, and he has offered the following definition. "A value is an enduring belief that a specific mode of conduct or end state of existence is personally or socially preferable to an opposite or converse mode of conduct or end state of existence."[1] Thus, honesty may be stated as preferable to dishonesty, happiness to unhappiness. A further important observation which Rokeach makes is that values function in many ways. A value "is a standard that guides and determines action, attitudes towards objects and situations, ideology, presentations of self to others, evaluations, judgements, justifications comparisons of self with others, and attempts to influence others. Values serve adjustive, ego-defensive, knowledge and self-actualizing functions."[2] In brief, values are expressed both as preferred behaviours and as standards that guide our actions.

In considering moral and religious values, it is important to recognize that morality and religion are not the same thing, and that morality is not merely a sub-set of religion nor religion a sub-set of morality. While it is true that a particular religion includes within it an approach to morality, it is also true that morality does not need to be based on religion. It is possible to discuss morality, to make moral judgements, and to behave morally without being related to a particular religion. Because of the different ways in which people understand and use the words 'morality' and 'religion', it is necessary to offer some definition of them before discussing the moral and religious development of children.

Morality

In this century considerable attention has been given by English speaking philosophers to the meaning of moral language. This concern for what counts as moral language does not attempt to define norms or standard of behaviour but only attempts to define what one is doing when using moral language. A.J. Ayer claims that moral language is not about propositions which are true or false. Moral language does not describe anything, it is more like an exclamation. Thus declaring that something is 'right' or 'good' in a moral sense is to express approval for an action.[3] C.L. Stevenson agrees with this, but goes further in suggesting that when we are approving actions we are also, by implication, trying to persuade people to behave in the same way. Thus, moral language is an expression of approval, but also a mode of persuasion.[4] R. Hare has taken the view that moral language is prescriptive, that is to say, it is an attempt to prescribe behavour.[5]

Other approaches to morality attempt to define criteria for establishing norms or standards for moral behaviour. Of two long-standing interpretations of morals, one has focused on consideration of consequences and the other on consideration of obligations. The former argues that morality is a matter of calculating the consequences of one action rather than another, and opting for that action which is likely to produce a greater good, however the good may be defined. The latter argues that moral obligations are such that we should fulfil them regardless of consequences.

In practice we do not opt for either consequences or obligation as if we are forced to consider one or the other. We tend to make decisions without much conscious effort, and for the most part we tacitly accept principles such as truth-telling, promise-keeping, and honesty as appropriate ways of behaving in relationships. In some cases we deny principles because of possible consequences. In doing so we may be acting out of our own interests and not out of the interests of others, although our own interests and the interests of others cannot always be clearly distinguished. If morality has as an essential component of regard for the interests of others, then acting in a purely self-interested way may be considered prudent, but not moral.

Two other aspects of morality are the relationship between law and morality and the relationship between custom and morality. Some acts, for instance murder, may be judged both legally and morally wrong. Others, such as parking offences, may be illegal but not immoral. Still others may be morally wrong, but not legally wrong, for example deception in interpersonal relationships. There is an overlap between law and morality. Much of our legal system is an embodiment of behaviour that is morally disapproved and socially disruptive. Changes in understanding morality also bring about changes in law. On the one hand, we have witnessed changes in the law with respect to the decriminalization of some aspects of homosexuality. In this case the move is towards a moral rather than a legal situation. On the other hand, laws have recently been passed to make it an offence to discriminate, with respect to employment on grounds of sex. In this case the move is towards legal sanctions to support a moral position.

There is an overlap between custom and morality. Confusion exists when these are identified. One of the major causes of relativism has been the identification in different cultures of modes of behaviour accepted in one culture but seen as morally offensive in another. This has led to the naive assumption that morality is merely culture-bound and therefore a matter of opinion. The diversity in our society may tend to reinforce this notion. In practice, we do not really believe this. In our own culture the burning of so-called witches, the use of child labour in mines, and the keeping of slaves were all accepted practices in their day, but today we condemn these acts as immoral because we believe these are not appropriate ways to treat people. The fact that this behaviour was accepted previously in our culture does not mean that it was ever morally appropriate. The only possibility, in fact, for moral advancement is a continual reworking of our understanding of what it means to be human and to respect human beings. This involves examination of both interpersonal and broader social issues. Focus on matters such as alienation, poverty, discrimination by sex, race or colour call attention not only to personal problems, but also to social structures.

Whereas the general proposition that morality has to do with what is fitting for persons individually and collectively may be acceptable, there is by no means agreement about the grounds on which morality and moral decisions rest. Some considered or assumed view of the world underlies a person's approach to morality. Morality may rest for instance on a religious, ideological, or philosophical basis. Thus, for example, Christianity (as a religion), Marxism (an ideology), Existentialism (as a philosophy) all have implications for morality, that is, for what is considered fitting for persons individually and socially. However, there is not necessarily agreement about moral issues nor about moral decisions among Christians or Marxists or Existentialists. In Christianity, for instance, criteria such as 'the Will of God' or 'the Love of God or neighbour', do not give clear directions on specific moral issues, such as abortion or involvement in war. It is of the essence of morality that it involves choice in situations of conflict and these choices are not always clear cut however much we would like them to be so. "The moral of life is an adventure not only in detail, but also in principle."[6]

Religion

Religion is a persisting phenomenon in history and culture. It is easier to define the marks of a religion than to define religion in a generic sense. In recent years, particularly through the writings of Ninian Smart, the use of the number of categories to define the characteristics of a religion have been widely adopted.[7]

Religions can be seen as having six dimensions. The first is a set of *doctrines* or beliefs which represent the intellectual expression of the religion. Thus, in Christianity, the doctrine of the Trinity is an attempt to formulate the Christian understanding of God. Secondly, religions have *myths*. In ordinary usage, to say something is a 'myth' is to say it is false. In religion the word 'myth' has quite a different meaning. It is meant to depict in some way the relationship between the human realm and the realm of the transcendent. In Judaism, the deliverance of the people of Israel from Egypt functions as a myth in that it symbolizes the relationship of the people to the purpose of God. Thirdly, religions have a *moral* dimension. In Christianity this is not worked out in any systematic way, but can be found in the teachings contained in the Gospels and other New Testament writings.

Religions have a *ritual* dimension which is expressed in forms of worship and in associated rites related to major events in life such as birth, marriage and death. Religion has an *experiential* dimension in that the intention of a religion is to involve people in feelings and experiences which confirm their attachment to the faith. The other dimensions contribute to the experiential dimension and the experiential dimension in turn modifies them. Finally, religion has a *social* dimension in that it gives rise to a community of some kind in which the meaning of the rites, beliefs, myths, and moral perspectives are experienced and shared.

The six dimensions described are also useful for examining ideologies which are 'world views' in competition with religion. Thus Marxism, although it is not strictly speaking a religion, in that it does not have like most religions an other worldly transcendent reference, can be looked at from the point of view of the dimensions of religion.

The definition of a religion by the six characteristics is useful for descriptive purposes. However, it is more difficult to offer a definition of religion itself. The description of religion as 'ultimate concern' based on the writings of Paul Tillich has been widely used. The problem with the definition is that it is too all-embracing because any ultimate concern becomes incorporated into religion by definition. It is possible to conceive a person's ultimate concern being the accumulation of money, or the pursuit of political power, or the single-minded search for a cure for cancer. It is difficult to conceive how these ultimate concerns can bear the description of religion. It is possible only by such a stretching of the definition as to render it unusable.

In some definitions of religious education a spin off from the idea of 'ultimate concern' has been the description of religious experience as "ordinary experience interpreted in depth". This phrase suffers from the same problem of generality as the term 'ultimate concern' itself. What is one to include under the term 'ordinary experience'? Is developing friendships an ordinary experience? Or doing schoolwork? Or playing sport? What would it mean to interpret these experiences in depth? What criteria is to be used to give definition to the word 'depth'? It is by no means clear that the idea of religious experience as ordinary experience interpreted in depth is meaningful. One possible way of rescuing the idea of religion as 'ultimate concern' is to draw some kind of limits in order to save the expression from being trivialized. The term may be useful if it is meant to convey the way in which religion functions in providing a framework for interpreting human existence.

One thing which religions have in common is that each, in its own way, offers a view of the meaning of life in the face of major 'boundary situations'. This has been expressed in the following terms:

> We take it as widely assumed that religion 'functions' to resolve certain distinctive problems in the lives of individuals and social groups. These problems are experienced as anxieties about certain 'boundary situations' in human life and experience, and they are encountered at at least three points: (1) in trying to make sense out of the obstinate inexplicability of the natural world, its existence and purpose, its processes and events; (2) in trying to cope with the obdurate presence of human suffering and death; and (3) in trying to live with and manage the irresolvable ambiguities and puzzles inherent in human conduct.[8]

Thus, these boundary situations have to do with perennial questions, such as: Who am I? What are we here for? What is life all about? Why is there suffering? Is death the end? How should I live?

How are moral and religious values acquired?

Whatever position one may take in the argument concerning the biological determinants of human behaviour, the moral and religious values acquired result from the interaction of the person with other persons in a particular environment. There is a wide range of social relationships which influence the moral and religious values of children, but it is inappropriate to conceive children as simply being passive recipients in this process. The child constructs his own world, and is not simply acted on by others.

The family is profoundly influential.[9] All families are engaged in the development of moral values in their children whether they are aware of it or not. Rewards and punishments are handed out for behaviour which is approved or disapproved by parents, by other adults, or by older brothers and sisters. Some of this is in the nature of learning social graces and etiquette. Some of it has a clear moral component. The standards of parents with respect to such things as truth-telling, promise-keeping, honesty, and concern for the welfare of other are evidenced by the way in which parents endeavour, through example and through reward and punishment, to guide children's behaviour. Most of this is done as a matter of course without much conscious thought or planning.

The pattern of family relationships itself is a powerful influence on moral development. Thus, if concern for each other is expressed within the family this begins to be internalized in the child. If rules are applied without consideration of circumstances, then the child begins to internalize that rules are absolute. If rules are applied but modified according to the circumstances, then the child begins to internalize that rules are not absolute. If there appear to be no rules, and parental behaviour is capricious, then the child begins to internalize that morality is subject to whim. It is in the intimate relationships that the child begins to learn compassion or callousness, prejudice or tolerance, generosity or meanness.

With respect to religion, it may not be quite as evident that all families are engaged in influencing religious values. If the broad definition of religion as 'ultimate concern' is used, it must be conceded that children are in some way exposed to family values about what is ultimately important, and this may be seen as money, position, concern for others, or something else. However, since the broad definition virtually leaves nothing out, it is not very useful. If religion is concerned with boundary situations, then the way in which families handle these may be seen as influencing children's religious values. The extent to which particular families are exposed to suffering and death, or consider openly matters of perplexity concerning life and conduct, varies greatly. It is possible for a child to have little or no exposure in the family situation to religious values arising from encountering boundary situations.

Outside the family, the school occupies more of a child's time than any other group or organization. In recent years it has been increasingly recognized that schools influence the development of moral and other values in children not only through what is taught in formal lessons, but through the whole structure of organizational life and patterns of social relationships. Thus, schools influence the development of attitudes, beliefs and values by the way in which they establish and enforce rules, hand out rewards and punishments, distribute authority and decision-making powers among staff, students, parents and administrators, express concern for individuals, stress conformity, encourage experimentation.

Specific attention to moral education in schools in Australia varies greatly and has not been characteristic of schools in the past, particularly government schools. While moral issues relating to personal and social problems have always been present in some areas of study, such as social studies and literature, teachers have not usually sought to deal with the moral aspects consciously. This is an area undergoing considerable change and an area of increasing debate.

As to religious values, the denominational school has an unequivocal right to influence the religious values of the children attending. Where parents choose to send children to these schools, whatever particular reasons they may have for sending them, they accept, at least implicitly, the religious purposes for which school is said to exist. Until recent years, it has been customary in government schools for clergy and laity of the various churches to conduct religious instruction within the framework of the laws and regulations for each state. From the point of view of influencing religious values, traditional religious instruction has been a two-edged sword. While some good results may be claimed, there are also children who have been negatively influenced about religion.

The influence of mass media, particularly television, on the development of moral and religious values in children is not well documented. More is known of the viewing habits of children than of the actual effect of viewing. Many children are regular viewers of programmes portraying violence and sex. They are exposed to advertisements promoting the desirability of the consumption of products of one kind or another. Such constant viewing may influence attitudes and values, often in ways which are undesirable. There is growing awareness of a need to improve the quality of children's television, and renewal of licence hearings in Australia have lead to the setting of higher standards for children's programmes in the late afternoon. However, what children watch is determined in the home, and that cannot be legislated by licence tribunals.

Moral development and moral education

The view taken thus far has concentrated on some of the social factors which influence moral and religious development. An influential theory of moral development at the present time is that of Piaget.[10] This approach considers stages of moral development related largely to cognitive development. Before examining it, it is worth noting that in considering moral values, moral development and moral judgement we are considering not simply a person thinking but also a person feeling and acting. Norman Bull, whose work springs from Piaget, makes the point that moral judgements are not purely cognitive, but that moral thinking is emotionally toned. He comments: "The responses of children of all ages to moral situations involving what they regard as the greatest evils are far from being coldly cerebral." A boy aged nine years, describing guilt, says, "Your mind goes all sort of beating fast". A boy of 15 years give a terse definition of conscience: "Every rotten thing you do sticks in your mind."[11]

Piaget's work in moral development was published in 1932. His interpretation of moral judgement is related to his general theory of cognitive development. The young child is egocentric and therefore not able to think in terms of social consequences. From about age seven the child is able to recognize points of view different from his own, and in the field of interpersonal relationships begins to take the role of the other. Thus there is an increase in social awareness. The adolescent can reflect on human relationships and consider principles.

The main features of Piaget's theory about moral judgement centre around what he describes as the two moralities of children. The first of these is moral realism, the morality of restraint. This is characteristic of the young child. Moral rules are external and rooted in authority with the consequence that their application tends to be literal and socially insensitive. The second morality is the morality of co-operation or reciprocity. It is clear that this is not possible until there is an awareness of other points of view and the growing realization that moral rules grow out of human relationships. Thus, as this morality develops it brings with it the realization that morality is not a matter of obeying authorities but of developing mutually agreed principles. These two moralities are different and in the view of Piaget they exist side by side in the growing child. He sees moral realism as necessary but not desirable, and considers that this form of morality is a hindrance to development. Growth towards moral autonomy springs from the morality of co-operation.

Currently the most influential work in moral development is probably that of Lawrence Kohlberg.[12] Kohlberg's studies in moral reasoning have covered a wide age range of children and have been applied across different cultures. He has arrived at a sequence of developmental stages based on Piaget but differing in some important aspects. Kohlberg identifies six stages of moral development which can be broken down into three different levels, each of which has two stages. In brief, his levels and stages are as follows:

Level I Moral value resides in external, quasi-physical happenings, in bad acts, or in quasi-physical needs, rather than in persons and standards.

Stage 1 *Punishment and obedience*: Follows rules and defers to superiors to avoid trouble.

Stage 2 *Personal usefulness*: Follows rules and conforms in order to obtain rewards.

Level II Moral value resides in performing good or right rules, in maintaining the conventional order and the expectancies of others.

Stage 3 *Approval seeking*: Good boy–good girl orientation. Pleases or helps others to get approval or avoid disapproval.

Stage 4 *Law and order*: Orientation to doing duty and to showing respect for authority and maintaining the given social order for its own sake. Moral decisions justified on the basis of fixed rules.

Level III Moral value resides in conformity to moral principles that seem true or valid apart from the authority of the person holding those principles.

Stage 5 *Social contract*: Duty is defined in terms of contract, general avoidance of violation of the will or rights of the majority will or welfare. Laws can be challenged when they violate more general principles.

Stage 6 *Conscience or principle*: Orientation to principles of choice involving appeal to logical universality and consistency—general ethical principles that apply everywhere.

Kohlberg believes that these stages are progressive, universal, and invariant, but that not many people reach stages five and six. It has been argued, however, that there is insufficient evidence to substantiate the universality of the model for all cultures.

Kohlberg movea from theory to practice, and educational programmes in moral education are being devised on the basis of his research. In general, the educational process involves group discussion about moral dilemmas. The teacher or parent needs to be able to recognize children's responses as reflecting their level of moral reasoning. Discussion is so arranged as to encourage students to raise their level of moral reasoning by one stage.

Because of the growing importance being given to Kohlberg's theory and its educational implications it is worthwhile to note some of the objections which are being raised. Firstly, he takes the position with respect to moral principles in that he chooses justice ("treat every many equally") as his ultimate moral principle which, he believes, is universal. His opting for justice as the basic universal moral principle can only be done at the expense of ignoring other possible alternatives such as utilitarianism. Secondly, it has been argued that the universal nature of the principle of justice is problematic, but that even if it were to be acknowledged we do not have any accepted content defining what it means to 'treat every man equally'. Thirdly, he ignores the affective side of morality in his concentration on the cognitive. Fourthly, it is not clear whether he is claiming that higher stage reasoning is not only different, but morally better than lower stage reasoning. Finally, since most people do not get beyond stage four it would seem important to get as many people to that stage as possible rather than attempting stages five and six which seem unattainable by most people. In listing objections to Kohlberg the intention is to show that there are unresolved issues which indicate the need for caution in adopting the theory into educational practice.

While not identifying stages of development, a contemporary approach to moral development which has influenced educational programmes in recent years is the values clarification movement. Values clarification had its origins in the work of Louis Raths in the United States and has been carried on particularly by Sidney Simon, Merrill Harmin and Howard Kirschenbaum. In the book *Values and Teaching* a theory of values is proposed which focuses not on substantive values such as honesty, truthfulness and so on, but on the process of valuing.[13] This process is based on seven criteria, all of which must be present if something is to be defined as a value. The seven criteria relate to the activities of choosing, prizing and acting.

Choosing	(1)	freely
	(2)	from alternatives
	(3)	after thoughtful consideration of consequences
Prizing	(4)	cherishing, being happy with the choice
	(5)	willing to affirm the choice publicly
Acting	(6)	doing something with the choice
	(7)	repeatedly, in some pattern of life.

Attitudes, beliefs, goals, aspirations, hopes, purposes, feelings, and interests are not themselves values but point to values. While the approach is about values in a general sense, the major thrust is in the area of moral values.

A wide range of strategies and techniques have been devised to enable children and adolescents to express their beliefs, opinions and feelings, and to be exposed to the viewpoints of others. Again, because of the wide influence of this movement some of the objections to values clarification should be noted. One objection is moral relativism. The approach does not overtly promote substantive values, but sets up procedures through which people can clarify their own values. This approach is potentially completely relativistic. Stewart comments about values clarification being a case of absolute relativism.

> The basic values clarification premise can be fairly and concisely presented as: All value statements are relative—except the following: (1) this basic statement; (2) those essential for values clarification theory and methodology; (3) those proclaimed by values clarification writers; (4) those deemed absolute by groups or organizations which want to use values clarification but keep their own values systems intact, e.g. Christian educators, schools, and others.

A second objection is that values clarification is superficial in that it rarely leads to an indepth examination of values, but looks at opinions and feelings and frequently deals with trivial matters. Thirdly, values clarification is concerned too much with techniques and strategies with a focus on issues and too little with the crucial matter of the underlying structure of thinking and valuing. Fourthly, there is an emphasis and reliance on peer pressure which tends to coercion and is therefore counter-productive to the intention of values clarification.

One of the difficulties in using values clarification is the extent to which the techniques and strategies are suitable for use with children as against their suitability for adolescents. Kirschenbaum in rethinking the seven processes originally put forward believes that there are five dimensions to values clarification—thinking, feeling, choosing, communicating, acting. These five dimensions, however, do not represent a theoretical justification for values clarification, they merely describe a set of human activities.

Who should be responsible?

Who should be responsible for moral development in children? In our society the primacy of the family is not likely to be challenged as being the chief setting where children's moral values should be developed. If this is so, it raises the question about ways in which the family might be helped to fulfil its purpose. Opportunities need to be provided for parent education in the moral development of children. While recognizing the problems and limitations in both Kohlberg's approach and Values Clarification, parents could be taught to understand and use these approaches. One problem is by whom, and with what resources is such a task to be undertaken.

The role of organized religion and the church are less clear. In our society the Christian church has traditionally been seen as a moral force in the community. Within the churches and other religious groups there are many points of view on moral issues. That these groups should influence their own members with respect to moral issues is to be expected. That they should attempt to influence the wider community is legitimate, in that any groups in a democratic pluralist society should have the right to be heard, to endeavour to persuade others to their point of view on moral and other issues.

The role of the school in moral education in a formal sense is not clear. There is no agreement as to whether schools should be directly involved. On the one hand, a combination of factors such as fear of indoctrination, of intrusion into areas seen as the prerogative of the family, of doubts about the ability of some teachers to handle controversial issues, lead some members of the community to wish to keep moral education out of the schools. On the other hand, a combination of factors including doubt as to whether families are taking responsibility for moral education, and acceptance of the school as fulfilling a broad educational role lead others to promote the role of the school in moral education. Teachers and administrators in schools find themselves under great pressure as they face conflicting demands for greater emphasis on literacy and numeracy, retention of traditional subject areas and the introduction of new areas such as health education, legal education, career education, religious education, consumer education and so on.

The school is engaged in moral education indirectly through the human relationships and structures of the institution. Issues relating to personal and social morality cannot really be avoided in the study of society and environment. The issue is whether schools should be encouraged to move in a more planned way into areas related to moral education, and if so in what ways this might be done. Who is to decide how far a school should go in moral education? Should moral education be taught as a separate subject or should issues be dealt with in the context of other subjects? How does one determine what is suitable for children in the primary school and what is suitable for adolescents in the secondary school? Is a teacher to endeavour to maintain a neutral position while encouraging discussion of moral issues with students? Is neutrality possible? To what extent should the school be concerned with moral reasoning and moral judgement? With expressing feelings about moral issues? With encouraging action? To what extent should schools treat all moral points of view as acceptable?

This last question raises the matter of moral relativism. Are there any moral values which all people should hold? Are there particular moral values which schools should aim to foster? Many individual schools and school systems publish statements of aims which often include specific reference to particular values. It is assumed that these values have wide acceptance in the community. It is a large step, however, from a statement of aims, even if these aims are accepted, to the translation of these aims into the structure and programmes of schools. It is at the point of translation into practice that parents are likely to express their approval or opposition, rather than to the general principle that there are certain moral values such as honesty and compassion which are worthwhile.

Religious development, like moral development, is concerned with the whole person thinking, feeling and acting. The most influential study in the field of religious development from the point of view of cognitive development continues to be that conducted by Ronald Goldman in the 1960s. This study, like that of Bull and Kohlberg in moral development, is based on Piaget's model of cognitive development.[14] Adopting the method of clinical interview, Goldman used three pictures and three biblical stories with a sample of 200 children aged 6, 9, 13 and 16 years. The three pictures were of a family entering church, a child praying beside his or her bed, a child looking at a mutilated bible. The three stories used were Moses and the Burning Bush, the Crossing of the Red Sea, and The Temptations of Jesus. Goldman concluded that the stages of religious thinking followed the Piagetian scheme, but he identified two additional stages, one between the pre-operational and the concrete operation stages, and the other between the concrete operations and the formal operation stages.

Michael Grimmitt has characterized these five stages as follows.[15]

The first to about age seven is a *stage of pre-religious thought* in which the child thinks of religion on the same level as fairy tale. God, Father Christmas and fairies are on an equal footing; prayer is magical. The second stage, *Sub-Religious Thought Stage I*, occurs about ages 7–9. God is seen as superhuman; Jesus and God are confused; prayer is egocentric and materialistic; the Bible is literally true. *Sub-Religious Thought Stage II* covers ages about 9–11. God's external appearance is less important, physical ideas about God persist, but a supernatural emphasis is emerging; there is intellectual confusion over God being everywhere and in one place at the same time; and there is awareness of conflict between religious ideas such as miracles and the day to day world. Stage four from about age 11–13 is *Personal Religious Thought Stage I*. The problem of dualism remains; this world and the world of religion are different; there is still a tendency to think of God in Heaven. The final stage, *Personal Religious Thought Stage II*, from about age 13 onwards marks the period of abstract thought. Thus, God is unseen and unseeable; there is a growing recognition of metaphorical and poetic truth.

The study illustrates that there is a developmental sequence in religious thinking; but there is no guarantee that everyone will arrive successfully at the stage of abstract thinking about religion. Children have difficulty developing religious concepts and the stage of formal operations is late in developing in this field. Why is this so? Some of the failure may be attributed to poor teaching. While some allowance can be made for inadequate teaching, a major difficulty arises from the nature of religious language itself. Goldman has been criticized for drawing conclusions about religious concepts on the basis of responses to three pictures, and in particular, responses to the three biblical stories. He has shown the difficulties children have in coping with the symbolic meaning of biblical stories. The inability of children to distinguish the literal from the symbolic and the possible rejection of religion because thinking is frozen at a concrete level is a salutary warning to those who are engaged in religious education.

Religious language poses special problems. Ian Ramsey speaks about the "logical oddness" of religious language.[16] It has the same grammatical structure as ordinary language but it carries it in the meaning of 'discernment' and 'commitment'. There are two reasons for dwelling on the problem of religious language. The first is to indicate that the nature of religious language poses special problems associated with the religious development of children from the point of view of cognitive development. The second is to show that religious language having to do with 'discernment' and 'commitment' is expressive of the whole person thinking, feeling and acting.

It was suggested above that the domain of religion includes

attempts to come to terms with the boundary situations of human existence. While these boundary situations can be approached from the point of view of psychology, sociology or any other form of thought and knowledge, the religious explanation has its own power. That is not to say that everyone finds the explanatory or convincing power of religion satisfying, but those who do see it as a holistic interpretation involving thought, feelings and action. It is the importance of feelings and action in religious development which frequently get overlooked if attention is exclusively focused on cognitive development. Violet Madge gave attention to the affective component in religious development in *Children in Search of Meaning*.[17] Drawing on her own experience as a primary school teacher, on reports of student teachers, and autobiographical reports, she indicated the importance of feelings of trust, security, awe, and wonder in the religious development of young children. N.K. Paffard, in England, using a questionnaire with 400 sixth form students and university undergraduates, found many instances of respondents recalling "transcendent experiences", such as feelings of "oneness", "ecstacy", "joy", "awe". Most of the experiences reported were from adolescence rather than childhood. In view of the emotional heightening at the adolescent stage, such experiences may not be surprising. Nevertheless, just how these experiences are to be interpreted is a matter of dispute. There appears to be little study of the religious development of children and adolescents from the point of view both of the development and sustaining of religious emotions such as awe and reverence, and of religious commitment.[18]

The development of a sense of wonder and awe in young children is often accomplished by parents and teachers who are themselves sensitive to life and its mysteries. This is often achieved by using the experience of natural phenomena such as contact with plants and animals and by the encouragement of imagination, and empathy in relationships. What we do not know in any detail is why these religious emotions fail to develop further.

As our culture is dominated by science and technology, and pervaded by materialism, it may very well be that the widening experience of children leads them to an acceptance of this dominant view of the world, as this may appear to them to be what life is really about. While confusion within religion itself over the literal and the symbolic contributes to the confusion of the growing child, the whole situation is exacerbated by the assumption that religion is to be measured against its conformity or otherwise to a scientific world view. Children are confronted by and large with a unidimensional world which excludes the religious dimension. But it is evident from the growth of interest in sects, cults, and a wide variety of religions, that people are not satsified with this unidimensional view. Unfortunately, their education and upbringing give many people little in the way of clues for making sense of religious values.

Who should be responsible for the development of religious values? As with moral values, the initial responsibility could be seen by most people as residing primarily in the family. Again, the same problem emerges with responsibility for moral development. What kind of help do parents receive to carry out this responsibility? For the most part, there is a significant difference in the discharge of parental responsibility for religion as compared with morality. The difference is that parents who see religious values as important tend to be associated with the local congregation of their particular persuasion. There is, therefore, an existing frame of reference from within which parents can operate. The extent to which they are actually supported in their task is important. In addition, these parents are unlikely to separate religion and morality. On the grounds that a particular religion has within it an approach to moral issues, parents concerned with religion are more likely to bring these two elements together in some relationship.

To what extent should the church be responsible for the development of religious values? In this context the term 'church' needs to be understood to include any group of persons of a particular religious persuasion be it Christian, Mohammedan, Hindu or other. Any church in this sense is concerned to influence the religious development of those who belong to it. Induction into a particular faith is carried out through the participation of children in the rites, educational programmes and other activities of the church. The broader question is the extent to which any church should expect to be able to influence the development of religious values of the rest of the community. The same applies here as in the area of morality. As voluntary organizations, churches have a right to persuade others to their point of view within the framework provided by society and its laws.

To what extent should the schools be involved in the development of religious values? As with the area of moral values this is a matter of considerable dispute. Denominational schools have that right by virtue of their religious affiliation. The situation is different with government schools. In Australia, the separation of church and state has traditionally excluded the use of schools to foster the development of religious values in the sense of fostering the establishment of a particular religion. In the general sense of the development of religious emotions, such as awe and reverence, the school has not been excluded as this has not been seen as the fostering of a particular religion.

A common pattern in Australia until recent years has been for clergy and laity to give religious instruction on the school premises, in some cases in official school time. This instruction had tended to be denominational in character. In recent years a significant change has begun to take place, in principle if not in practice. Official inquiries into religious education in government schools have been conducted in almost all Australian states in the past decade. Most have recommended the offering of religious education as part of the normal school curriculum.

It is generally conceded that government schools should not influence students to adopt a particular religion but should expose students to religion as a phenomenon of society. The descriptive and empathetic approach to religion in government schools is not as problematic as the curricula which focus on the view of religion as 'ultimate concern'. The problem with this definition has already been alluded to. In practice it leads to inclusion under the rubric of religion of any studies related to self-knowledge and human relationships. Such studies are clearly not the exclusive prerogative of religion. Religion is a legitimate component in these studies but they should be undertaken from an interdisciplinary point of view.

The debate about how far government schools should be involved in religion and the development of religious values is not finished. The next decade is likely to produce further changes in the role of schools in the development of both moral and religious values. A major issue in the area of both moral education and religious education is the decision about what is appropriate for children in primary schools as distinct from what is appropriate for adolescents in secondary schools.

Practical Possibilities for Parents, Teachers and Planners

David R. Merritt

For people involved in the practical everyday business of being parents, teachers, or planners of services to children, the forces which shape children's values are frequently matters for bewilderment and even resentment. Adults are influenced by most of the same factors that impinge on children. Adults, however, are more aware of change, insecurity about old certainties, and the influence of such recent social forces as television, radio and films which are very much beyond their influence or control. To be an adult is not to be in a position of command over the forces shaping values, either one's own or those of children in family, school or community. Today children are exposed to a much wider range of alternative values than in previous generations. Technology expressed in mass media is probably the major new factor. This is a relatively recent development and has introduced a new situation not yet understood. For example, the debate about the influence of television on children is far from conclusive.

On the basis of studies and contemporary theory, no one can be more than mildly confident in suggesting practical programmes to shape or strengthen values. Using available theories and looking back from adults or adolescents to their childhood, it is possible to describe a development process, but that is a far cry from being able to plan for children in one's family, school class, or community, confident that significant values education will take place. Education generally and values education in particular is a much more tentative enterprise than that. It is not surprising that some parents and teachers have chosen to opt out of major attempts to influence values. Australian state education has generally been reluctant to include socially contentious issues in school courses. An unfortunate consequence has been that most politics, religion, morality and sexuality have been removed from school subjects—a practice likely to make education seem anaemic and irrelevant to much of what concerns young people and gives life richness. Parents sometimes feel out of their depth with children's and young people's fashions, fads, and morality, and either wring their hands silently on the side lines or put a bold face on 'leaving them to make their own decisions'.

It is important, however, not to exaggerate the actual position of most children in our society. While it is true that there is an increased range of values in Australia today compared with earlier in this century, most children still grow up with their early and most formative years strongly influenced by a very small group of significant adults, usually one or two parents, who express a limited range of values for a child. It is true that there is greater diversity in the total social environment and this impinges on very young children extensively, for example through television programmes. It is not necessarily true, however, that a child's immediate values environment does not have a coherent shape. An analogy with language will illustrate the point. Since the Second World War there has been a big increase in the number of languages spoken in Australia. But this does not mean that any particular child necessarily grows up in a linguistically pluralist environment. Indeed, few Australian children learn to speak two or more languages. In the broader values area we simply do not know yet how influential this early selective environment is for people who will live their adolescent and adult lives more conscious of the alternative values held by others in the world around them.

On the whole the evidence seems to favour the view that continuity factors are stronger for most children and young people than discontinuity factors. In other words, most children share most of their parents' beliefs and ideas of what is desirable and what really matters in life. However the specific problems parents and educators face about values are largely of two kinds. The first is the difficulty of maintaining one's own beliefs and standards of behaviour in the face of the different ideas and practices of other people. The second is the problem of deciding what attitude to adopt to views and practices that differ from one's own. Examples of areas of widespread confusion and perplexity are sexual practices and standards, the use of drugs, and the practice of religion.

There has been strong recognition in recent years that most of children's values are not taught but learned. They are acquired through participation in groups of people significant to the child—family, other relatives, same-age friends, church, clubs. In schools this insight has strengthened the conviction that teachers, the school as a system, and classes as groups, provide examples or models of value positions. There is a curriculum much broader and more pervasive than the subjects listed on daily school timetables. Similarly, the place of children in the church's total activities has been recognized at least as significant as participation in a special programme established for education in religious faith. Sunday schools have an educational role but they are to be seen as significant as a particular learning opportunity within a broader educational strategy that is about people sharing their beliefs and expressing a faith in their worship, fellowship and community service. In families, parents are recognized as the first and most formative teachers of children, not because of formal teaching skills but because the nature of their relationship to young children is profoundly influential. Everything a family or a church or a school is and does teaches—not just those programmes labelled education. Children learn values whether or not adults set out to teach them values.

Thus attention to social environments, the formative influence of significant adults, and the expression of roles in groups to which a child belongs, must continue to be matters of priority attention for anyone concerned with the values of children. In addition there are a number of strategies that can be carefully planned as values education. There seem to me to be three lines of action that are useful as guides to people concerned for children's values in Australia at this time.

1. *To express and affirm one's own values.* It is part of the development of one's own life as an adult and a valuable contribution to children to express or support some things that are held to be important for our lives. Such ideas of what matters will influence the choices we make, the way we spend our money, the groups of people we associate with, the causes we support, the things that make us angry or enthusiastic. Our society generally, and our children in particular, will be poorer if adults as parents, teachers and citizens do not actively embody and promote ideals. Bland, characterless, apathetic adults are a greater threat to children's development than those whose lives express commitment to some significant values.

2. *To provide information about a range of values important in our society.* Every parent, teacher and citizen knows that his or her values are not shared by everyone. Our children have to live in a world of such differences. However much we want them to be persuaded of our particular values, it is clearly essential for them to have some understanding of and tolerance for the different views of others. Indeed in our society there is a range of views on almost all important matters—politics, religion, sexuality, morality, and personal tastes, for example. These differences are an integral part of our cultural and intellectual heritage. It is difficult to conceive of

education in families or schools that did not introduce children sympathetically to a variety of value positions. Some of the fears parents have of this kind of approach could be reduced if the purpose was clearly expressed as understanding others' positions combined with encouragement to affirm and support their own family's values.

One of the objections to this approach has been that there is a virtually limitless range of viewpoints that could be explained. Is it possible to cover the world scene on morality, religion and politics for example? The practical need of children, however, is not to know all the possible alternatives there are, but to know that there are alternatives that are important to others in their immediate environment. Thus a limited range of value positions likely to receive substantial support in our community is a reasonable guide for such values education and provides a feasible and politically acceptable approach for government schools.

There have recently been major advances along these lines in Australian school curricula and in courses for religious education and Christian education. The approach suggested here would allow schools to take a more constructive role than has often been the case in Australia. It would focus attention both on a limited area of consensus about values and on the need to actively teach understanding of a variety of value positions on important issues on which our society is divided. It allows debate about values to continue with attention being given to the content of values and not just to the processes of valuing. These matters are important for our society generally and for the quality of education young Australians receive in particular.

3. *To provide assistance in clarifying values.* It is part of the experience of most adults and children that there are parts of life that are confusing and in which ideas of what is desirable are in conflict. Such areas of life are value rich but unclear. How can people take increasing responsibility for their own lives or choose satisfying lives if they do not sort out in some way what is most important *to them*? It is primarily because this is an acute need that the term 'values clarification' has become so widely used. The term refers to an approach to values education which sets out to help people to become clearer about what is important to them. This approach contrasts with traditional approaches which set out to pursuade a student to accept what is important to the instructor or parents or some group in society.

Taken on its own, values clarification would clearly be an inadequate approach. Children and young people need a great deal of help in discovering what our society's value heritage is. They need to feel the pursuasive force of some of the greatest minds in human history arguing for particular values. Values clarification is not proposed as an alternative to such approaches but as an addition to them. Few people, if any, claim that values clarification is in itself a comprehensive approach to values education. The claim is rather that it is a desirable and effective addition to other approaches—an addition which is especially important in a society which offers so many confusing alternatives. Values clarification provides assistance with the processes of valuing—how people decide what is important to them.

There are clearly powerful pursuasive forces already operating in our families, community organizations, churches and schools that must be recognized as in existence when any parent or teacher considers adopting clarification strategies. Indeed, it is precisely because there are so many conflicting pursuasive forces at work that clarification strategies are needed. Provided this framework continues to be recognized, the theoretical objections to values clarification strategies do not and should not diminish their importance for parents and teachers.

As a parent I could respond to my child's expressed intention about a particular action in one or more of four ways. First, I could attempt pursuasion about better ways of behaving. Second, I could avoid any active response and leave him to his own decisions—and thus refrain from offering assistance on what may well be a confusing and important matter. Third, I could point to examples of people involved in a particular way of behaving and hope that there are also useful 'models' in the lives of parents or other significant adults who may influence the child's decisions. Finally, I could actively assist the child to sort out what is important to him, what his range of possible choices are, and what the consequences of making a particular choice are—that is, I could adopt a clarifying approach. It is simply a fact of experience that the first and third approaches (pursuasion and 'modelling') are in some measure part of the experience of all children, and that the fourth approach (clarification) is a constructive addition to the child's values environment. The clarification approach is supportive of a child, respectful of his or her own dignity and esteem, and frequently has very positive results both in decision-making and building relationships of trust between adults and children.

In summary, practical possibilities for parents and teachers in relation to the values of children are to be found in four courses of action: first, recognition of the strong influence of significant adults and institutions such as family, school and church upon children; second, encouragement to express and affirm one's own values; third, provision of information about a range of values important in our society; and fourth, provision of assistance in clarifying values.

These are useful approaches that deserve priority from parents, teachers of school classes, church education programmes, and workers in other community groups. They deserve support from social planners. These approaches are positive and hopeful. They recognize the diversity of our society without paralyzing action. They are both respectful of our social heritage and open to change. They involve a healthy modesty at a time when there is no solid basis for more grandiose strategies of values education for children. Increasing attention to these priorities by people involved in planning and delivering services to children will be a significant contribution to the development of children in our changing society.

PART 5

Children's Health

Basil S. Hetzel and *Graham V. Vimpani*

The improved health and quality of life of children in the Western world is one of the striking characteristics of the twentieth century.[1] In Australia the most dramatic improvement had largely occurred before 1940, and was mainly due to a reduction of infant mortality (deaths in the first year of life) from more than 100 to around 30 per thousand live births. Deaths of older children had also been more common previously. For instance, in the 1880s of the 90 out of every 100 children born who had survived the first year of life, only 85 reached school-going age and only 78 reached adulthood.[2] The decline in mortality was largely due to improved educational standards amongst mothers, better nutrition, housing and sanitation. It largely preceded the introduction of mass immunization, antibiotics and post-war medical technological advances.[3] Today only about 1.3 per cent of children die during infancy and all but 2 per cent reach adulthood.

The major health problems facing Australian children today are not the infectious diseases of the past but developmental difficulties, congenital defects, behaviour problems, accidents and nutritional disorders, which are influenced by the quality of the child's most intimate environment, whether this is the uterus, the place of birth, the family or the school. Accidents now account for over half the deaths in children of school-going age. Behaviour problems of sufficient severity to require management by professional services probably affect one in ten Australian children. Obesity—one of several major health problems which derive from unhealthy lifestyles—predominantly affects the health of adults, but has its roots in childhood.

In this chapter we examine some of the issues raised by the existence of these contemporary health disorders. To what extent are non-medical and medical influences interwoven as causal factors? Would improved education, better nutrition and altered lifestyles have a greater influence on child health than further refinements in medical technology? How important are health services to the improvement of children's health? Can health services sometimes have a harmful effect on children's health? Do inequalities of access to our health services contribute to some of these problems? Is the traditional personalized medical approach necessarily the most appropriate choice from the available strategies to solve these present day disorders? What other strategies should be considered?

Ecological imbalance is a common causal factor linking many present day problems. There is good evidence that by better application of existing knowledge of the factors causing child 'illth' much more could be done to improve the health of children. We believe that preventive programmes must be broadly based and directed at bringing about health promoting changes in all components of the child's ecosystem if the gap between knowledge and its application is to be closed. This requires directing programmes aimed at reducing harmful interactions between children and their environment at both the individuals at risk—parents and children—and at the community generally, through education and various forms of social and political action.

Strategies of prevention

Preventive programmes are generally thought of as operating at three levels—primary prevention, in which disorders are prevented from occurring at all; secondary prevention, in which attempts are made to detect disorders as soon as possible, particularly at a stage before they cause permanent damage and often before parents have suspected anything is wrong; and tertiary prevention, where the effects of established illness are minimized by effective treatment and rehabilitation of the whole person.

Primary prevention

Illness may be 'prevented' by favourable demographic changes brought about by many related social, economic, political and biological factors which are outside the sphere of influence of traditonal medical intervention. For instance, there is evidence that the decline in deaths in early infancy is partly attributable to a reduction in family size and a decline in the proportion of mothers over the age of 35 giving birth.[4]

Illness can also be prevented by a variety of interventions directed at both an individual and social level which have as their goal the fostering of harmonious, health-promoting relationships between individuals and their environment. An educational strategy aimed at parents and children is often the basis of such programmes, and there is evidence that these programmes can change attitudes. What is less clear, however, is their ability to change behaviour.

Individuals receive many powerful messages from the mass media and particularly the advertising industry which glamorize illness-promoting behaviour; and preventive strategies will remain relatively ineffective unless they counteract these influences.

There is historical evidence to support the efficacy of health education. In the early 1900s, the Infant Welfare movement developed as health workers began to realize that infant deaths from malnutrition and gastroenteritis could be prevented by education of mothers in hygenic feeding practices. Death from these causes is now relatively rare in non-Aboriginal Australian infants. Another example of a primary prevention strategy is immunization. Although many infectious diseases had declined both in frequency and severity before the introduction of specific mass immunization, the virtual elimination of conditions such as poliomyelitis and smallpox can be credited to the effectiveness of immunization.

Secondary prevention

Secondary prevention, the presymptomatic detection of disease, has been one of the most successful strategies of traditional medicine, and it has had important benefits for the health of children. Preventive programmes rely on screening apparently healthy populations known to be at risk for particular disorders by examinations or tests designed to uncover various problems. The most useful definition of screening is "any medical investigation that does not arise from a patient's request for advice for specific complaints".[5]

According to North, to be a suitable target for a screening programme disorders should meet the following criteria:

(i) They must be functionally important health problems
(ii) They must have specific diagnostic criteria
(iii) They must be treatable—not necessarily curable but something can be done to alleviate the problem
(iv) Earlier treatment is more effective than treatment begun later on the basis of discovery through symptoms
(v) Detection is possible soon enough to allow effective treatment
(vi) Adequate diagnostic and treatment facilities are available
(vii) An effective screening test exists which is of low cost and high accuracy (that is, it usually correctly identifies both those with and without the condition)
(viii) The costs to those who are incorrectly classified by the screening test must be minimal.[6]

North reviewed some twenty conditions ranging from phenylketonuria (a disorder causing mental retardation) to abnormal behaviour, for which such screening programmes have either been advocated or introduced. Whilst many improvements in child health can be attributed to the successful implementation of screening programmes during pregnancy, the new-born period and later childhood, the importance of some newer screening programmes which have been advocated or implemented has yet to be determined. Some conditions do not satisfy all of the criteria for screening since there are still unanswered questions about the natural history of the condition and the effectiveness of treatment. Issues related to some of the more controversial programmes will be discussed later in the sections on perinatal health and child development.

Tertiary prevention

Tertiary prevention is concerned with reducing the effects of hospitalization on young children, as well as reducing the social and psychological effects of chronic illness and disability on the child and his family. Thus there is a growing awareness that bereavement suffered by parents following a stillbirth or the death of a child, if incompletely resolved, can interfere with their ability to care for other or subsequent children.[7] Health professionals are becoming more involved in helping parents to work through the mourning process to prevent such sequelae.

Problems of perinatal health

The perinatal period extends from the twentieth week of pregnancy to the end of the first month of life. About 18 in every 1 000 Australian children born die during this interval, either before birth or shortly after it. This is more than the number who die in the whole of the next 25 years. Over the past 40 years the number of perinatal deaths has fallen consistently, with the most dramatic decline being registered among older children. To what extent can the improved outlook be attributed to demographic changes in the child-bearing population? To what extent is it due to improvements in medical care? How important have preventive programmes been? What are the prospects for future improvement?

Improving mortality experiences have been accompanied by an increased concern for the quality of life of the survivors—a significant but gratifyingly decreasing proportion of whom are left with residual and often permanent handicap resulting from congenital abnormalities (present in about 2 per cent of all births) and abnormal pregnancy or delivery, or other illness arising in the first few days of life.

Demographic changes

Demographic shifts in the characteristics of child-bearing women and families in post-war Australia have been considerable. In South Australia, for instance, women are in general postponing the start of their families, giving birth to fewer children and completing their families earlier than in former years. In 1977 only 4 per cent of all births were to women aged over 35 compared to 8.6 per cent a decade earlier. In 1977 only 1 per cent of births were to women with five or more previous legitimate births compared to 4.4 per cent in 1966. Birth rates, apart from an initial rise in younger women following the Second World War, have declined steadily in all maternal age groups—except the youngest—to levels which in 1977 were between 9 per cent (in women aged 45–49) and 70 per cent (in women aged 20–29 years) of the rates 30 years earlier.

Both medical and social factors have contributed to this decline. The widespread practice of effective contraception, and the ready availability of therapeutic abortion, have been partly responsible for the rapidity of the most recent decline, particularly in younger women, but it is clear that family size had been declining for many years prior to this. An equally important factor, has been the wish of many women to pursue a career other than motherhood. Many reasons underlie this; they include a growing desire among women to be allowed to exercise their rights to self-fulfilment, rising educational standards, and the pressures placed upon families to conform to the living standards of their neighbours in a materialistic society. There is evidence from mortality studies in several countries that the demographic changes of themselves have resulted in a declining number of perinatal deaths, and that they have contributed to the reduction in numbers of children with long term handicaps.

There have been other demographic changes in the last decade which are more worrying, since from available evidence they are more likely to work in the opposite direction and cause increased death and sickness rates. These include a rising proportion of illegitimate births, particularly in adolescents. In South Australia the total exnuptial (illegitimate) birth rate has doubled since 1962—from 48 to 98 per 1 000 total live births. Despite a decline in birth rate for all other age groups, that for 15 to 19-year-olds was the same in 1977 as it was 30 years earlier. Although total births in South Australia have declined, the proportion of exnuptial births to older teenagers has increased from 2.9 per cent of all births in 1968 to 4.2 per cent in 1977. Accompanying these changes has been a decline in teenage marriages and a decline in the number of first births occurring within eight months of marriage. These statistics confirm that pregnant, unmarried girls who decide to continue with their pregnancy are increasingly deciding to remain single rather than taking a chance with an unwanted marriage.

The health implications of adolescent pregnancy have been long recognized. Early ante-natal care is known to be associated with a more favourable outcome for both mother and child, yet recent studies show that teenagers are later in entering such care. They also have a greater risk of suffering from several serious complications of pregnancy, such as toxaemia, and an unduly high proportion of low-birth weight infants, regardless of their socio-economic status. Children born to adolescent mothers have also been shown to have a high accident rate. Canadian studies have suggested that adolescent mothers give birth to children with an increased prevalence of handicaps.[8] Baldwin reported that 11 per cent of children born to girls aged less than 16 years scored less than 70 on I.Q. tests at the age of four compared with only 2.6 per cent for the general population.[9] Adolescent girls are often deserted by the baby's father which is likely to have untoward effects on child development.[10] The pregnant adolescent is also subjected to further psychological, economic and social hazards arising from her developmental immaturity. "She is usually economically dependent, forced to interrupt her schooling, and engenders anger, distress and often rejection by her own family."[11]

Medical advances in ante-natal and perinatal care

In recent decades there have been major advances in perinatal care. Earlier this century medical care was directed mainly at reducing the mortality and morbidity of mothers during pregnancy and childbirth from causes such as puerperal infection, haemorrhage and obstructed labour. Today the focus of obstetric care has shifted from these concerns to an emphasis on the outcome for the newborn child. The concern is not limited to a reduction in perinatal deaths but to an improvement in the quality of life of surviving children.

There has been, for example, a reduction in the severity of handicaps arising at birth, probably due to a combination of demographic changes and medical advances. Although gross intellectual and physical handicaps resulting from difficulties during pregnancy or childbirth may have become less common, some children suffer from multiple minimal handicaps such as minor visual and hearing impairments, and subtle disorders of the nervous system such as disturbed perception and muscular control, hyperactivity and emotional instability. These tend to impair children's ability to concentrate and learn efficiently at school. Most—unlike many more severely handicapped children—can cope with varying degrees of difficulty, with a normal pre-school and school environment. But they need sympathetic understanding and management by teachers and parents who should be aware of the origin of their difficulties if their problems are not to be aggravated by a constant sense of failure, brought about by their being labelled naughty, difficult, stubborn or lazy. This is the essence of tertiary prevention.

Thus whilst advances in medical care during pregnancy and the new born period have brightened the outlook for the new born, there are still opportunities for improvement by extending the range of preventive activities. For instance, it seems probable that the most effective way of reducing perinatal deaths would be to reduce the absolute numbers of low-birthweight infants. At present about two-thirds of all perinatal deaths occur in infants weighing under 2.5 kilogrammes. Low-birthweight babies probably comprise around 6 per cent of all births in Australia, although the proportion is higher in adolescent pregnancy and in women from lower socio-economic groups, and it may be as high as 13 per cent in Aboriginal women. In Sweden, only 3 per cent of infants are this small. Although the Swedes have not managed to achieve the same survival rates in low-birthweight infants as in the best North American centres, they have the distinction of having the lowest perinatal mortality rate in the world since they have so few high risk (low birthweight) babies born.[12] Their success can be attributed partly to effective primary preventive programmes aimed at improving the nutrition of pregnant mothers, the reduction of cigarette smoking and alcohol consumption in pregnancy (both of which reduce birth weight and increase perinatal deaths and illness), ensuring adequate financial support of families through generous maternity benefits and privileges, and making sure that antenatal care is accessible to all sections of the population.

Nevertheless since the pattern of an individual pregnancy is probably largely determined at the time of conception, attempts to prevent low birthweight—and congenital abnormalities—may well be too late by the time the woman first sees a doctor at 12 weeks. Diabetes is a classical example. The chance of congenital abnormalities in the offspring of diabetic mothers is much higher in women whose diabetes is poorly controlled at the time of conception, and some specialist centres are now advising that diabetic women planning to conceive have their clinical condition carefully monitored and controlled before conception.[13]

In Australia there are opportunities to extend the content and coverage of parent education programmes during pregnancy. Other countries, notably Finland and France, have gone even further than Sweden to ensure that primary preventive and antenatal screening programmes achieve high penetration. In Finland, for example, payment of the maternity allowance—currently worth about $160—is conditional upon women presenting for antenatal care before the sixteenth week of pregnancy. In 1968, 91.2 per cent of all women attended for the first examination by this time.[14] In Britain it is estimated that 25 per cent of women do not receive antenatal care until seventeen weeks or later. The proportion in Australia is unknown. Although many other changes have occurred in living standards in Finland since the end of the Second World War, it is pertinent to note the marked decline in infant mortality which accompanied this aggressive social policy. The rate has fallen from 68.6 per 1 000 live births in 1944 to 11.3 per 1 000 in 1972. Over the same period the rate in England and Wales had dropped from 44.5 to 17.3. In France, the infant mortality rate has fallen from 25 per cent above to 25 per cent below that of Britain during the past ten years, which is believed to be the result of a sustained campaign to improve the quality of antenatal care and to attract women to clinics. Since 1975 all women have been required by law to have antenatal examinations at different stages of pregnancy; the generous maternity grant of $600 is dependent upon such attendance. Only 5 per cent of French women have not visited antenatal clinics by the sixteenth week of pregnancy.[15]

As evidence pointing towards the success of more intensive monitoring of pregnancy and childbirth in at-risk women has accummulated, many obstetricians have come to believe that universal fetal monitoring during labour would also provide another opportunity to improve perinatal outcome. At present the evidence for such a policy is inconclusive. However the strength of the evidence showing its benefits in at-risk cases, allied with the fact that about one-third of the women who develop complications during childbirth cannot be predicted beforehand, has been sufficient to persuade health planners in some parts of the United States to progressively phase out financial support to obstetric units delivering fewer than 2 000 children a year, the minimum number required to make economic use of the capital intensive plant and to ensure the maintenance of a high level of competence in the medical and nursing staff. Not surprisingly, such developments have met with opposition from smaller hospitals and from parents who do not believe that the benefits (of a small gain in safety for themselves and their baby) compensate for the disadvantages of sacrificing the intimate atmosphere of a small community hospital for a large impersonal institution.

Signs of a reaction against high technology perinatal medicine—which many, including Illich and Carlson, perceive to be an example of the "medicalization of life" by health professionals[16]—are to be seen in a rising number of home births. Because some women unpredictably develop complications during childbirth which can only be safely treated in hospital, it is difficult to justify planned home births in a society which places such a high premium upon optimal perinatal outcome. Moreover, one of the most disturbing aspects of obstetric care in Britain is the poor selection of women for home delivery on the basis of 'at risk' criteria. Cox *et al* found that 19 per cent of women delivering at home in a London suburb should never have been accepted as candidates for planned home delivery because of the presence of high risk obstetric factors.[17]

There are signs that progress is being made towards a compromise on this issue which accommodates the needs of parents and the concerns of professionals. This is seen in the movement towards "individualized maternity care" in Australia. In some cities maternity hospitals are being remodelled to produce an atmosphere which not only simulates the privacy and intimacy of the home but allows older children as well as fathers to stay with the mothers during childbirth. Some hospitals now give prospective parents a check list of choices about the method of delivery, the people to be present and the form of pain relief to be used. Such individualization has further advantages since there is evidence that it is likely to promote attachment ('bonding') between new born children and their parents and thus facilitate healthy child development.

One of the difficulties in measuring the success of any health programme directed at improving the outcome of the new born in Australia is the lack of data to serve as a basis for evaluation. That this is a widespread problem in Australia was indicated by the recent report of the Senate Standing Committee on Social Welfare on the Evaluation of Health and Welfare programmes in Australia.[18] Birthweight distributions, for instance, are known only in two Australian states, and race is not recorded on statutory birth or death certificates. Without such data it is impossible to determine how effective preventive and other health care programmes have been in improving the outlook for high risk pregnancies. There are signs that this deficiency will soon be overcome following the decision by the Federal Government to establish a National Perinatal Statistics Unit, and to assist the states to set up their own perinatal data collections where these do not already exist. Such collections will also enable the possible effects of environmental hazards (such as the chemical 2, 4, 5-T) on unborn children to be carefully monitored.

There is evidence that with the various tools at our disposal perinatal outcome could be significantly improved. The extent to which these opportunities for prevention will be grasped in Australia depends upon many factors, not least the value we as a community place upon the life of unborn and newly-born children, particularly when at the same time we adhere to values which may not always be in the best interests of the child.

Later deaths in infancy—Sudden Infant Death Syndrome

No review of contemporary child health would be complete without mention of the Sudden Infant Death Syndrome (SIDS) which, with the declining number of deaths due to perinatal causes and infectious disease, now accounts for over half the deaths of children between the beginning of the second month and the end of the first year of life. In Australia about two in every 1 000 children die from this condition, the cause of which is unknown. SIDS is defined as "the sudden death of any infant or young child which is unexpected by history and in which a thorough port-mortem examination failed to demonstrate an adequate cause of death".[19] There are many theories as to what causes SIDS. It seems likely that none will be able to entirely explain all cot deaths, but each may be applicable in a few cases. SIDS probably results when a variety of different factors interact, with a fatal outcome in some children as they pass through a sensitive stage of development. Some children are known to be at higher risk than others.

Current research in trying to identify causes is adopting several approaches. Some workers are exploring the influence of sociological factors, others are trying to identify infants at increased risk of SIDS, others are looking at differences in the way in which children with SIDS respond to infection, and others at the possible role of abnormal breathing patterns and disturbed heart rhythmns.[20] There is a need to identify which high-risk factors are relevant in an Australian context. If a high-risk group of children can be identified at birth or shortly afterwards, it may be possible to prevent many cases from occurring—as they appear to have been in Sheffield—by increased health surveillance, despite ignorance of the basic causes. There is also a great need for sympathetic counselling of parents who have lost a child in these circumstances—yet another form of tertiary prevention. Parents "need reassurance, explanation of the cause of death and an opportunity to talk through their tragedy to help dispel guilt, calm fears, restore relationships and rebuild parental confidence".[21]

Disturbances in child development

The complex process of child development in all its aspects—physical, intellectual, emotional and social—is affected by many influences both internal and external for individual children and their families. Two issues are currently the subject of debate. The first is the extent to which developmental disorders should be regarded as 'medical problems' to be detected, diagnosed, treated and prevented; and the second, which is related to it, is the extent to which professional involvement in the prevention and treatment of developmental disorders is justifiable and effective.

The first issue has arisen because of a broader understanding of the nature of 'health'. Health is no longer regarded simply as the absence of disease but "a state of complete physical, mental and social wellbeing". Whilst under the older definition none would have questioned the legitimacy of labelling poor physical development as a medical problem, the validity of regarding inadequate social development due to ecological factors such as poverty, neglect or oppression by parents, as such would have been questioned. The broader definition places medicine under no such limitations. Indeed "if anything can be shown in some way to affect the workings of the body and to a lesser extent the mind then it can be labelled jurisdictionally a medical problem",[22] irrespective of the capacity of medicine to deal with it.[23] The danger of this approach is the tendency for medical solutions, which involve a process of personal intervention, to be prescribed for social problems with a multiplicity of causes, the solutions for which should accordingly be sought by broader approaches. A further effect of labelling these problems as illnesses is the resulting dependency of those affected on professionals to provide a solution.

According to this view it is not so much the fact that "modern day medical problems" have many causes, but that the approaches which doctors in particular have devised for their treatment have often been inappropriate because the treatment plans have originated in a system dominated by the "germ theory" of disease. This theory developed in the latter half of the nineteenth century and identified discreet, specific and external causative agents for disease processes, which were usually thought of as acute and shortlived. It gave support to the idea of specific therapies for particular conditions.[24] Undoubtedly this theory applies to the treatment of some medical conditions, e.g. appendicectomy for appendicitis, antibiotics for meningitis, but attempts to widen its application to all human disorders indicates a failure to appreciate the genesis of many contemporary health problems. Thus since many factors contribute to developmental disorders, many strategies are necessary to tackle them—individual treatment, family therapy, community development programmes, and social and political activism to reduce the increased frequency of these disorders in disadvantaged sections of the community.

Despite the doubts of those who question the wisdom of professional intrusion into the normal processes of child development, health and allied professionals are engaged in many preventive and intervention programmes. There are numerous examples of both parent education programmes designed to promote healthy parent–child relationships and optimum child development (primary prevention) and secondary preventive programmes aimed at early detection and treatment of developmental disorders. There is also concern amongst parents and professionals aimed at minimizing the maladaptive behaviour which may occur in young children admitted to hospital, or in those with chronic physical illness (tertiary prevention). Professionals can marshal cogent arguments to justify their involvement in programmes aimed at increasing knowledge of child development amongst parents and other care takers. Firstly, much experimental work identifying important influences on child development has only been done in the last 25 years and, because of its importance for all parents, it needs to be widely disseminated in the community. Secondly, with the breakdown of the extended family network, perhaps accentuated in Australia more than elsewhere by immigration and large, widely dispersed metropolitan areas, the intergenerational transmission of cultural customs and values occurs less frequently than formerly, which causes parents to look elsewhere for information on methods of child rearing. Thirdly, with increasing participation of mothers in the work force, professional caregivers need to be properly prepared for looking after young children by being well informed about child development. Finally, professionals would argue that educational programmes do not necessarily encourage dependency. They may encourage parents and potential parents to develop responsibility and to adopt behaviours which promote healthy child development.

A variety of educational strategies are advocated. They include programmes with universal application such as antenatal parent education classes, parent effectiveness training and child development courses in secondary schools. Other programmes have been devised for children with special needs such as developmental stimulation programmes for socially disadvantaged children, parent–child centres for children at risk of child abuse, and training programmes to enable parents to modify the behaviour of handicapped children.[25] Many believe that programmes which presently provide information about infant development, infant care and the economic realities of child rearing, for both boys and girls in some high schools, should be more widely available.

One of the problems common to many of these programmes is the difficulty one encounters in trying to evaluate their effectiveness in the absence of specific measurable programme objectives and adequate data by which to evaluate programme performance. This is not a difficulty confined to this area of health practice or to this country. Bronfenbrenner recently reported that only a handful of the several thousand programmes launched under the umbrella of "Head Start" in the United States had been adequately evaluated.[26] In a time of increasing economic stringency we should heed the warnings of the recent Senate Social Welfare Standing Committee report which suggested that there will be increasing pressure on the advocates for such programmes to offer convincing evidence of their success if funding is to be maintained.

Some influences on child development

Although there are many factors which influence child development, one which has been a centre of attention recently, both in the lay press and in parent education programmes, is the importance of attachment between mother and infant.[27] There are probably several reasons for this. The first is that advances in the care of the sick or premature new born had until recently tended to separate all mothers from their new born children until such time as they were certified as normal, but the recent recognition of the importance of maternal–infant attachment, has caused policies which encouraged this to be reviewed. Bonding theory has thus provided the straw which could be grasped by those who were opposed to the medicalization of birth and the emotionally sterile atmosphere which has often accompanied the advanced technology of present day childbirth. A second reason has been the recognition by professionals that bonding failure could result in a variety of disorders—ranging from failure to thrive to physical abuse.

Australian and overseas studies have shown a high incidence of child abuse in children with a history of neonatal illness, and have led to a re-appraisal of the criteria governing infants' admission to and discharge from special new born care.[28] Several studies have shown that some low-birthweight babies can be as well cared for at home as in hospital, provided adequate backup facilities are available, and that the risks of infection are not increased by mothers participating in the nursing care of their infants.[29]

Studies by Klaus and Kennell and Lozoff *et al* compared the subsequent behaviour of mothers and children who were encouraged to have extra contact with their new born infants immediately after birth and over the next few days, with those who experienced the usual hospital routines—a glimpse of the baby in the labour ward, a six to twelve-hour separation, and subsequently a twenty to thirty-minute period of contact every four hours of feeding.[30] It was found that mothers who had the extra contact showed more affectionate behaviour for their infants, and by the age of two were speaking differently to them. The infants were also found to behave differently; those with the extra contact smiled and laughed more and cried less. There is no evidence of effects of these experiences on other areas of individual child development; for instance rates of psychomotor development are similar.

Perhaps one of the most important findings emerged in a study of 300 low-income mothers, who having just had their first baby, were randomly assigned to different post-delivery experiences. One group had the usual four-hourly feeding contact with their babies, and the others were given up to an additional eight hours of daytime rooming in. Over a 12 to 20 months followup period, only one incidence of disturbed parenting which required hospitalization was noted amongst the 134 infants who had roomed in. In contrast 9 of the 143 infants who had received routine care were subsequently admitted for parenting disorders such as failure to thrive, child abuse, neglect or abandonment. These studies show that the amount and timing of contact with new born babies in the hours and days after birth have a significant influence on early maternal–infant attachment and child development.

The present over-emphasis on bonding has the signs of being not only a transient reaction against years of previous neglect, but of being grasped as the new magic which will forever banish disturbed parent–child relationships. One danger of placing such marked emphasis on the importance of physical contact between mother and child in the first few hours after birth is the neglect of other influences on child development including an under-emphasis of the importance of fathers, and the creation of anxiety in those parents who for a variety of reasons including general anaesthesia and adoption, have been unable to experience physical contact with their babies during this period. Adoption studies show that parents can develop satisfactory relationships with infants and children who are adopted at older ages. Furthermore, the capacity of parents and infants for continual adaptation to shifting social circumstances probably over-rides the paramount importance of any single time period for the formation of social relationships.[31]

Klaus and Kennell, who have done much to popularize 'bonding', gave explicit recognition to the importance of other factors in the process. These include the mother's own genetic makeup, the way the baby responds to her, the quality of relationships she has experienced with other members of her childhood family, her experiences with previous pregnancies, the values and practices she had absorbed from the surrounding culture, and not least—as recent research is beginning to show—the quality of relationships existing between her and the child's father.[32] It is now clear that fathers are just as nurturing and just as involved as mothers in interacting with their infants and just as sensitive to infant cues. Furthermore, it has been found that fathers play a significant role in early intellectual development. No longer can it be said that Margaret Mead's famous claim that "fathers are a biological necessity but a social accident" is valid.

Screening for delayed development

Some of the most controversial aspects of childhood screening programmes are those aimed at the detection of delayed physical and intellectual development. They rest on the belief that early identification of developmental delay allows for more effective early intervention. Such intervention programmes may, for example, consist of language stimulation for children with severe mental handicap, injections of growth hormone for children with short stature when it arises from deficiency of growth hormone, or physiotherapy for children with cerebral palsy. They are justified on the basis that without them children with these problems would not be detected soon enough to receive optimum benefit from treatment.

There is evidence to support this logic. A longitudinal study in France has shown that the ability of parents to detect developmental abnormalities depended very much on the nature of the underlying condition.[33] In a large study of 10 000 ten-month-old infants in Paris, it was clear that parents were much more likely to detect abnormalities affecting limb movement, such as cerebral palsy, than those affecting language development (such as hearing loss). In a Scottish study which sought to identify the shortest 1 per cent of children in the second and third years of primary school in three cities, it was apparent that the parents of only 45 per cent of these very short but apparently otherwise healthy children had been concerned about their child's physical development. Only 18 per cent had sought advice from their doctors. Although about 5 per cent of the children were found to have a treatable condition (growth hormone deficiency) two-thirds of these children had remained undiagnosed before screening.[34]

The controversy surrounding developmental screening programmes arises for three reasons. Firstly there is some disagreement about the efficacy of early intervention of such disorders. Secondly there is concern about whether 'developmental delay' meets the criteria for a screening programme and finally there are further doubts about the effectiveness of many available screening tests.

Whilst there is clear evidence of the efficacy of growth hormone in the treatment of short stature due to growth hormone deficiency, recent experimental evidence from New Zealand has failed to confirm the value of language stimulation programmes for children with moderate language retardation who have been detected during developmental screening.[35] Whilst the benefits of language stimulation for severely retarded children was not thrown into question by this study, it was clear that such children would have been detected even in the absence of a screening programme. More evidence on the efficacy or otherwise of similar early intervention programmes from other centres is clearly needed before a definitive conclusion can be reached.

There has been similar questioning of the effectiveness of early intervention programmes for children whose delayed development is largely a product of environmental disadvantage. Whilst family-centred intervention has been found critical to the success of these intervention programmes—without it any cognitive benefits are rapidly eroded once the programme ends—no strategy of intervention has been found effective in the most deprived groups in society in the absence of adequate health care, nutrition, housing and employment.[36] Again it is this group of children whose delayed development is largely contributed to by poor environmental circumstances who are those most likely to be detected by screening programmes. More severely retarded children, who usually have an organic basis for their retardation, are brought to the attention of health professionals without the implementation of a screening programme.

Developmental delay may occur in several areas of development either separately or in combination. Delays may be confined to physical development, motor development, language development, the cognitive area, emotional and behavioural development, or involve multiple areas. What norms should apply to the diagnosis of emotional, behavioural and social developmental delays? Those applicable to the Upper North Shore, Toorak or Burnside, or those found in Mount Druitt, Fitzroy or Hindmarsh? When is a 'disorder' merely a value judgement in the eyes of a middle-class professional? What happens if delayed development in any of these areas is left untreated? Whilst it is generally believed that the outcome is poorer in the absence of treatment, the evidence still remains inconclusive, particularly with respect to less severe delays. Because of these doubts and the lack of rigid diagnostic criteria, some people question the worth of screening, even though none question the functional importance of these problems and their potential effects on an individual child's capacity for achievement.

What are the costs to individuals of being incorrectly classified? What happens to children who are wrongly labelled by the test as being abnormal? Could they suffer the ill-effects of self-fulfilling prophecy? To some extent this depends on the availability of diagnostic referral centres which permit the screening test result to be confirmed or refuted by thorough investigation. There is evidence that present demands are being inadequately met and to embark on widespread screening without planning for an increase in such centres would be irresponsible. Whether children suffer from being 'labelled' depends in part on whether parents also perceive such children to have delayed development, in which case they may lose interest in or even reject a child. Such loss of interest might be manifested, for example, by their playing less often with and reading less frequently to the child. What happens to developmentally delayed children who are missed by such a test? Do they suffer preventable developmental handicap by being denied access to the advantages of effective intervention programmes?

Such questions highlight some of the unresolved issues. Because of these difficulties some people are convinced that developmental screening which so categorically defines children as normal and abnormal should be discarded in favour of a less rigid system of developmental monitoring and observation which can be incorporated into a more broadly based health surveillance programme. There are still gaps in our knowledge of this subject which can only be filled by further research.

Behaviour disorders

Whilst isolated abnormalities of behaviour in older children, e.g. thumb sucking or bed wetting in ten-year-old children, may be regarded as examples of delayed development in that they consist of the persistence of normal but immature behaviour beyond the normal age, the appearance of multiple behavioural symptoms is often indicative of underlying emotional disturbance arising from ecological disequilibrium. Consequently many question the appropriateness of using an individually orientated 'medical' approach to provide solutions to disorders caused by unsatisfactory social relationships.

The prevalence of behavioural disorders varies with social class and the degree of urbanization. Using a questionnaire which had previously been found to be a reliable means of detecting disturbed behaviour, Mawdsley and Graves, in a survey in the Westernport region (Victoria), showed that the prevalence of behavioural disorders in a Housing Commission estate (36 per cent) was more than twice as high as in the rural area of the same region (15 per cent), and higher than in a middle class area (18 per cent).[37] This survey was similar to Rutter's Isle of Wight study, which found that almost half of the parents whose children were disturbed, did not see the problem as serious, and did not consider their child needed professional help.[38] Both studies indicated that few parents had sought help for their children. Inaccessibility to sparsely provided services was a contributing factor. A recent study in one Australian state has suggested that the manpower resources of Child Psychiatric Services are not able to deal with more than 5–8 per cent of the children with disturbed behaviour or other psychiatric abnormalities.[39]

Effects of hospitalization on child development

The growing understanding of child development has heightened awareness of the needs of sick children and infants. Bowlby's classic description of the long-term psychological and physical affects of maternal separation and deprivation, followed by the subsequent work of Robertson and the Platt report in Britain, led the present movement aimed at reducing the emotional consequences for babies and children admitted to hospital.[40] Application of this research has seen marked changes in attitudes, policies and practices in children's wards and hospitals. Prior to the mid-1950s, for instance, parents were restricted from visiting their children in the Adelaide Children's Hospital more than twice a week.[41] The reason given was fear of infection, but one wonders how much the practice was influenced by the inability of staff to cope with the emotionally distressing sights of tearful children being separated from their parents, and their lack of understanding of the origins of such behaviour.

Staff are now more aware of their role in ensuring that vulnerable children are not harmed by the experiences of hospitalization. In many hospitals, parents are now allowed free access to their children at all times. They are encouraged to participate in the nursing care of their children, particularly during the initial settling in process. Mothers of very young children are actively encouraged to live-in for the duration of their child's admission. About 14 per cent of all children under the age of one year are now accompanied by their mothers at one major Australian teaching hospital. Children's hospitals and wards are doing much to make their atmosphere less threatening and more child-centred by more adequate preparation for admission through the use of books, films and play equipment and visits by hospital personnel to neighbourhood schools and kindergardens. Unfortunately, the parents of country children who have illnesses which can only be adequately treated in large metropolitan referral centres, and the parents of disadvantaged children living in outer suburbs are still inadequately catered for by existing transport subsidy arrangements.

Social effects of chronic illness

Advances in the prevention and treatment of many childhood disorders have meant that many children who in former times would have died in infancy or soon after the onset of a serious illness are now surviving into adolescence and adulthood. The recognition that children with severe chronic illnesses were often anxious and afraid led to awareness of the need to create a 'climate of security' in which the sick child could function most effectively.[42] Chronically-ill children are now faced with a task of coping with their illness over much longer periods. According to Burton, "There would seem little value in offering good quality physical life if one cannot also offer viable psychological survival."[43]

Parents not only affect but are affected by their chronically-ill children. Faulty parental attitudes or marital dysharmony can limit the child's emotional and physical functioning. Parental ability to cope with a seriously-ill or disabled child is also influenced by many social factors—attitudes of their other children, their own parents and other kinsfolk, their social class, religious affiliation and financial status. Their reactions are also influenced by the special meaning they attach to the sick child.[44] Although family disintegration can be a consequence of having to care for a chronically-ill or disabled child, many writers have gained the impression of family strength rather than weakness in the face of trouble. Others are less sanguine about the prospects for the child and family. In a recent survey of parents of intellectually-disabled children in one Australian city most respondents said that having a handicapped child had had a deleterious effect on their families' economic position and relationships.[45] Burton suggests that perhaps the secret lies in a combination of "maintaining a sense of hope, emphasizing sick children's personal worth and encouraging them to use their intact facilities, thereby transcending their infirmities". Such a health promoting approach is not only important to attitude and lifestyle but also to the progress of the disease.[46]

Childhood accidents

Accidental injury is the major cause of death in children over the age of one. During the school-going years accidents account for over half the deaths of children. Accident mortality rates of Australian children compare unfavourably with those in Sweden, and despite a decline in both countries the gap between them is widening. The death rate in 0–14-year-olds from accidents in Australia in 1954 was one and a half times as high as in Sweden, but by 1971 the Australian death rate was double that in Sweden. In some categories of accidents, for example drowning of pre-school children, death rates have risen in recent years.[47] This tragic waste of life and the

Figure 1: Model of the social process for accident prevention using epidemiological data

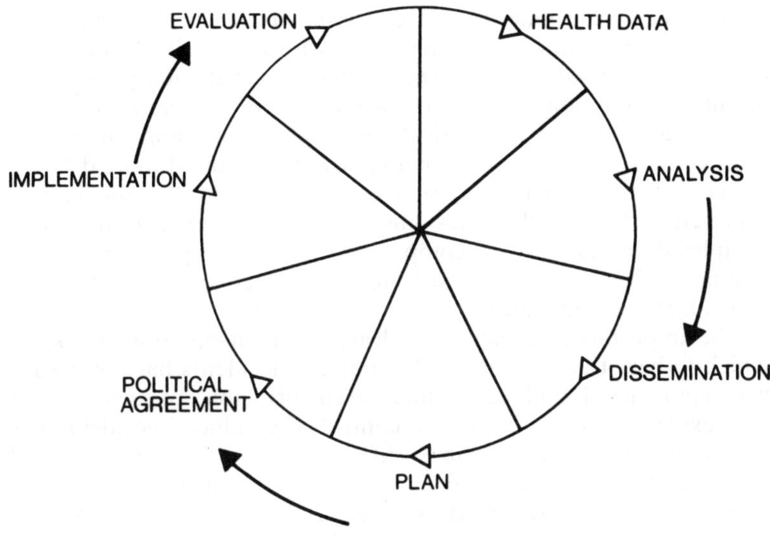

Source: B.S. Hetzel, 'A Model for Public Learning in Health Care: Administrative Application of Epidemiology and Health Statistics in Australia', in *Epidemiology as a Fundamental Science*, ed. K.L. White and M.H. Henderson (Oxford University Press, New York, 1976).

sometimes life-long incapacitation of survivors was a focus of attention during the recent International Year of the Child, and has led to the establishment of a National Child Accident Prevention Foundation which receives financial support from government, industry and the community.

However, whilst there is wide consensus in the community about the need to promote healthy familial life and child development, there is much less agreement about strategies to be adopted to tackle serious childhood accidents. Hetzel has developed a model to describe the relationship between the various components of the social process associated with health improvement (figure 1).[48] The model is relevant to the control of childhood accidents. The process begins with the collection of *health data* which may include mortality and morbidity data and other information related to health but usually of an epidemiological character. The next step is *analysis* and consideration of the meaning of the data. The third segment involves its *dissemination*—not only through the scientific community, but even more important through the mass media to the community at large. Eventually a plan emerges for discussion between the epidemiologists, administrators and other professionals involved. The plan has to received *political agreement* which required widespread community consultation. Eventually the plan can be *implemented* following the achievement of political agreement. After implementation must come *evaluation* which involves the collection of more data for a review of the plan and any necessary modifications in the light of experience. Hetzel illustrates how this cyclical process has been completed in the case of compulsory seat belt legislation, where evaluation has clearly demonstrated the effectiveness of the plan which had been introduced.

The importance of having a clearly-thought-out framework on which to base the prevention of childhood accidents has not always been appreciated. Failure to adhere to the principles of such a model may explain why success in the control of childhood accidents has been less marked here than in Sweden.

There have been many deficiencies at each stage of the social process cycle. Firstly the data base has been inadequate. Whilst accident mortality rates are known, little is known epidemiologically about the long-term outlook for accident survivors. There is also insufficient information about the victim, and the circumstances leading to accidents in many cases. Without data, analysis is clearly impossible. But of equal importance has been the lack of analysis of the data which is available (e.g. mortality statistics). Results have often been inadequately disseminated. The extent of the problem has not been widely recognized by the community, whose attitude to childhood accidents is often one of fatalism. The community has yet to learn the lesson from Sweden that many fatal childhood accidents can be prevented. Dissemination of results alone is insufficient as a strategy to prevent accidents—an intensive media campaign in Brisbane highlighting the risks of private swimming pool drownings had no effect on fatal incidents.[49] Without data, proper planning cannot take place. Accident prevention campaigns have been well motivated but often have lacked specific objectives. The most successful campaigns—for instance those aimed at the prevention of burns caused by the wearing of flammable clothing, or fireworks—are notable successes because of their well-defined objectives. Plans must also take into account the need to make parents aware of the limited capacity of young children to perceive and assess risk

Figure 2: Model illustrating the relationship between the effectiveness of a preventive strategy and the frequency of action required by individuals

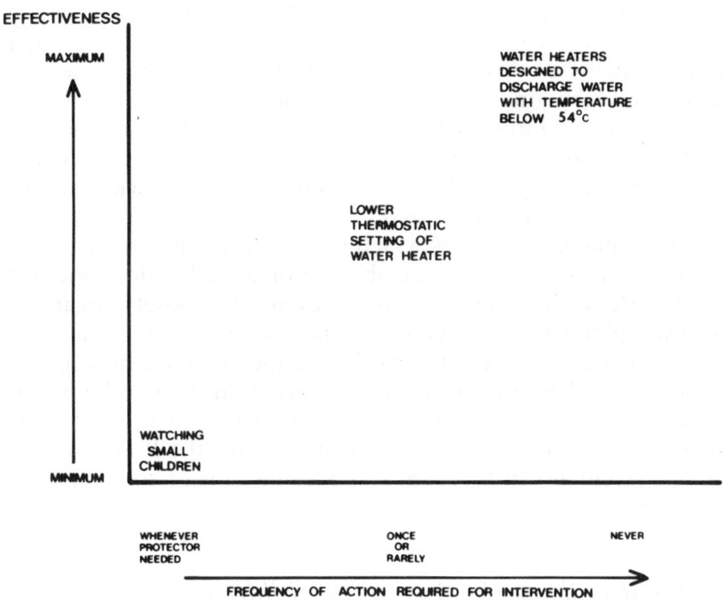

Source: After C. Baker, 'Preventive Options' (Paper presented at the International Year of the Child National Conference on Childhood Accidents and Prevention, Brisbane, 1979).

situations. Sandels in Sweden has shown that until children reach the age of ten to twelve years, they do not have the ability to perceive and assess risk in traffic situation.[50] Plans have often not received political agreement, as in the attempt to have legislation introduced in Queensland for the compulsory fencing of swimming pools. Plans requiring political consensus must be realistic and take into account the frailties of human nature. Although one can legislate for compulsory installation of childproof medicine cabinets in homes, one cannot compel their use. Finally, adequate data must be available to evaluate accident prevention programmes. This is frequently unavailable. For instance, the risks of a child drowning in a private swimming pool depend on the number of unprotected pools in the community, and yet this information is unknown in at least one state which has compulsory fencing legislation, which makes it difficult to evaluate the effectiveness of this legislation.

Baker, at the first Australian National Conference on the Prevention of Childhood Accidents, introduced a useful model which illustrates that the effectiveness of a preventive programme is inversely proportional to the need for action on the part of individuals in the community (figure 2).[51] In applying the model to the prevention of scalding (caused through the supply of boiling water from domestic heaters), she showed that the least effective strategy would be one based on advising parents to constantly supervise their children, whereas the most effective method of intervention would be to design a hot water system which could never deliver water hotter than 54°C. This model has wider application than is presently recognized.

One of the major difficulties which has hindered effective accident prevention in this country is the absence of co-ordination amongst those working in the field—whether they be child safety organizations, town planners, architects, product designers or researchers and epidemiologists. Without this, it is difficult to see how agreement can be reached on priorities for prevention. It is to be hoped that the Child Accident Prevention Foundation will follow the example of the Joint Consultative Committee for the Prevention of Childhood Accidents in Sweden, and become a major co-ordinating influence in Australia.

Nutritional problems in Australian children

Nutrition is one of the most important determinants of health. Both McKeown and Powles attribute much of the historical decline in death rates to the elimination of malnutrition.[52] Yet nutritional problems are common in Australian children. It is hardly surprising therefore that by generally accepted health standards, Australians are "one of the unhealthiest peoples amongst those to which they belong by tradition and standard of living".[53] Both under- and over-nutrition occur in Australian families.

As has been pointed out many times, the Aboriginal population provides the most glaring example of under-nutrition in Australian children which contributes to their often defective growth, high susceptibility to chest and bowel infection, and their generally higher disease and death rates.[54] The background to under-nutrition in Aboriginal communities is complex and varies from place to place. Important factors include the general level of community development, standards of housing, hygiene and education, job opportunities for parents, as well as the availability of food supplies. Aboriginal malnutrition is an example of the way the human organism suffers as a result of ecological imbalance. Many different strategies are necessary for its resolution.

At the other end of the nutritional spectrum, obesity is a growing public health problem particularly in urban Australian children and adolescents. A survey of children attending metropolitan and rural high schools in Victoria showed that 8 per cent of adolescent girls and 5 per cent of adolescent boys were severely overweight (i.e. more than 20 per cent above their expected weight for age) and similar proportions were moderately overweight.[55] Inner surburban children tended to be more overweight than those living in the country and children from a Southern European background were more overweight than those of Anglo-Australian origin. In an earlier survey, Court *et al*, found evidence suggestive of high blood pressure in 55 per cent of obese children which they believed had relevance to the development of coronary heart disease in later life.[56] Others have found frequent elevation of blood cholesterol levels in otherwise healthy Australian adolescents.[57] Obesity is not a problem confined to children; a recent study in Busselton in Western Australia showed that about 25 per cent of apparently healthy adults were obese.[58]

Why is obesity so prevalent? From dietary surveys it is apparent that Australians consume far more food than they need. One study of migrant and Australian-born children in Perth showed that many children consumed excessive amounts of high energy foods and protein and that the consumption of empty calorie "junk" food was also high.[59] The causes of over-eating are complex. Whilst individual psychodynamic factors contribute, social influences exerted through the media are probably equally important. Thus many different strategies involving intervention by legislation and education at a socio-political, group, or individual level need to be used to prevent or eliminate obesity. As in the control of childhood accidents, the "social process model" is relevant to an understanding of how improvement can be brought about. At an individual and small group level, educational strategies appear to be most relevant. One promising programme, introduced as part of the routine school health service in New York, may be a useful model for Australia. This is the "Know Your Body" programme.[60] Children are screened for the presence of factors known to be associated with an increased risk of coronary heart disease in adults—such as obesity, high blood cholesterol, high blood pressure and poor exercise tolerance—and when these are found they and their parents are counselled on the dangers associated with these abnormal findings and given the responsibility of making the appropriate changes. The effect of these changes on risk factor prevalence can then be monitored.

In Australia some promising results have been observed in primary school students who were randomly assigned during a 14-week intervention period to either an endurance fitness programme, a skills programme, or a non-intervention (control) programme.[61] A significant amount of body fat (as measured by changes in skin fold thickness) was lost by the end of the study in children who were classified as overweight at the outset and who had been assigned to the "fitness" programme compared to those in the other two groups.

Australians are greatly misinformed by the mass media as to what constitutes healthy eating habits. Young children in particular are subjected to a barrage of junk food advertising during their peak viewing hours. Should such advertising not be controlled? There is widespread ignorance about nutrition in Australia. In the United States a Senate Select Committee on Nutrition and Human Needs reported in 1977 that:

> The eating habits of this country represent as critical a public health concern as any now before us. We must acknowledge and recognize that the public is confused about what to eat to maximize health.... We have an obligation to provide practical guides to the individual consumer as well as set national dietary goals.... Such an effort is long overdue.[62]

The same is true for Australia. The Senate Committee set out six dietary objectives which could well be adopted in Australia:

1. Carbohydrate consumption to be increased to between 55 per cent and 50 per cent of total energy intake
2. Reduction of fat consumption to 30 per cent of energy intake
3. Reduction of saturated fat content to 10 per cent of total intake (presently about 16 per cent in Australia) the balance coming from polyunsaturated (10 per cent) and monosaturated (10 per cent) fats
4. Reduction of dietary cholesterol to 300 milligrams per day
5. Reduction of refined sugar consumption to 15 per cent of energy intake (currently about 17 per cent in Australia)
6. Reduction of salt intake to 3 grams per day.

The reality of the economic pressures militating against the adoption of healthy nutritional practices in Australians must be confronted. The future health of the Australian community will have to be balanced against such economic considerations. This issue has been faced in Norway where agricultural production policy is now being modified to produce dairy foods of lower fat content.[63] Norway is also reducing sugar consumption by the abolition of subsidies and cereal consumption is being encouraged. Consideration of these and similar measures suggested earlier in Scandinavian countries has led to advocacy by the Federal (Australian) Department of Health of guidelines for a Food and Nutrition

Policy. These guidelines include encouragement of breast feeding, nutrition education for the community, decreased consumption of total fat, refined sugar, salt and alcohol and increased consumption of complex carbohydrates.[64]

Penetration of preventive health programmes

The message is clear. Prevention—through the adoption of health promoting life-styles, the early detection of disease and the harmonious adaptation of individuals to the limitations placed upon them by illness—offers the best prospects for the improved health of Australian children. "The doctor of the future will be a teacher as well as physician, whose real job will be assisting people to learn how to be healthy."[65]

We are concerned that this message does not reach all sections of the community. What potential does health education have to serve those who need it most, those who come from the poorer socio-economic groups, and who suffer disproportionately higher rates of perinatal death and illness, developmental disorders, accidents and obesity? Does it ever do more than preach to the converted? Chapman believes that successful health education programmes for low income groups have been those that have:

> involved strategies that organize and empower people to challenge and change the agents and institutions of ill health in addition to attempts at influencing change at legislative and public policy levels. The minimal aim of health education should be to broaden the range of options available to people and to make health promoting choices easier.... The beginning of the process must be to arouse or develop interest or concern at both mass and local community levels.[66]

Chapman suggests health educators could become involved in the following areas:

(i) Formation of pressure groups to influence local government in matters such as child minding, recreation facilities, safe town planning, use of pesticides, etc.
(ii) Formation of local consumer groups to influence stocking of food stores, school tuck shops and canteens
(iii) Development of participation and representative control of community health centres by local residents
(iv) Organization of lobbying, petitioning and boycotting
(v) Collection of relevant health and illness data to help local residents substantiate their arguments.

We are also concerned that screening programmes are not universally accessible. Accessibility is determined both by social factors in individuals (such as knowledge of available resources, resourcefulness and mobility) which affect their ability to communicate with the services available, and the locational characteristics of the service provided. There is evidence both here and abroad that the parents of socially disadvantaged children use preventive child-health services less often. Murrell and Moss, found that 25 per cent of Anglo-Australian children living in a socially disadvantaged Adelaide suburb had never attended a child-health clinic during the first six months of life compared to only 3 per cent of children living in a nearby well-off suburb.[67] Other studies have shown that some preventable and treatable conditions are found more frequently in disadvantaged children. Booth and Oates, found dangerously low levels of immunization in some disadvantaged children in inner Sydney suburbs, particularly within newly arrived non-European ethnic minorities. Nowotny and Stretton found a significantly higher incidence of dental caries, unrecognized medical conditions, and a tendency towards higher rates of hearing loss and language disorders in disadvantaged Victorian children. These findings mirror those of the National Child Development study in Britain in which 1 in 3 disadvantaged children born in 1958, had by the age of 11 never attended an infant welfare clinic (compared to 1 in 5 ordinary children), 1 in 7 had suffered a burn or scald (1 in 12), 1 in 25 had received a flesh wound requiring 10 or more stitches (1 in 100), 1 in 35 had marked hearing loss (1 in 140) and 1 in 22 had some speech difficulty (1 in 66).[68]

Could we do more to reduce the differences in access? Some countries (e.g. France) whose governments have appreciated the cost benefits of preventive programmes which reduce later needs for institutional care, have introduced legislation which recognizes the rights of the child to health protection. It is generally accepted, for instance, that the costs of a screening programmes for the detection of phenylketonuria at birth (a condition accompanied by severe mental retardation) are more than balanced by the costs of a life time of institutional care for one severely retarded individual. Similar advantages were considered by the French to justify a universal screening programme aimed at the early detection of childhood deafness. To ensure universal coverage of these programmes, the French government introduced a requirement for all children to undergo compulsory medical examinations at eight days, nine months and twenty-four months. Certificates of health which were completed at the time of these examinations had to be presented before the full amount of family allowances was paid.[69] In the United States many states require evidence of up-to-date immunization status before children are allowed to be enrolled in primary school. In Finland and elsewhere health authorities have laid down regulations governing minimum staffing levels in preventive child health clinics.

No legislation of this sort exists in Australia. Would it be acceptable here? Do we really need further data collection and analysis to prove beyond all doubt that disadvantaged Australian children have poorer health and diminished life prospects compared to those more fortunate? Or is our inactivity related to the same sort of ambivalence—which arises from conflicts between our values and the rights of children—which is so clearly apparent in some of our attitudes to the control of childhood accidents?

In the final analysis the health of children depends upon the balance between health-promoting and health-destroying forces in their ecosystem. Our children's health will reflect whether the way in which we resolve some of the present value conflicts in our society is indicative of wise or foolish stewardship.

Children's Health, Parents and the Community

Deane Southgate

In discussing children's health in Australia this paper will refer to the relationship which exists between the community, the children and their parents. Four areas in which the community could take a more useful role in the interests of children's health will be discussed: pregnancy, early parenting, development assessment and services for sick children.

The community has increasingly shown itself unhappy to leave the affairs of health to individuals and their chosen professional advisers. Almost without noticing, we accept the benefits of the sanitary revolution in daily life, a testimony to the value of community action for individuals. Perhaps without noticing its significance, our community has required a gradual intervention of the state providing services for the health of children separately from parents. There is a long tradition of health care services through School Health services and Infant Welfare services, which are examples of priorities in provision of services. These have been frequently truly community initiated. They are community initiatives in health promotion. More dramatically there has been community intervention to save life (for example when parents have sought to withhold treatment such as blood transfusion on religious grounds).

Pregnancy

The success in Australia of imported cars compared with locally manufactured cars has often been attributed to quality control in manufacture. There is much that can be done before birth to determine a higher standard of health in a new born infant. That standard of health, determined by influences during conception and pregnancy, as well as care during delivery, may well determine the quality and health of a lifetime. In Australia we have spent resources on a high standard of high technology care at the time of birth; in other countries, notably Scandinavia, the emphasis seems to be on a high standard of care during pregnancy. There is much we could do in this area to improve the potential health, not only of the new baby, but also the subsequent child and adult. Additional resources to promote welfare in pregnancy seems much more likely to produce significant returns than increasing high cost care at delivery.

Some factors in early pregnancy

The well-read Australian lay person, educated by the thalidomide disaster, is aware of the effects of drugs on pregnancy. Such is that understanding that it is sometimes difficult to persuade a pregnant mother to take well-established and safe drugs for the alleviation of vomiting during pregnancy. Similarly, there is a growing understanding of the place of smoking in producing small-birthweight infants. There is less understanding in the community of the effect of low birthweight on survival and the occurrence of disease. There is increasing medical understanding of the effect of alcohol on infants but this understanding has so far not been shared with the community. The 'foetal–alcohol' syndrome of low birthweight, facial deformity and mental retardation has received a deal of recent attention.[1] It only occurs in babies born to mothers using alcohol at and around conception.

It is important therefore that this information become community folklore; that all people who have the potential to become parents should be aware of these three important factors in possibly determining their child's health and its chances of survival in the first year of life, and the quality and length of life thereafter. In all three cases advice during pregnancy is too late. These factors operate from the time of conception and only by having a well-informed public, principally possible mothers-to-be, can they be eliminated as causes of foetal damage. The effective resistance of pregnant women to the taking of drugs is concrete evidence of the significant contribution an informed community can make to its own health.

Obstetric care

The new trend which has emerged in obstetrics in Australia is one of fragmentation. Promoted by the drama of modern deliveries, and the differential fees of the Gorton Government's health scheme, an increasing number of pregnancies are managed by specialist obstetricians, people with whom the mother-to-be had had no previous contact, who may not be present at the birth of the child, and will not be present afterwards. An increasing proportion of deliveries, for good reasons, take place in larger centres. In such situations it is less likely that there will be consistency in providers of treatment and the mother is likely to meet a number of people (during pregnancy, labour, and after delivery) with whom she has not been able to establish a working relationship. Yet in Australia, as part of prenatal preparation, we often show a film made in Britain to describe the process of pregnancy and labour. In that film there is a recurring face—the face of the midwife who has seen the mother in pregnancy, and who sees her in hospital, both at the time of labour and after delivery. Until recently in Australia that relationship was provided by general practitioners; there was a continuity of care which extended not only through the pregnancy, but frequently before it and well after the delivery.

We need to increase the quality of pregnancy, to raise standards of nutrition, to educate mothers and to establish a supportive and instructive relationship for them throughout pregnancy, delivery and postnatal care. This is an admirable role for the community health nurse and one which should be promoted especially in areas of high risk and social disadvantage, with a likely improvement not only in the health of the new born but in the bonding which is established between mother and child. The diminishing returns from increasing expenditure on technological medicine do not indicate great opportunities for improving the well being of the new born by more successful technical management of labour and delivery.

The parent–child relationship is perhaps one of the most important areas to which we should address ourselves. Evidence is beginning to accumulate which suggest that the lack of this relationship has much to do with subsequent illness. Studies among adults have shown that social dissonance is a significant factor in the determination and the distribution of ill health.[2] There is probably a close relationship between that and the initial bonding of child and parent. The move in Australia to have babies at home is evidence that the lay community believes in the importance of bonding with the father and family. The present time has given strength to their voice. The relative oversupply of hospital beds for all sorts of purposes has produced a sensitivity on the part of hospital administrators and professionals to the needs and interests of patients. It is likely that we shall see an even greater opportunity given to fathers and mothers-to-be to 'conduct' their labour with their own flavour, and with the hospital playing a standby and resource role.

A new threat

Recent evidence points to another problem which presents a threat to the new born. Prematurity has always been, and still is, associated with sickness and death. Prematurity occurs more commonly in pregnancies following termination of pregnancy, another increasing phenomenon. In responding to a social need we have jeopardized the well-being of subsequent children.[3]

Effective parenting

It is possible that no single factor will determine the outcome in terms of health and welfare as much as the early establishment of a warm, comfortable relationship between mother and child. Whether the child is normal, gifted or handicapped, its acceptance by its parents for its own sake is critical. Acceptance of a role because of duty, honour, guilt or a need to provide, is associated with trauma. We ignore factors known to affect bonding at the peril of the new born.

There has been a call for increased child-care facilities, but there has been a loss over the last 15 or 20 years of child-care facilities in the community. The huge increase in numbers of working mothers must imply a loss in terms of hours of caring for small children. There are many arguments to say that a mother is more effective if she is happier and fulfilled. These must weigh heavily. However, we must accept that the total volume of people caring for children has probably been significantly diminished during this change. At the same time there has been increasing lack of experience in parenting as the two-child family means that parents themselves will have less experience as observers of children being parented when they are young, and will have less children themselves to practise upon. In larger towns young people, and therefore small children, live at the periphery. Poor public transport means that the young mother is often separated from the experienced members of her family who could indicate appropriate action and give support. The experience of new towns in England shows that people in these circumstances use doctors four to five times as often as those in established areas.[4]

There is a need for a supporting, informed person with whom a satisfactory relationship has been established. This further strengthens the case for the community health nurse who can play a significant role with the young mother throughout pregnancy and early childhood. Motherhood introduces women to the 24-hour day shift on a 7-day week basis. For many their first period of leave does not occur before long service leave many years later. One could advance forceful arguments for paid holidays for mothers!

Developmental assessment

Should developmental screening be offered to all children in all schools or should it be offered to all children between infancy and before going to school? Will early remediation be effective? Are our tests precise enough? Are we able to respond in a way that will correct the problem? Do we have sufficient services to do that assessment and to meet the needs that it will generate? Would such a service be more effective than the present response to noticed deviations? It cannot be said that the present system does identify all infants and school children in their early years with developmental deficiencies, particularly those which are not of a measurable, physical variety. Neither can it be said that all those that are detected are adequately dealt with. Follow-up is poor, in terms of seeing that effective management takes place. Services in this area are dependent upon the kindergarten teacher, school teacher and child-care worker. They may recognize difficulties which are either difficulties for them or for children. We cannot say we always know about these problems, let alone provide a service which is effective in remedying them.

Some would say developmental assessment is a useful tool of health surveillance. As a screening tool this may not be achieved in the near future. We are unlikely to have the resources. There is a need to see that whatever screening is done has adequate follow-up and effective management—not completion of the paper work, but completion of the child care. This implies a closer relationship between health services in kindergartens and schools and its entry into child-care services and other health services in which professional hierarchies do not prevent effective communication.

Sick services

Australian medical care is of a high standard. This also applies to care for children. But the inverse care law of Tudor Hart which states that "care is provided inversely as to its need" also applies in Australia. Nowhere is this more true than in services for children. The disadvantaged child is not able to provide or find these services for himself. There is a higher proportion of undetected disease in those who do not attend health clinics than those who do.[6] It is to these that we should move services. The movement of health professionals is determined more by their career opportunities than by the needs of those they service, and the services that are provided are frequently coloured by the needs of the provider.

Increasing lay activity is a testimony to this fact. Probably nowhere does this apply more than in the care of children, especially the mentally retarded. Services offered by lay organizations have been particularly active in child care. The emotional needs of parents who are unable to find help for their children often leaves them dependent on those who profess to help. The fees that can be charged are testimony to how dependent parents can be. As in all health services, consumers should have the means to make clear their needs and the deficiencies they see in services. Reference has been made to the way in which consumers now can choose to some extent the nature of the obstetric service which will be available. They need also to be able to determine something of the services that will be available for children. Frequently programmes to teach parents are unrelated to parents' present knowledge, attitudes or need. The parents' motivation and interest are related to the problems that they see and service for those problems may only be part of a package. It is important that the services should more clearly be seen by the patient as being related to their problems. Counselling services and parent training should start where parents are, not where the provider is.

New directions

There must be an increasing relationship between health services and other child related services, especially education. The child-care worker, kindergarten and school teacher play an increasingly significant role in the life of the child. Importantly they are the professional observers who have most contact with children and the relationships between them and health professionals is therefore a critical one. Health is a changing adaptation of the individual to his or her environment. Teachers not only observe the child, they also control and constitute a significant part of the environment. They need support and guidance from health professionals as to the problems they should be looking for and the ways in which they should be responding to those problems. Except in small communities, in Australia this relationship is usually no more than a nodding acquaintance. It should be strengthened to the benefit not of each, but of the children they are concerned with.

There must be an increasing relationship between health services and parents. The intervention of health services on behalf of children separately from parents may leave the latter less able, less sure and uninformed. The role of the third member of the eternal triangle is to increase the autonomy and the health of both parent and child. The health care system should listen to non-professional, parent and lay opinion and involve them in decision-making and management. The Australian health care system is singularly devoid of consumer participation or other evidence which suggests that parents may be able to have a responsible and competent role in the management of their children's health (or their own). While professional services take all the decisions it will remain that way.

Research

Health education is directed especially at children. This is done within the school curriculum and by other groups, either within or outside of the school, directing their messages to children. Most of these messages are anti-health and widely and effectively spread through the media. We need data about the effects of the information we attempt to give to children. The South Australian Royal Commission on Drugs has told us of some unfortunate effects, particularly when a programme is provided as an isolated exercise directed at what the community says is a problem.[7] Research is needed to evaluate whether changes in knowledge and even attitudes are sufficient to ensure changes in health. That research is needed to convince lay people (school committees, parent–teacher associations) to press for the inclusion of proven material and methodology in the school curriculum.

Even more, we need research which will tell us about the effects of intervention in behaviour problems in children. Any large school will testify to the number of children who are having problems in achieving and problems in behaviour. Any general practitioner can testify to the numbers of occasions they have seen malfunctioning families. What intervention will bring about changes that are useful in these situations? Some say that certain behaviour disorders are best left alone, that notification to 'helping professions', be they medical, psychological or psychiatric, brings disruption, activity, discussion and meetings—but no improvements. We should identify those situations where this is so and those in which we can help. Any programme that is supported by state resources should have with it sufficient funding to demand its evaluation. There has been a dramatic increase in community programmes over the last four to five years. We know much of what they have done. We have little knowledge of what they achieved.

PART 6

The Child and Education

Malcolm Skilbeck

Primary education in Australia has reached a challenging point in its development. The general aims of individual personal development and integration into society are widely proclaimed. Yet we are not sure how programmes relate to these aims, or how stated goals are being achieved. Moreover, the primary school has become the focus of public debate over 'progressive' versus 'traditional' methods, a debate which raises basic questions about the purposes and priorities of the school, its curriculum and the standards it sets itself.

Primary education must foster skills, knowledge and attitudes that will facilitate children's adaptation to an unknown future. Cognitive skills alone are insufficient for this purpose: social, aesthetic, motor and other skills are also important, as are interpersonal relationships and the development of a value system. Whilst education must aim to prepare children for future life, the primary school is a major part of the child's present life. The quality of that life is often overlooked in debates about economic trends, social needs and what the community expects.

This chapter first examines ideas on personal, social and cognitive development, which form the basis of much current educational practice.[1] New developments in practice in recent years, such as open education and community involvement, are then discussed in relation to ideas and theories about the socio-cultural role of the school and the needs of the individual child. The last section raises discussion points which highlight issues for educators and others. Although there are large areas of agreement between parents, community bodies and schools about what education is for, there are significant differences. It is upon these differences that much public and professional discussion has been focused during the seventies. The education of the child has become and is likely to remain an arena of controversy in Australia.

The role of the school in society

The school as a universal social institution has a relatively short history and its development has been closely related to social perspectives of childhood as illustrated in Part 1 of this volume. The socio-political rationale for the education of children has always powerfully shaped school policies and practice, as have the economic assumptions and resource base of the social system. From the days of Socrates onwards, however, philosophers and educational reformers have sought to moderate prevailing *social demand* approaches with a view of the child itself as an active agent in its own growth and development. The essential differences between the social demand approach and that of many educational theorists relate both to the ends and the means of the educational process. Society expects and children need appropriate schooling to equip them to fulfil a productive role in the economy and to subscribe to the prevailing social norms and values. Educators are expected to achieve such goals as efficiently and economically as possible, and most of them seek to do just this.

There is, however, an alternative view of children's education and of society itself. This view is, basically, that the life and interests of the child are not reducible to the demands of political, social and economic utility and that it is one role of education and educators to foster critical, creative and reconstructive approaches to the social order. For convenience this will be called the *human and social developmental* as distinct from the social demand approach to schooling. The developmental approach sees each child as an unique individual who has the right to develop to the fullest extent possible his or her interests and talents. It treats society as a creation of human intelligence and will, not as a blind and dominating force. Educational researchers and practitioners, administrators and parents, whose personal philosophy of teaching is based on these beliefs, direct their attention to an understanding of child development and the structuring of learning situations which will enable each child to reach his or her full potential, academically, aesthetically and socially. Moreover, they seek to understand and appraise forms and processes of social change and the interrelationship of social and psychological factors in the child's education.

These two approaches need not be seen as contradictory. Indeed, it is one of the requirements of educational policy that the interests and perspectives they represent be reconciled in school programmes and practices which satisfy a wide range of social and individual needs. Much of the debate in Australian education is unduly polarized. In the clamour of ideological warfare it is necessary for schools to keep clearly in mind their ultimate responsibility, which is to educate the child as a complex individual who lives in but need not be entirely of the social world.

Within the policy framework of state departments and other authorities, primary schools in Australia have shifted in recent years somewhat towards a developmental approach. Social demand, however, has not been ignored, for example the demand that schools foster basic literacy skills in all children. Schools have endeavoured to broaden their approach to satisfy an increasing range of social requirements and professional understandings of the educational process. This broadening has created its own problems. At pre-school level, for example, the general concern is to support the family in its child-rearing role. However, when translated into action, broad goal statements which promulgate a philosophy of individual development and social competence produce a diversity of school situations which are both professionally very demanding and a subject of significant public debate.

The school is itself a social institution, through which socialization takes place, and part of a wider social order which changes and influences it in many ways. Increasingly in Australia, as in other countries, the school is being looked to as an educational agency both in a narrow sense of training in so-called basics and as a vehicle for a wide range of public concerns and demands. The inevitable interweaving of social issues and concerns with the outcomes of schooling is strongly evident in the public concerns expressed by the media. Issues such as children's moral and physical health, youth unemployment, the rate of technological and social change, the growing recognition that Australia is now a multicultural society, and part of the international community of nations, and public debate over standards of literacy and numeracy are influencing perceptions and understanding of schooling.

The prominence of these issues, and the accelerating costs of providing educational services, have led to an emphasis on public accountability of aspects of educational practice once regarded as a professional preserve. We lack not only adequate techniques of accountability but also the broad framework of agreed goals, curriculum methods and resource standards which is necessary if accountability is to be more than a shibboleth.

The movement for accountability has yet to come to terms with the fundamental as distinct from surface manifestations of education. The essence of the change in contemporary views of education is towards learning to think and to display competence in managing diverse and novel life situations. The educated intelligence is flexible; imaginative, creative, adaptive, exhibiting strengths that are both theoretical (ideas, concepts, thought structures) and practical (skills, competence in everyday situations). The regurgition of facts and information and the routine performance of skills are of little benefit unless the child is able and wishes to use that information and those skills to solve problems in his personal and social worlds. It is easier to make objective judgements about content—how much the child knows—than it is to evaluate process—the way in which a child approaches a problem and attempts to solve it. Hence much of the debate about basics is obscured by lack of clarity—and agreement—about just what is *fundamental* in the child's education for an uncertain future. It is clear that educators have not yet succeeded in demonstrating either the meaning or the value of the newer approaches to a sceptical public.

The concern expressed by educators for the development of each child's individuality is paralleled in changing attitudes in other social sectors towards children and their rights. The recognition that Australia is now a multicultural and plural society in which ethnic and other social groups have a right to their chosen identity within the overall fabric of a national culture, and that those who may be intellectually or socially disadvantaged should be protected and supported, poses considerable problems for schools. We must come to terms with the complexity of devising a system of education which will equip children with the best foundation for their active participation in shaping their futures in a world undergoing rapid and often unforseeable changes. Cultural pluralism, it seems, entails a social conflict model in which the management of difference must become a major object of policy.

It is the general policy of education authorities to encourage community discussion and participation in education matters. Throughout Australia, the state administration of education is being focused on regionalization; flexible patterns of support permit direct and relevant responses to educational needs within different communities. School curricula are being diversified within guidelines to ensure the maintenance of common standards and to more fully accommodate the talents and interests of individual students. Closer relationships are being developed between schools and community-based educational activities; and specific attention is being given to disadvantaged schools and communities and to those with special needs. The pitfalls which accompany a desire to recognize the diverse interests and needs within society and yet retain a universally recognized set of standards, such as those provided by the public examination system or state-wide testing of particular skills, illustrate the dangers of pursuing fundamentally different goals without clearly specifying the relationships between them. The following sections endeavour to clarify some relationships between personal, intellectual and social development, general development of skills, knowledge and abilities, and the ways in which schools are attempting or might seek to articulate their goals and develop programmes to achieve them. Whilst it is recognized that social demand requirements have to be met, the emphasis in the remainder of the chapter is on the developmental approach since this is still inadequately understood by the public and unevenly applied in schools.

Children's intellectual development: an overview

Two major spheres of theories have shaped current thinking about the nature of childhood and the role of the school in the formation and growth of the child. In both the child is seen as an active agent in his own learning, and in neither have research and theory building reached the point where practical applications in classrooms are clear. Indeed it is questionable, given the ineluctable value structure of education and schooling, whether research and theory ever will of themselves produce direct classroom applications. Yet research and theory do illuminate our understanding of how children think and develop.

The first area of research and theory relates to the personality and social development of the child and the second to fundamental intellectual development. Each will be considered in turn.

Personal and social development

The view that the child is either a semi-passive organism who is acted upon and shaped by environmental events or is trapped by subconscious forces created during the earliest experiences of infancy and childhood, is inadequate. The person, both individually and through group effort, is capable of influencing the effects of subconscious and of environmental influences. Regardless of the social order, personal choices can be made which substantially modify behaviour. Reinforcing this psychological construct is a whole range of philosophical beliefs about the role of the individual in assuming responsibility for his own life. These beliefs are an essential part of the democratic heritage, although the particular form they take is a function of the ideological cast which is given to that heritage in different societies and at different periods. Australian democracy has, of course, a historical scope and direction but is not so precisely and rigorously defined through institutions or policy goals that schools have a clear notion of the context in which individual responsibility is to be exercised.

Research on children's development proceeds within particular societies and usually takes their values for granted. In western societies, belief in individualism, including individual rights and responsibilities and the sacredness of the individual personality, has had an overwhelming impact on educational thinking and research. Thus, in our kind of society, the belief that one is personally responsible for one's own destiny is of central importance for an understanding of the autonomy of the person and learning processes. Curiosity and the need to explore and solve problems are powerful forces possibly associated with the desire for a sense of mastery and competence in dealing with the environment. They have a high status in our culture and are closely associated with the ethic of achievement and fulfilment through personal effort which are rewarded with social success, status, praise, and money.

The strong motivating force of success has been clearly demonstrated in a wide range of studies, as has the importance of believing that success is attributable to one's own efforts rather than to chance or luck. If children are placed in a situation of continual failure, despite their use of a variety of attempts to meet adult-determined expectations, a state of 'learned helplessness' may be induced. Repeated frustration may lead to a sense of apathy which culminates in withdrawal, listlessness and apparent indifference to further failure. The experience of helplessness apparently interferes substantially with normal learning and unfortunately schools provide many examples of this phenomenon. Educators need to be particularly alert to the 'growth of helplessness' in the period of late primary and early secondary school, a time when some learning curves appear to dip, and a time of crucial importance for entry into the workforce and the assumption of early adult roles. Success for all students in well-structured and meaningful learning tasks is essential and ought to be one of the major goals for teachers.

Perception is another aspect of personality and social functioning whose importance has been inadequately appreciated in schools. The individual perceives and interprets the world using a unique set of 'personal constructs' described by George Kelly in this way: "Man looks at his world through transparent patterns or templates (constructs) which he creates and then attempts to fit over the realities of which the world is composed."[2] Through interaction with the cultural and social environment the individual builds up a unique set of personal constructs through which information is filtered and changed so that it fits previous experiences, or is rejected because it will not fit. It is then organized and interpreted so that a response can be made. The forming and remaking of these constructs has long been recognized as crucial in the growth of the self, the acquisition and use of personal knowledge and the achievement of personal autonomy and self-reliance. Jean Piaget has documented the development of such constructs within the intellectual sphere. Kelly tended to concentrate on social perception.

The uniqueness of individual perception and understanding is given unity, coherence and pattern through culture and socialization. Perception and motivation are themselves mediated through relationships, interactions and other kinds of experiences in the social world. Hence the extreme importance of home and school environment for the future life of the growing child.

Events in the infant's world are patterned by basic drives, the satisfaction of needs, and by parenting behaviour. They are gradually reorganized and integrated with appropriate response patterns to other people. Patterns of reinforcement, the language and non-verbal communication processes used, and cues from the situational context in which interactions occur, help focus the infant or child's attention on the salient aspects of a rapidly expanding environment and provide him with means and forms of expression. The infants and primary schools are amongst the most decisive institutions in this environment and therefore demand attention as crucial agencies in any national policy of human resource development. Such attention, however, has been focussed in recent years on the late adolescent, a necessary but quite insufficient basis of policy.

At present Australian child-rearing and educational policies lack clarity and direction. Frequently, in the form of public policy documents, they read like well-meaning incantations; they lack the bite and precision which show that issues have been addressed and choices made. Unless educational, political and other authorities responsible for the well-being of the child in society are able to come forward with incisive policies and guidelines, schools will increasingly become the prey of whatever lobby or interest group is able to seize the stage and affirm its prescriptions.

Educational policies are, however, improving in at least one important respect: their acknowledgement that development is continuous and not divisible into our traditional levels of schooling, from pre-school to tertiary education, each with its own narrow set of assumptions about what is educationally appropriate. Our understanding of the overall development of the child has been strongly influenced by the work of the psychoanalyst Erik Erikson, who proposed a 'stage' theory of growth through expanding human relationships.[3] Each of his proposed eight stages represents specific problems; and the way in which the individual addresses these problems determines the kind of person he or she will become. The focus is on the broad social and cultural forces with which the individual interacts and which help shape human development. Erikson's work, in the neo-Freudian tradition, has implications for schooling as profound as Piaget's cognitive theories. A longitudinal, culturally-based approach to development in which non-cognitive development tasks are emphasized is crucial to our understanding of children's activity and in devising appropriate learning situations. This approach has been given too little attention in the preparation and continuing education of teachers.

Parallel to Erikson's proposed stages of development are those postulated by Kohlberg for the development of moral reasoning, to which reference has been made in Part 4.[4] Moral development proceeds from an orientation towards punishment and obedience, with deference given to superior power, to decisions of conscience, and self-chosen, abstract ethical principles that are logical, comprehensive, universal and consistent. They are governed by universal principles of justice, equality, human rights and respect for the dignity of others. Few people reach the highest level, most remaining at about the level where 'right' behaviour consists of upholding social order for its own sake, and rules and authority are paramount.

Educators have always held as an ideal, the transformation of individuals and even whole societies to a higher stage of morality than prevails at any given time. Thus they argue that schools should introduce studies focused on personal values, ethics, morals, and social and environmental issues which could lead towards the progressive attainment of higher stages of moral reasoning.

Cognitive development

Current views about the process of intellectual growth in children are based largely on the ideas of the Swiss psychologist, Jean Piaget. Piaget's central thesis is that fundamental knowledge is gained through action and interaction—transactions—with the environment. Essentially, this view of knowledge as a *construction* of reality underlies the whole tradition of progressive education, from Socrates to Dewey. Since it is frequently dismissed as 'soft pedagogy', the emphasis it gives to the growth of knowledge and understanding needs to be appreciated. Cognitive development, according to Piaget, occurs in stages or levels accompanied by qualitive changes in the capacity of the child to think and act on his environment. The stages proceed from the first operation, of the infant through sensory impressions and motor actions, to the manipulation of symbols, and the analysis of abstract ideas and theories by the intellectually mature adult. Each level is assumed to be intrinsic to the developing person and to be actually or potentially characteristic of most people. The person's ability to comprehend and interpret increasingly complex kinds of information is held to depend on the cognitive stage reached, with each stage relating to the development of knowledge and understanding of relationships and processes. Skills and facts can be learnt without the acquisition of such fundamental knowledge and schools frequently tend to be more concerned with the former. A skill-and-fact-based schooling may be to the detriment of the child's intellectual development rather than an enhancement of it.

The major processes through which learning occurs are termed "assimilation" and "accommodation". Piaget argues that new information, to be understood, must be readily assimilated into existing cognitive structures. Information which does not fit readily will be distorted or rejected unless the schemata themselves undergo accommodation or change so that they can accept the new information. For accommodation to occur, new information should diverge only slightly from that which can already be assimilated.

The biological maturation theories of Piaget have been challenged on various counts. Evidence from cross-cultural studies emphasizes the importance of the roles of experiences provided by the pervading culture in determining levels of development. More recently it has been argued that the ages at which the various levels of fundamental knowledge analysed by Piaget are attained depend to a large extent on the structuring and sequencing of learning experiences. Nevertheless, recent cognitive research although critical is still largely within the Piagetian paradigm which remains of fundamental importance in understanding contemporary approaches to schooling. Apart from its value in helping the teacher and parent to understand the level at which learning tasks may be undertaken with understanding by the child, Piagetian theory provides ideas for the direction of learning. At the primary school, learning may be regarded both as having value in its own right and as contributory to the development of intellectual and other powers in the child which come to fruition at a later stage.

Theory and research on development: implications for schooling

If schools were to direct more attention towards the student's construction and reconstruction of knowledge and his understanding rather than the acquisition of skills and facts, many of the community criticisms of schooling might diminish. But this would require both the development of new curricula and substantial inservice programmes for teachers, and consequent increases in education budgets.

The child's interactions with the physical and social world are essential for the progressive construction and reconstruction of its own cognitive schemata through which the world is interpreted and understood. Active learning involving extensive use of concrete materials is required, not only in early childhood education but throughout the primary school years. These interactions need to be guided by principles of development and well-designed, systematic, sequential curricula. Too often in practice they are spasmodic, repetitive and dominated by inappropriate text material or the predilections of individual teachers and schools.

The dynamic nature of human cognitive structures illustrates the active role played by the individual in both creating and adapting to a physical and social environment. The reality of that environment is dependent on social experience and consensus rather than being objectively given: it is created and discovered by and not merely transmitted to the child. Shared perceptions give a sense of reality to our social world. Hence the need for a free and rich exchange of experiences, communicated for example through spoken and written language. Reality is that which is constructed by individuals and groups and has gained, or can succeed in gaining, social endorsement. Truth itself is a construct, that for which we have a warrant, and 'evidence' is relative to the current state of knowledge. These propositions about knowledge, truth and reality have dramatic implications for the education of the young child. This dynamic conception of knowledge, human and social development and reality is disturbing to people whose picture of the world and of school is one of a fixed order of things, summed up in their admonitions to "teach the kids as we were taught". The present era is one of confrontation between fixed and dynamic views of the nature of schooling.

Learning is an activity of the person comprising a wide range of specific processes. These include, for example, perceiving a problem, issue or question, identifying tasks of problem resolution, practising skills and other performances, memorizing information and ideas, reviewing and reflecting, constructing, modifying and otherwise acting on selected aspects of the environment, and many others. Any one act of learning will not necessarily involve all these but a learning process carried out over time, in some complex areas such as communication skills, or interpersonal relationships, or mathematical reasoning, involves many different processes and a wide range of tasks in which the learner is doing things with material and symbolic data. Learning tasks need to be selected which are interesting, challenging, and within the power of the child to undertake. 'Failure' in learning is a function of the tasks set and the conditions surrounding its performance as much as it is of the attitude and application of the child. The design of learning situations in classrooms involves selection and simplification of available materials and tasks, providing cues and selective reinforcement. The management of a learning environment, with 30 children or more and a wide array of resources, is a high level professional challenge.

In recent years a virtual explosion in the variety and availability of teaching aids and materials has occurred. They can be introduced quickly and efficiently and are often used to individualize learning. It should be noted, however, that their use generalizes on teaching techniques and the organization of curriculum materials, and as such they are not custom-built for each individual child, nor do they introduce much in the way of labour saving for the teacher. The promised revolution through computer-managed learning has yet to arrive. Teaching is still highly labour intensive.

Few schools are able to take into account each child's unique perception of the world and mode of interpreting and relating to it. It is difficult to teach to each child's level of cognitive development, skills and abilities, level of social development and degree to which its non-rational and emotional responses to the physical and social world affect its behaviour. To do all this, each teacher would require a range of skills in evaluating the needs of each child and interpreting them in an appropriate sequence of classroom activities, and resources, facilities and time—all of which at present are largely unattainable. Some educators would even question whether the school as we now know it could ever be adequate for such an ambitious educational regimen.

Without the necessary and demanding structuring of educational experiences, child-centred teaching may achieve little of the learning that its exponents intend. Choice, for the child, could become confusing. Without leadership, guidance and knowledgeable understanding from the teacher, the child could retreat to the safety of a small range of activities within which he felt secure. Teachers, if not confident and skilful in the theory as well as the practice of child-centred pedagogy, likewise retreat to tried and traditional practice—the safety of the customary.

Open education: concept and ideology

The term 'open education' denotes one of the most significant innovations in educational thought and practice, expecially but not exclusively at the primary school stage. The term refers to two distinct concepts which are often blurred—the openness of the education programme and the openness of the architecture.

Open-area schools have frequently been built to provide physical conditions which would favour greater diversity of educational programmes and more attention to individual differences. State departments of education in Australia have avoided identifying open-area schools with progressive education, yet educators in other countries have deliberately related the two. In Britain, open-plan primary schools have been designed to promote child-centred approaches to education, and in the United States team teaching and openness of working relationships among teachers and between teachers and students are associated with open-plan architecture. Overall, designers have emphasized the flexibility of open-area schools which would give teachers a greater choice in teaching strategies, learning activities and school organization.

Open-area schools are loosely defined to include contemporary and recent architectural designs not based on the traditional structure of a set of more or less homogenous classrooms used for a wide range of instructional and learning activities. A variety of arrangements of spaces fall within 'open' designs. The Australian Open-Area Schools Project describes a number of different arrangements, whose distinctive feature is a general learning area which is a space occupied by two or more teachers and a commensurate number of students.[5] In addition, these schools may incorporate other special purpose areas such as practical areas, withdrawal areas for small groups, quiet areas for individual work, resource areas for library materials and teaching aids, and a space that may be used as a home base for a teacher and single class of students. The keynote is diversity and flexibility of space.

Open architecture has been associated with improved design of furniture and storage space, carpeted floors, bright colour schemes and outdoor learning areas. These features could, of course, be incorporated in schools of conventional design. Australian school systems have now focused on designs consisting of two-teacher units rather than the barn-like structures of some of the earlier open schools, following evaluation projects which highlighted the difficulties inherent in the operation of larger units.

According to its exponents, open plan design will: cater better for the individual differences of pupils and teachers; foster teacher co-operation; provide scope for different groupings and interaction of pupils; provide a more pleasant, stimulating environment for learning; and allow for change in educational practice. Unfortunately, many teachers have found themselves in open-plan schools, lacking specific preparation or rationales relevant to these situations. Since economy has been a factor in some decisions to build open-plan schools, the resources needed to make them work well have not always been available.

Sharp definitions of open education are impossible to extricate from concepts such as individualized education, activity-based learning, co-operative teaching and informal education. In general, open education is an approach that is receptive to change and new ideas in curriculum, scheduling, the use of space, and the honest expression of feeling between teachers and students. It is characterized by a classroom environment in which there is a minimum of teaching to the class as a whole and provision is made for children to pursue individual interests, to be actively involved with materials and to exercise initiative and responsibility.

Open education favours the emergence of new patterns and forms of pedagogy, teacher–student relationships and student activity. It is both an affirmation of long-established ideas of progressive education and a reaction to instructional orthodoxies. Much of the unease about contemporary schooling, including the 'back to basics' movement, is attributable to uncertainty about what open and progressive education is about. Educators need to achieve clearer definitions in this area, to affirm the educational and social values and purposes of open education, as they understand them, and to respond positively to criticism.

Community participation

The traditional classroom organization is that of one teacher working with 'her' class. Few other adults enter and children interact with other teachers and adults only in activities in the playground, through medical services, on sports days and excursions, and so on. This picture is gradually changing, and despite some resistance, more adults are entering the classroom to work with the teacher in a team.

In a study of four 'integrated day' primary schools, carried out by Bristol University in Britain, it was noted that each school had a thematic approach to integrate the curriculum for a major part of the school week and each child had a programme designed to meet individual needs and interests.[6] The success of the programmes was dependent on the class teacher having time to talk with each child; for which assistance in the classroom was necessary. Moreover, teachers needed to be trained and retrained more effectively in the efficient deployment of teaching assistants and other ancillary helpers. In each of the schools studied all teachers had an aide. The situation of a teaching aide for each teacher does not apply in Australia, except in special circumstances such as in Aboriginal schools where aides are needed to interpret the local culture for teachers and help bridge the gap between home and school, Primary teachers, with a full timetable, are in particular need of assistance. It is paradoxical that it is in tertiary institutions, where students ought to achieve maximum self-direction, that teaching loads are lightest and support staff most numerous. Research needs to be supported of course, but the education of the younger child is no less vital to the well-being of our society.

There are good reasons for community involvement in curriculum decision-making in schools. Firstly, although students spend a significant proportion of time in their formative years at school, schooling is only one of a number of agencies which affect the child's educational progress. The family, peer group and media have a considerable influence on the student, both directly as part of the community and indirectly by shaping attitudes to school. The school should aim to work in association with family and community, to enhance student attitudes and performance in school and to overcome the traditional separateness between schools, and between schools and the wider community.

Secondly, schools should be conducted in accordance with democratic principle of maintaining authority through consensus and participation in decision-making. Students, even young children, need to develop a better understanding of such processes. Parents and other members of the community will participate more actively in decision-making at school level if they have a significant influence on the outcomes. To encourage effective participation, schools and teachers need to be clear about what they are doing and to explain their aims and their curriculum to the community. Without this understanding, lay people cannot contribute adequately to decisions on school policy, curricula and methods. Equally, teachers must learn to take account of parent and community views.

By making the involvement of parents a condition of funding in its disadvantaged schools programme, the Australian Schools Commission has provided an impetus for the establishment of school–community links in areas of high migrant density and low socio-economic status where parents are commonly reluctant to visit schools and talk with teachers. There are some outstandingly successful programmes which have altered the whole school climate by involving parents in a variety of school-based activities.

While there are many examples of successful school–community co-operation, there are also many schools in Australia where crucial decisions affecting school–community relations are made entirely by the principal and, usually but not always, the teaching staff. There are many barriers to community participation, some of which are the difficulties in defining the role of the community and the sorts of decisions in which parents can play a part. Other barriers are the attitudes of parents who are either apathetic or reluctant to become involved because they are uncertain of their reception by teachers or of their ability to discuss educational issues, the difficulties of reaching agreement among parents, the need to avoid undue pressure by small vocal groups, and teachers' attitudes which may be both negative and defensive.

The movement towards community participation is still in its infancy. It suggests interesting and challenging new models of education. It is a reminder of the old view of the 'educative society' where professional and non-professional roles are redefined. The freeing of primary school curricula and teaching which has accompanied the relaxing of tight controls, for example by examination and inspection, has created many problems. Nevertheless, it provides ample scope for constructive community involvement in the life of the state school—something on which some independent schools have long prided themselves.

Issues and trends in education

School practice seems frequently to fall short of what theorists offer as appropriate structures for learning, curriculum design, organization of learning situations, and the aims of education. Likewise, there is a considerable gap between school practice and what many community groups see as proper directions for Australian education. There is a fine balance between schools feeling demoralized by these gaps and inspired to improve performance. It must be borne in mind that the world of the practical provides a unique form of knowledge against which research, educational theories, and community demands must themselves be tested.

Traditions and past practice, however, no longer provide adequate guideposts. Although teachers often feel uncomfortable about child-centred education (too loose, too demanding) and the social demand approach (an intrusion of adult demands before children are ready for them), it is a major task of our time to redefine the primary school curriculum in recognition of the large strides taken in theory and research, new techniques and resources, and the rapidly changing social context. Schooling appears to many commentators to have many of the features of a protected social orthodoxy. Like all other social processes it must meet challenges to its assumptions, structures and policies and its relationships with other social institutions. The concept of the community as educator and as resource offers challenging issues to explore. The school is but one agency, and frequently a very limited one, affecting children's learning. The education of children requires a concerted community effort if appropriate structures and a cohesive policy of education involving the community is to be developed. The school itself is not and should not be a static institution. It must renew itself and redirect its programmes and resources to meet emerging needs from a variety of sources.

How different from today will the school of the year 2 000 be? Pedagogy is subject to many extravagant claims, to fashions and to often naive confidence in gadgetry. Nevertheless, much of the stock (buildings and professional teachers) in existence today will be in service in two decades' time. Materials, equipment and resources may not change as rapidly as it is sometimes assumed, particularly if constraints within the governmental funding of education continue. We cannot assume, therefore, that change will come from the injection of new resources and massive numbers of young teachers as happened in the sixties and seventies. We need now to question how relevant the school of the future will be to changing societal needs. As a universal institution schools have had a relatively short history. Can we even assume that they will remain the major formal educational vehicle? In Australian primary education today there is disturbingly little evidence of a radical reappraisal. Indeed, there are plaintive cries that the pace of change has been too great and that the schools' greatest need is for a period of consolidation. We may question whether consolidation of the status quo is an adequate response to either the developmental or the social demand orientations identified earlier in this chapter as major determinants of educational policy.

Multiculturalism has emerged as a significant political and ideological force in the late seventies in Australian society. It provides an opportunity either to create a new, more equitable and satisfying society, or to segment society into well protected interest groups. The challenge of multiculturalism is a powerful one which needs to be translated into guidelines for, and critiques of, educational policy and practice. It poses many unanswered questions to the primary school. Should the school assist in affirming ethnic identity? What do children need to know about the multicultural nature of Australian society? Should ethnic languages be introduced into the curriculum? In an increasingly diverse society, to what extent is a core curriculum of shared perceptions, values and experiences necessary? Individual differences and needs remain postulates of educational theory, and the organization of schooling today only partially recognizes them. Is it paradoxical for a democratic society to seek to acknowledge the uniqueness of the individual and yet strive for social integration at the levels of, firstly, the ethnic subculture and, secondly, the whole society? This cluster of issues alone is sufficient to rebut the view that the schools need to consolidate rather than embark on further changes.

Conclusion

This chapter began with a distinction between two broadly-based orientations to the educational process, namely *social demand* and *human and social development*. It said that there is no necessary contradiction between the two and that it is a task of educational policy and practice to achieve reconciliations between them. Emphasis in the chapter has been given to the developmental approach in which the child as a dynamic and constructive being is of central concern. This is because this approach has come under severe and often ill-informed criticism in recent years as part of a reaction to what are thought to be extreme progressivist ideologies prevalent in schools, and because it is necessary to affirm that the developmental view is not a new-fangled innovation but lies at the roots of Western educational theory based, in its historical origins, in ancient Greece and, in its modern research form, in the theories of developmental psychologists. Nevertheless, the practicalities of everyday life require us to acknowledge that society has legitimate demands of education. Our schools must aim to meet these and our teachers need to be so educated as to learn how to recognize and satisfy these demands. Their professional expertise must be extended and given strong community backing.

In the last part of the chapter, a number of issues have been raised. These include the claims of a multicultural society, the relation between core curriculum and individualized courses, and the relationship of the child's school learning to his total experiences. In each of these, one may detect social demands on the school. The issues are only a few amongst the many confronting teachers of children today, and they are selected because they are, at present, open and controversial. They illustrate a basic proposition of this chapter that the developmental needs of the child must be addressed in a social context where diversity of view and belief and uncertainty about the future prevail. The child's education must be mapped firmly and clearly within and as part of this context.

The Unending Challenge

Roy F. Smallacombe

Although there have been times of significant social and population changes in Australia's history, the decades since the Second World War have brought unprecedented attention to school education. Other levels of education have experienced similar or greater expansion, but for this discussion we consider education to the end of the primary stage.

The reader of the history of schooling in Australia will be aware that schools have been the servants of society, responding to events rather than influencing them. The egalitarian tone of the Australian school indicates the attitude of a young nation that developed mateship rather through historical accident than by immigration for religious freedom or as a result of war. Particularly since Federation in 1901, Australia's history has strongly influenced the development of schools. The centralist view, perhaps determined by geographical as greatly as by historical factors, was reflected in government activities in general, and in educational administration in particular. Large Australian education systems have contrasted markedly with the local school districts of the United States and England. Uniformity of educational practice, aims and funding was acceptable to a nation with equality of opportunity as a main goal. Isolation through distance was a strong influence towards a common curriculum, uniform levels of achievement and dependence on centralized systems for new ideas. Schooling in Australia, then, until quite recent times showed the influence of utilitarianism, geography and history. Two other factors, economics and politics, have been historically important, and to an increasing degree in the last two decades.

This is not to claim that the place of the child has not been important or that children's learning has not been effective. But the child's role in learning and questions of personal growth and development have been implicit in the process of schooling. Few committees of enquiry address themselves to these matters. Dr

Skilbeck discussed above a number of theories of learning and human development which have resulted from research in recent decades. These discoveries have raised issues which were unknown or irrelevant to educators of the past. Many of these questions have yet to be accommodated in curriculum planning and classroom teaching: these should be the key issues in the future. Cognitive development with the main aim of assisting children to remember and apply quantities of facts has been a feature of schooling. An underlying assumption has been that, within broad limits, children have similar capacities to learn facts and to organize and apply them to life situations. Indeed, the accumulation of information has been held to be an educational aim in itself. It has been most easily managed by teachers and most demanded by parents. Furthermore, it has been assumed that cognitive development is the most valuable of all; our social system has bestowed approval and material rewards on it, and progress through the school system has depended on it.

Teaching methods in schools, which long remained persistently didactic and based on a stimulus-response theory of learning, have begun slowly to take more account of the work of educational psychologists: the work of Piaget and his identification of stages of individual development are well known. To translate research findings into effective classroom practice is no easy task, particularly when they challenge existing methods and school organization. For instance, it is difficult to reconcile the practice of promotion of children by age with acceptance of the need to cater for individual differences. Exponents of humanistic psychology (Erickson, Bettelheim and Maslow are representative) have been influenced by psychoanalytic theories. Many new terms have crept into the daily usage not only of teachers but of us all as a result: such terms as 'awareness', 'freedom', 'self-understanding', 'conflict', 'maladjustment' and 'permissive' are linked with these theories. Counselling and guidance services and curriculum emphases on health education reflect the influence of psychoanalyis on education[2].

Psychological theories have extended our knowledge of child development well beyond the cognitive. They have been eagerly taken up by teachers of young children. In many instances, these theories have explained new modes of learning or difficulties of children that impede learning. The importance of assisting children to develop a positive self-concept is the basis for many modern teaching approaches.[3] Combs, Rogers and Maslow variously have stated characteristics of a person whose self-development is adequate. Modern practices in early childhood education have won a high reputation in this aspect of child development. Similarly, the influence of the behavioural psychologists (Skinner and Gagné being representative) has been significant, but Australian teachers, in a climate where 'self-realization', 'discovery methods' and 'creativity' have been regarded highly, have had fundamental objections. Reconciliation of behaviourist and humanist theories at the classroom level is still a long way off for most schools.

In summary, there are apparently conflicting views about children's learning which provide a dilemma for today's parents, teachers and administrators. Children develop in stages at individual rates: cognitive development should be balanced with that of self-concept and receptiveness. Educators at all levels should understand that schooling should reinforce positive attitudes and eliminate the negative personal assessment that occurs in too many classrooms.

Differences in social growth of children are as important as differences in any other area. Schools reveal their attitudes to this question by the ways in which classes are organized, by teachers' views on discipline and control and by the physical appearance of class areas. The inter-relatedness of these aspects led, in the early 1970s, to the development in South Australia of open-plan teaching areas in primary schools and flexible-plan in secondary schools. These planning efforts, since they aimed at providing education outside the narrowly intellectual, were courageous. They are likely to be misunderstood because unobtrusive social and attitudinal growth is difficult to measure in any statistical sense. The flexible-plan school has shown that teacher co-operation, detailed planning and organization, and a willingness to develop new modes of teacher–student relationships have been required to a greater degree. These developments were accompanied by acceptance by education systems that local autonomy assumed local competence to handle new situations.

But what were the new aspirations of 1970 which were to increase as the years passed? An official report in South Australia listed 15 assumptions about the secondary school of the future.[4] Some should be mentioned because they have been commonly accepted in schools and are relevant for primary students. They included: an increasing awareness that learning is essentially an individual process and that individuals vary in their abilities and rates of progress; an increased emphasis on self-directed student involvement; the encouragement of the enquiry or discovery approach, so that the teacher more frequently adopts the role of guide rather than that of instructor; considerable oral work and more physical activity both in the classroom and in movement to different school areas; school buildings designed as a tool to facilitate teaching and learning; and, as part of the learning process, more frequent contact between students and their immediate social, physical and cultural environment. Here was an example of an education system about to develop a new generation of schools on a stated set of beliefs about teaching and learning.

These proposals raise a number of educational issues, such as learning as an individual activity and the need for motivation and learning through discovery. Bruner acted as advocate for the child as well as for a learning method with the claim that "discovery is most often a matter of rearranging evidence in such a way that one is enabled to go beyond the evidence to new insights".[5] That is not to claim that discovery methods are suitable for learning in all situations. Jacka states that "there is very little research evidence that supports their use over other methods".[6] Why, then, is this approach adopted? A simple answer is that it enables the child to develop abilities to handle information in a world where the quantity might otherwise be overwhelming.

A decade later, Bruner admitted that his earlier views were based on a belief "that learning was what students wanted to do.... Their motivation was taken for granted."[7] In other words, cognitive learning is not enough. One danger with new developments is that they may be expected to be a panacea for shortcomings. Balance is needed, and selection of the most effective learning methods is an everpresent question for a teacher. Jacka has described the discovery–expository debate well for the general reader.[8] Other aspects of children's development have been given considerable attention in the 1970s. Statements of the aims of primary education from the 1950s have been influenced by psychologists such as Maslow and Rogers who advocated self-actualization (Maslow) and the fully functioning person (Rogers) as desirable aims of schooling. Educational aims began to be stated in terms of assisting children to develop according to their abilities and interests, and the like. This was a far cry from a decade or so earlier when children in most states sat for an external examination at the end of the primary stage.

Dewey's influence began to be felt in Australian primary education in the post-war period of the 1950s.[9] It was a slow process here as it was in England where, Bennett notes, the so-called progressive education "was legitimated by the Plowden Report (1967) which was strongly prescriptive" of it.[10] It reiterated the words of the 1931 Hadow Report that "the curriculum is to be thought of in terms of activity and experience rather than knowledge to be acquired and facts to be stored". Bennett's findings about different teaching styles and their effects on children's progress make interesting reading.

In the 1970s attempts were made in Australian school systems to accommodate the most useful and effective theories into school practices. In doing so schools have been criticized by both reformers and conservatives, and by the lay community and the professionals. But these developments contributed to the redeeming outcome of placing children and their many-sided development in the centre of the aims and activities of the primary school.

The curriculum reform movement forced a realization upon educators that curriculum development is very much more than the arrangement of subject matter. Discoveries about human development and the nature of the learning process and new understanding about the organization of knowledge itself were all considered as parts of the learning process for children. Whereas the problems of facilities, finance and staff have demanded most attention in the post-war years, questions of the aims of education, teaching methods, and student performance—curriculum issues—are likely to dominate in the 1980s. The aims and objectives of a school programme, the needs of students, decisions about the most suitable materials and methods and the most meaningful means of the evaluation of a student's development or the effectiveness of a programme are all contributing factors in a complex curriculum process. Other chapters in this book have focused attention on the problem in modern societies of determining the role of the school, the family and the state in fostering the welfare of the child.

Much has been written about the role of the school in fostering the welfare of the child. As social institutions have expanded their roles, so the helping professions have increased in number. The school has been expected to assume many roles beyond those of providing intellectual and character training. Schools might be excused for thinking that a rapidly changing society is expecting them to be a last hope in solving its children's problems. Schools and systems appear to be under pressure from social forces that educational theories have not allowed for. And schools in Australia have not articulated their roles with clarity or confidence and have found themselves accepting new obligations with disconcerting haste. The issues of the social role of the school, of moral and personal development, of physical health—to name a few—have come to rest in the school. School systems also have been late in articulating the purposes of schools. Committees of enquiry and state departments have produced statements of aims quite recently. These broad aims have to be translated into specific programmes at school level and community participation in this work is now encouraged by most systems.

In 1977 the New South Wales Department of Education, restated the aims of primary education thus: "To guide individual development in the context of society through recognized stages of development towards perceptive understanding, mature judgement, responsible self-direction and moral autonomy." The Purposes of Schools statement current in South Australian government schools mentions 11 main purposes from the child's viewpoint. It draws implicitly distinctions between cognitive learning and the acquisition of understanding of oneself and of habits, attitudes and appreciation. A Victorian statement proposes the general aim "to promote maximum development of each student within the limits of his or her capacity." Other states have similar general goals of education. These broadly reflect the theoretical discoveries referred to earlier in this chapter.[11]

The challenge of developing courses and methods to match these aspirations is considerable and schools will need advice and resources to make this work possible. Curriculum development is a task whose complexity is not always understood both inside and outside schools. We have mentioned the exposed position in which Australian schools have often found themselves, lacking clear aims and policies. Bowker has pointed out that changes in education in Australia until the post-war period were very slow "since no national policy in Australia was possible since the six states were the sovereign authorities in educational matters". The 1970s have seen great changes in the support of governments for schools and in their influence over the curriculum.

We noted earlier the events which aimed to place the child at the centre of education; education too, however, has its centres of power. Centralized systems in most states have begun to share control and authority. The innovations and disadvantaged schools programmes of the Schools Commission have encouraged initiatives by individual schools and teachers. Independent development of tertiary institutions of teacher education and proliferation of organizations and institutions have led to new pressures on schools. To these we may add employing and funding authorities, buildings departments and commercial producers of classroom materials. At least two other groups exercise control over schools. Teachers unions have won significantly improved conditions and an influential voice in educational decision-making. The most recent arrivals on the power-sharing scene are parent groups who are likely to become more prevalent in the eighties. Whatever the group that influences the education of children, a risk is that the child's development may be overlooked in the effort to build administrative structures, introduce new programmes or establish cases for better funding, larger staffs or better facilities.

The tendency to interpret education in terms of finance, organization and procedures is common in the reports of educational bodies in Australian education. The Schools Commission Triennial Report for 1979–81 illustrates this point in its reference to educational and financial contexts, recurrent resources, capital facilities, and initiatives supporting devolution. The 1971 Karmel Committee Enquiry report in South Australia reflected similar emphases. The collected views of outstanding educators and administrators in 1974 had relatively little to say about children and learning.[13] Teachers unions, too, have developed a preoccupation with industrial questions. Professional associations of teachers have a commendable record of concern for learning. In general, however, we have persisted with a long-lasting tendency to import educational ideas.

Early childhood educators have been alert and successful in adapting research findings to school practices. The literature of junior primary education clearly places the child at the centre and supports varied means by which the yound child's self-concept is developed by teaching methods, a supportive school environment and links between the school and the home. We accept that the growing practice for schools to commit themselves to specific aims for older primary children will result in more effective education for those children. In Australia, in the face of criticism of educational bureaucracies, many changes in education have occurred as a result of administrative or political initiatives. New developments in career education, through multiculturalism, and in social, health and religious education—to name a few—have not arisen spontaneously from the schools.

What should be the future directions of children's education, given that each child is recognized as having individual needs, interests and abilities, and that intellectual learning must be accompanied by growth in values and attitudes? Changes are occurring in two directions. There is a better understanding of the total curriculum and its central importance. The importance of informal learning, determined by the attitudes, customs and environment surrounding the child, is being acknowledged. Most educational energy in the past has been spent on the former and it is properly still the teacher's professional area. But the latter is crucial. Notions like school–community co-operation are not slogans. Every citizen, parent or not, has a part to play in building the society in which good schools prosper. The education of boys and girls is too urgent, too lofty a task to be left only to administrators and teachers.

PART 7

The Economic Costs of Children and Child Poverty in Australia

Peter Saunders

The aim of this chapter is to consider those elements which constitute the economic costs of dependent children and their implications for policies aimed at providing income support to families with children in Australia. Particular attention will be given to the existence of child poverty in Australia, the efficacy of the existing policies aimed at combatting child poverty, and some suggested improvements to the existing system. Two questions are of interest in considering policies designed to provide income support to families with children. Firstly, the underlying rationale for the existence of such policies needs to be clearly spelt out. For example, are the policies designed merely to eliminate financial poverty amongst children, or is there a wider justification for providing assistance to all families with children? Secondly, there is the related question of the adequacy of existing provisions. Are they sufficient to compensate families for the full costs of children? Indeed, should they be? In order to answer such questions, an evaluation of the economic costs of children is essential. This can then be used as the basis for defining poverty lines and measuring child poverty in the first place. Thus the problems of measuring the costs of children, of determining the extent of child poverty, and of assessing the effectiveness of policies are inter-related and should be considered together.

In what follows, methods adopted to measure the economic costs of children, the problems they involve, and the evidence which has been produced for Australia over recent years are considered. The relationship between the costs of children and the definition of the poverty line are highlighted, and the evidence on the extent of child poverty in Australia is presented. The final two sections deal respectively with the existing income support provisions for families with dependent children, and some recommendations for improving the existing arrangements. The wider questions of the underlying rationale and justification for such policies are considered briefly in the remainder of this section.

Two distinct approaches have been taken by economists in the way in which children, and child-rearing activities are viewed. They can be characterized as regarding children largely in private consumption terms, or largely in social investment terms. The first of these represents a relatively new strand of economic research and is concerned with analysing the economic factors which affect the decision to have children. This approach views children as an economic commodity like any other, on which parents may freely choose to allocate their limited resources.[1] Children embody consumption elements, in that their existence contributes to the current satisfaction of their parents, and investment elements, in that the skills and education which they acquire will persist in the future and may produce a return to the parents during old age and retirement in the form of support and assistance. Of these two elements, the consumption aspects of children dominate. The emphasis is on benefits which accrue privately, i.e. within the family, as a result of the existence of children. A basic insight of these models is their emphasis on the cost of time involved in child rearing. Child rearing, particularly during the early years, is a very labour intensive activity and thus a major cost involved is the foregone earnings of those (usually mothers) directly responsible for caring for the children in the home. In general terms this approach provides little justification for the provision of financial assistance to families with children, at society's expense, because of the private nature of the benefits which children provide. For why should families who choose to devote their resources to the rearing of children be compensated as against families who choose to devote their resources in other ways to satisfy their consumption needs, by going on expensive annual holidays for example? Proponents of this view would not deny that adequate provisions should be made to ensure that poverty be effectively eliminated amongst all families, including those with children. Such a policy would be justified, however, on the grounds of poverty alleviation rather than any requirement that families with children should receive income assistance from the public purse irrespective of whether or not they are poor.

The second, and more dominant, approach views children largely in social investment terms. Children are a human resource whose development during their early years, which is a crucial determinant of their ability to realize their full potentialities in later life, is financed within the family itself. This process of investment in human capital contributes ultimately to raising the productivity of the labour force, hence raising economic growth in society, from which all can benefit. These benefits are wide ranging (i.e. social) whilst the initial costs, considered largely in terms of the costs of goods and services required to rear children, are internal to the family (i.e. private). Thus a strong case exists for the provision, financed from the public purse, of assistance to all families with children to ensure that adequate investment can take place. In order for such provision to be effective, the level of assistance must be closely related to the costs of children—in the extreme the two should be equal, although it can be argued that the existence of private consumption benefits from children justifies some part of the cost falling on the parents themselves, if their resources are sufficient. This explains the continued emphasis on estimating the costs of children which characterizes this approach. As Margaret Wynn, one of its leading proponents argues:

> ... the identification of people, and children in particular, as a *resource*, provides a new justification for devoting *resources* to their development, care and maintenance.... Most of the total investment in human capital is made by parents within the family and depends upon the resources made available to parents for satisfying the needs of their family.[2]

Within this later view, the costs of children have conventionally been expressed in terms of the expenditures on goods and services required by children. The implicit labour costs incurred by family members during child rearing have largely been ignored. In contrast, Apps has argued that the labour expended within the household sector of the economy is exploited since it receives no monetary compensation, even though it produces labour (by rearing future adult members of the labour force) which will ultimately form part of the production sector of the economy.[3] Thus the production sector gains directly at the expense of the consumption sector by using the latter's output as one of its inputs, and yet makes no contribution towards the development of this input. It therefore follows that labour expended on child care should rightly be viewed as a productive activity in its own right and should thus receive a wage payment as compensation. These arguments appear to be similar to those expressed in the first approach which emphasizes the opportunity costs of the labour employed within the family in rearing children. They are quite different, however, in that the opportunity cost arguments are based on the dichotomy between the household and productive sectors, and in fact relate the labour costs incurred in the household sector to the earnings which would accrue in the productive or market sector. Apps' approach challenges the basis for the continuation of this dichotomy, and argues that labour expended in the household sector should be compensated directly as productive labour, in the same way as labour expended in the market sector. All labour involved in child rearing would therefore receive the same wage payment, recognizing its direct contribution to raising productivity. The important point is that the arguments presented by both Wynn and Apps suggest that income assistance should be provided to all families with children and not just to those families in poverty, reflecting the social benefits which child rearing ultimately produces.

Measuring the economic costs of children

Before one can begin to consider and compare the economic circumstances of children in different families and the existence of poverty amongst children, some measure of the economic needs and costs of children must be developed. In general, the living standards of the members of a family including children will depend upon family income and the size and composition of the family which is dependent upon that income. Incomes which are sufficient for a family with one child, for example, may be woefully inadequate in providing acceptable standards of living for a family with six children. But how can one decide the increase in family income which is required to maintain living standards when an additional child enters the family? Until an answer to this question is obtained, it is impossible to compare the living standards of families with differing incomes and of differing size and composition. Is a single adult with an income of $100 per week better off than a two-child family with an income of $150 per week for example? Are the current levels of government assistance to families with dependent children sufficient to cover the economic costs borne by such families? The concept of family equivalence scales, or equivalent income scales as they are sometimes called, is designed to provide answers to such questions. As such, these scales reflect the economic costs of additional family members, and are thus a crucial element in measuring the extent of poverty amongst children and in assessing the adequacy of effectiveness of government policies which direct financial assistance to families with dependent children.

Family equivalence scales measure the relative incomes of families of differing composition which are required to maintain the family at the same standard of living. They are normally expressed in relative terms, and the childless married couple will be used here as the benchmark for them. The childless couple is conventionally given a scale of unity. The equivalence scales for other families then reflect the incomes they require, relative to the childless couple, in order to attain the same standard of living. If, for example, the equivalence scale for a family consisting of husband, wife and two dependent children is 1.25, this implies that this family requires an income which is 25 per cent higher than the childless couple, in order to maintain the same standard of living. In terms of measuring poverty, these figures imply that the poverty line for the two-child family should be 25 per cent higher than the poverty line for the childless couple. The family equivalence scales, then, reflect the economic costs of children in families of differing composition.

Early attempts to measure family equivalence scales in Britain can be found in Rowntree's studies of poverty and Beveridge's social insurance proposals, which related the payments to the costs of subsistence budgets for children.[4] Beveridge proceeded by calculating the cost of a minimally nutritious diet adequate for health, and added to this allowances for expenditures on clothing, fuel, light and various sundries. The basic problem with such an approach is the inevitable element of subjectivity that it contains. A more serious criticism is that they are based on what poor families ought to consume of particular goods, rather than what families actually do consume. There is broad agreement now that the measurement of family equivalence scales, and of poverty lines should be based at least partly, if not fully, on the actual consumption expenditure patterns of poor families.[5]

The derivation of family equivalence scales solely from observed expenditure behaviour requires the analysis of family budgets. An extensive study of pre-war British family budgets was undertaken by Prais and Houthakker, whose work stimulated subsequent work by Podder and Kakwani for Australia and by McClements for the United Kingdom.[6] The work by Podder and Kakwani analysed data derived from a Survey of Consumer Finances and Expenditures undertaken in 1967–68 by Macquarie University and the University of Queensland. The theory on which these studies are based views families as maximizing their utility (standard of living) subject to an income or budget constraint. The family utility level is dependent upon the flow of goods and services which it consumes, and the characteristics which determine the family composition, for example the number of family members, their age and sex. The model produces expenditure equations for goods and services which relate family expenditure to family income and the family composition variables, and from which the family equivalence scales can be derived.[7]

A somewhat simpler method of calculating family equivalence scales is based on the estimation of Engel curves. These curves relate expenditure on a particular good to family income. Engel's law derives from his observation that the proportion of family expenditure devoted to food declines as the standard of living of the family increases. This suggests that families which devote the same proportion of their income to expenditure on food have the same standard of living, a simplifying assumption which has been used by Podder to estimate family equivalence scales from household expenditure survey data.

Whilst the techniques used in the work of Kakwani and Podder are sophisticated, the results, as always, are only as good as the data on which they are based. Doubts about the reliability of the data they used have been expressed recently by Richardson.[8] Alternative data collected by the Australian Bureau of Statistics in its Household Expenditure Survey should allow the derivation of more-satisfactory family equivalence scales, although no such analysis has as yet appeared.[9] It was largely due to the non-availability of the Household Expenditure Survey Results for 1973 that the Commission of Inquiry into Poverty in Australia (hereafter the Henderson Report) based its poverty line calculations on family equivalence scales derived from a survey undertaken by the Budget Standard Services for New York in 1954.[10] These scales had been used in the earlier study of poverty in Melbourne undertaken by Henderson, Harcourt and Harper.[11]

It is not clear how useful these scales, derived for New Yorkers in 1954, are for analysing Australian conditions in 1973. The importance of this point should not be understated, for the equivalence scales are used to determine the poverty lines for families of differing composition, and are thus an important determinant of both the numbers of families living below the poverty line, and the

Table 1: Estimated family equivalence scales

Family Composition	Equivalence Scales		
	Henderson	**Kakwani**	**Podder**
Single adult	0.738	0.604	0.488
Married Couple (MC)	1.000	1.000	1.000
MC and 1 child	1.153	1.210	1.250
MC and 2 children	1.373	1.379	1.481
MC and 3 children	1.594	1.481	1.675
MC and 4 children	1.815	1.537	1.972
MC and 5 children	1.958	1.588	2.381
MC and 6 children	2.260	1.637	2.732

Notes: (a) The last family size for Kakwani and Podder also includes families with more than 6 children.
(b) The ages of the children in the 6 families in the Henderson scales are assumed to be 3; 3 and 9; 3, 9 and 12; 3, 9, 12 and 15; 3, 5, 9, 12 and 15; 3, 5, 9, 12, 15 and 16.

composition by family size of the poor. For comparative purposes, table 1 shows the family equivalence scales used in the Henderson Report, along with those derived by Kakwani and Podder.

As the table illustrates, the estimated family equivalence scales differ considerably depending on the method and data used to derive them. For example, if one considers a childless married couple with a weekly income of $100, the three sets of equivalence scales imply respectively that a four-child family requires a weekly income of $181.50, $153.70 or $197.20 in order to achieve the same standard of living. It is interesting to compare the Henderson and Kakwani scales, since both have been used to define poverty lines and measure poverty in Australia.[12] Compared to the Henderson scales, Kakwani's are higher for one-child families, the same for two-child families and substantially lower for families with more than two children. Thus the poverty lines used by Kakwani will be lower for families with more than two children, and higher for families with one child, compared to those used by Henderson.

Child poverty in Australia

The family equivalence scales presented in table I were used in the Henderson Report to derive the poverty lines for different families relative to the standard family. The standard family used in the report consisted of a working husband with a dependent wife and two dependent children. There remains the problem of deriving the poverty line for the standard family. This was based on the poverty line developed by Henderson, Harcourt and Harper in their study of poverty in Melbourne. They chose as the poverty line for the standard family the existing basic wage plus child endowment payments. This level was chosen on the assumption that it reflected community attitudes towards the normal needs of families in Australian society. Since the Henderson Report viewed poverty in relative terms, this figure was then updated to 1973 in line with movements in average weekly earnings. The resultant poverty line for the standard family was $62.70. Both the method used to determine the poverty line for the standard family in 1966, and its updating to 1973, have been the subject of criticism.[13] However, whilst the poverty line for the standard family determines the poverty lines for other families and hence the overall extent of measured poverty, it is the family equivalence scales which determine the composition of poverty amongst families of different sizes.

On the basis of their definition of the poverty line, the Henderson Report found that in 1973 10.2 per cent of income units, containing

8.2 per cent of the population, had incomes below the poverty line. Whilst these figures themselves provide grave cause for concern, the extent of poverty amongst dependent children is doubly serious, both because of their inability to improve their current situations, and because the poverty they experience during childhood will in many cases permanently affect their life chances. The figures indicated that just above a quarter of a million dependent children were living in families below the poverty line. This represents 7.9 per cent of all dependent children, or about 1 child in 13. Of these, 170 000 came from families with 2 parents and the remaining 84 000 from single-parent families. Poverty amongst single-parent families was particularly acute, with 37.5 per cent of fatherless families and 15.9 per cent of motherless families in poverty. Further disaggregated analysis of single-parent families proved impossible because of the small numbers involved. In addition, a further 207 000 dependent children were living in families whose incomes exceeded the poverty line by less than 20 per cent; in Henderson's terms these families were 'rather poor'. Considering only two-parent families, 5.8 per cent of dependent children were in poor families, and a further 7.1 per cent in rather poor families. The probability of a child being poor is positively related to the number of dependent children in the family. As the Henderson Report notes, "Of the children living in very poor families, 59 per cent were from large families, although only 29 per cent of all children were living in large families."[14] Children in families with five or more children have a probability of being poor which is more than six times the probability for a child in a one- or two-child family. The latter types of family are however about 15 times more numerous than the former, so that the number of poor children in such families was about two-thirds of the number of poor children in large families.

The results in table 2 are designed to indicate the sensitivity of the compositon by family size of the poor, to the family equivalence scales on which the poverty lines are based. Here the Henderson Report's findings are compared with those derived from the Survey of Consumer Finances data by Podder and Kakwani.[15] The equivalence scales used by Podder are those used in the Henderson Report although the data source differs, whilst Kakwani, using the same data source as Podder, employs the equivalence scales indicated in table 1. Thus, whilst the Henderson figures are based on the most comprehensive and reliable data, the Kakwani figures are based on a much more sophisticated and appropriate set of equivalence scales. In comparing these two sets of figures, the expected divergences appear. As compared to the Henderson figures, Kakwani finds poverty to be less serious amongst larger families.[16] Both studies agree that the overall incidence of poverty amongst dependent children is high and of a broadly similar magnitude.

Table 2: Alternative measures of child poverty in Australia

Family Composition	Percentage in poverty		
	Henderson Report	Podder	Kakwani
Married Couple (MC) and 1 or 2 children	2.9	4.4	3.8
MC and 3 children	3.9	5.5	3.7
MC and 4 children	8.9	6.9	1.9
MC and 5 or more children	18.6	9.7	6.2
Total number of dependent children in poverty	254 000	n.a.[(b)]	212 000
'Standard family' poverty line	$62.70	$36.10	$33.00
Year	1973	1966–67	1966–67

Notes: (a) $33 in 1966 is the same proportion of average weekly earnings in that year as $62.70 is in 1973.
(b) Not available.

What can be concluded from this bewildering array of statistics? Firstly, there is agreement that an alarmingly high number of dependent children in Australia are in poverty. The most authoritative figure, provided by the Henderson Report, puts the number close to a quarter of a million in 1973. Secondly, conclusions as to the size of families from which these children come are very sensitive to the family equivalence scales used to derive the poverty lines. This sensitivity itself reflects the fact that many families are only slightly above the poverty line, thus making the measurement of poverty very responsive to slight adjustments in the poverty lines themselves. Whichever results are used, it must be said that poverty amongst dependent children is widespread and represents a serious social problem. The far-reaching demoralizing effects which living in poverty has on family life and thus on the social environment within which children spend their formative years, are discussed in the following section.

Poverty and family life

To fully grasp the effects of poverty on family life and on children in particular, one must go beyond the statistics to the personal lives and circumstances of the poor. The family as an institution socializes children and prepares them for their roles in later life. The existence of poverty can seriously impair these normal functions, leading to harmful effects on children in both the short run and the longer term. There are strong social pressures to conform, particular in attitudes towards material possessions, to which the poor are unable to respond. Bryson quotes evidence which suggests that the attitudes of the poor towards the ownership of houses and consumer durables is no different from that of the affluent.[17] There is no apparent 'culture of poverty' in which the poor are alienated from the major institutions in society and behave according to a value system which is distinct from the values of the affluent and the dominating classes.

The inability of the poor to conform and respond to social pressures in society places great strains on family life. As a result, personal relationships within the family and between the family and other relatives, friends and neighbours are affected. However, as a recent study by McCaughey and Chew has noted, these personal networks of friends, neighbours and relatives are an important source of help to many families when crises arise.[18] Thus if these links are broken, families in poverty become isolated from their major source of informal assistance and support. Family life for the poor is one of constant struggle to make ends meet. Behaviour becomes determined by family circumstances and the need to survive financially, and important elements of choice and freedom are lost. Husbands work long hours, and wives join the workforce not by choice but by force of economic circumstance. Inadequate child-care provisions inevitably imply that the children do not receive the attention they require. In the continual struggle for the basic necessities, much of what is taken for granted by the non-poor becomes an unattainable luxury. This is particularly damaging for children, when the pressures to conform to peer groups is particularly strong.

Two recent books, one by McCaughey, Shaver, Ferber and others, and the second by Hollingworth, provide many striking descriptions of family life for the poor.[19] They show that poverty has many damaging effects on family life, the main sufferers being the children in these families. Not only do they suffer directly from the hardships which accompany living in poverty, but in turn their longer run prospects are also adversely affected. To the problems arising from the strains which poverty places on family life, a whole nexus of additional factors can be added which disadvantage poor children. Poverty increases the probability of malnutrition and ill-health amongst children whilst simultaneously restricting the ability of parents to provide adequate health care. Children from poor families on average undergo less formal education than other children and benefit less from the education which they do undertake. According to Jencks, "on almost any reasonable set of assumptions, family background explains nearly half the variation in educational attainment".[20] Low educational attainment in turn increases the probability that in adulthood poverty will be sustained; the Henderson Report found that poverty amongst those who left school at 14 or below was 13.8 per cent, whilst it was only 6.8 per cent for those who stayed at school beyond the age of 15. For all of these reasons, and many more, poverty amongst dependent children is a characteristic which unfortunately may persist in later life. To be born and raised in poverty substantially increases the probability that poverty will be a lifetime, rather than just a temporary phenomena.

Financial support for families with children: existing arrangements

Government support for families with dependent children takes the form of direct financial assistance, relief from personal income taxation through certain deductions for concessionable expenditures, and the provision of welfare services. Assistance is provided by Commonwealth, state and local governments, supplemented in many essential areas by voluntary welfare agencies. Attention here will focus on the cash benefit provisions made through the Commonwealth government's Department of Social Security. Figures presented in the 1979–80 budget indicate that total child-related expenditure in 1978–79 amounted to $1 087.9 million, or 13.4 per cent of total Social Security and Welfare Expenditure. The major expenditure item was family allowances ($997.6 million) supplemented by handicapped children's benefits and allowances ($18.2 million), maternity allowances ($3.2 million), children's services ($63.8 million), and other items ($5.0 million).[21] In addition, the author has estimated that about $196 million was paid to pension and benefit recipients in the form of child allowances.[22]

The provision of welfare services for children operates through the Children Services Programme, administered by the Office of Child Care within the Department of Social Security. Schemes in the programme include the provision of pre-school education, child-care facilities of various kinds, and projects geared to children with special needs such as aboriginal, migrant, handicapped and isolated children. In addition, the family support services programme was established during 1977–78, "to assist the development of a range of services designed to support families in the responsibilities in the

Table 3: Cash benefit provisions for children by the Department of Social Security, 1977–78

Provision	Terms and Conditions	Weekly Amount	Annual Cost in 1977–78 ($Million)	Date of Last Adjustment of Payment Level
Family Allowances	All families with dependent children. No income test; not taxable.	$3.50 (1st child) $5.00 (2nd child) $6.00 (3rd, 4th children) $7.00 (5th and subsequent children)	1038	June 1976
Child Allowances	Pensioners and supporting parent beneficiaries with dependent children. Income tested; not taxable.	$7.50 per child	126	November 1975
Child Allowances	Unemployment, sickness and special beneficiaries with dependent children. Income tested; taxable.	$7.50 per child	53	November 1975
Mothers/ Guardians Allowances	Pensioners and supporting parent beneficiaries solely responsible for dependent children. Income tested; not taxable.	$4.00 (aged over 6 years) $6.00 (aged under 6 years)	36	October 1965 October 1969

Table 3 (cont'd)

Provision	Terms and Conditions	Weekly Amount	Annual Cost in 1977–78 ($Million)	Date of Last Adjustment of Payment Level
Maternity Allowances	Paid to mothers on, or before, birth of children. Lump sum payment; not income tested.	$30.00–$35.00 depending on the number of children in the family aged under 16 years	7.2	1943
Handicapped Children's Allowances	Payable to parents of severely handicapped children, to allow them to be cared for at home. Not income tested; not taxable.	$15.00	16.3	January 1976
Double Orphans Pensions	Payable to the guardians of children whose parents are deceased or not traceable. Not income tested; not taxable.	$11.00	1.9	November 1974

rearing and development of children".[23] Total expenditure on children's services in 1978–79 was $63.8 million, which was $7.4 million less than expenditure in 1977–78. This represents a cut in nominal terms of 10.4 per cent, or a real decline of over 19 per cent after allowing for movements in the consumer price index. The estimated expenditure on children's services is forecast to increase to $69.3 million in 1979–80, a figure which, even in nominal terms, is less than expenditure in 1977–78.

The most recent detailed statistics on cash benefits refer to 1977–78, when total expenditure amounted to $1 278 million. Details of the various forms of assistance and their weekly amounts are shown in table 3. It is apparent from these figures that there is no consistent rationale underlying the various forms of assistance. Some are income tested, some are taxable, the child allowances for beneficiaries are both income tested and taxable, whilst others are neither income tested nor taxable. Most are paid at a flat rate per child, although family allowances are paid at rates per child which increase with the number of children in the family. This ensures some positive relationship between allowances and children's age, since the average age of children is greater in larger families, but the relationship is only a weak one. Furthermore, the existence of possible economies of scale with respect to the number of children is not allowed for. No explicit account is taken in any of the allowances of the extensive evidence discussed by Wynn for example, which shows that child costs increase with the age of the child. In fact the only benefit which does vary with the child's age, the mother's and guardian's allowance, actually declines once the child reaches the age of six.

It is also apparent from table 3 that successive governments have made little attempt to maintain the real value of benefits by automatic or discretionary adjustments in line with cost of living movements. The most recent adjustment to any of the benefits shown in table 3 was in 1976 when the new family allowances were increased over the child endowment payments which they replaced. The cost of living as measured by the consumer price index increased by 33 per cent between June 1976 and June 1979, implying an equivalent fall in the real value of family allowances over this period. All of the other benefits have fared worse, having remained fixed in nominal terms for longer periods. The allowances for mothers or guardians had not been altered for ten years, whilst the maternity allowances had not been altered since 1943.[24]

Whilst demand for the indexation of the personal income taxation system and the basic pension and benefit levels payable to adults have become major political issues recently, to which politicians have shown some willingness to respond, the same unfortunately cannot be said of the indexation of child-related allowances. This inevitably means that there has been an in-built bias against families with children as a result of wage, tax and pension and benefit indexation over recent years. Such arrangements have contributed towards maintaining the real living standards of adults without children, whilst those with dependent children have inevitably suffered falls in real living standards due to the fixed nominal payments in respect of their children. This can only mean that child poverty will inevitably increase amongst those families solely dependent upon cash benefit assistance from the government.

Since in revenue terms the system of family allowances represents the most important source of assistance to families with children, it is worthy of more detailed consideration. The family allowance system was introduced in 1976 and replaced the former system which contained two components: child endowment and personal income tax rebates for taxpayers with children. The latter was introduced in the 1975–76 budget and replaced the system of concessional deductions which was inequitable in that it benefited most those taxpayers whose marginal tax rate was the highest. This change therefore effected a substantial downwards redistribution to families with children, although it did not extend to those whose incomes were below the tax threshold. The redistributive effects were reinforced in 1976 when the tax rebates were abolished and replaced, along with child endowments, by the system of family allowances. Taken together, the 1975 and 1976 changes constituted a substantial redistribution of income to low income families with children. Unfortunately, the failure to index the new family allowances had lead to a significant decline subsequently in their real value. By not indexing family allowances, the government therefore ensured that the redistributive effects which accompanied their introduction would be removed with the passage of time and the rise in the cost of living.

The system of family allowances serves both as a means of income support for poor families with children, and as a means of achieving horizontal equity (the principle that income tax payments should reflect the number of individuals dependent on that income) as between all families. To effectively satisfy the former role, the allowances clearly need to be closely related to the costs of children. The attainment of horizontal equity, however, does not necessarily require that the allowances fully cover the costs of children, since it can be argued that part of the costs should be borne by the parents themselves, rather than by taxpayers in general. Thus there is some conflict implied by the two roles which family allowances serve. The Henderson Report argued that family allowances should be regarded primarily as a means of achieving horizontal equity between taxpayers with different numbers of dependent children. Additional support would therefore be necessary in the case of poor families, to ensure that the costs of their children are fully covered. Additional assistance is currently available in the form of child allowances, payable to pension and benefit recipients with children. In order to achieve this income support role effectively, the two allowances should in total cover the costs of children, which are implied by the family equivalence scales. In evaluating the adequacy of the existing income support provisions for families with children, the Henderson equivalence scales will be used as a benchmark. This allows the provisions to be assessed in terms of poverty lines which, being produced by a Commission of Inquiry, represent in a sense 'official' definitions of financial poverty in Australia.

The updated Henderson poverty lines are compared with the value of existing pensions, benefits and allowances in table 4. The major feature of these figures is the inadequacy of the existing provisions for families with children, particularly those in single parent families. Whilst the basic married couple pension or benefit is 5 per cent below the poverty line, the single-parent benefit is almost 24 per cent below the poverty line. In two-parent families, those with one child fall 11 per cent below the poverty line, whilst seven-child families fall 23 per cent below the poverty line. The shortfall is consistently of the order of 24 per cent in single-parent families, where the income tax clawback does not apply because child allowances are not taxable. The poverty lines imply that the costs of the first child is $18.70 per week, whilst assistance for the first child amounts to only $11 per week. This shortfall is reduced to some extent in larger families due to the higher family allowances, although this is more than offset in two-parent families by the effects of the income tax clawback on the child allowances. Thus for the fourth child, the additional costs implied by the poverty lines amount to $18.70, whilst assistance increases by only $11 for two-parent families and $13.50 for single-parent families. The continued failure to index child-related allowances will ensure that these shortfalls, alarming as they already are, will grow as inflation proceeds.

Financial support for families with children: some suggested improvements

It is clear from table 4 that existing provisions are inadequate and require improvement. All families would benefit from the raising of the basic pension and benefit levels to the poverty lines. This implies an increase of about 5 per cent in the married rate and an

Table 4: Poverty lines and social security provisions, April 1979 ($ per week)

Family Composition	Poverty Line	Basic Pension or Benefit	Child Allowance	Family Allowance	Income Tax Due	Net Income	Net Income as a Proportion of the Poverty Line (%)
Married Couple	93.30	88.70	—	—	—	88.70	95.1
Married Couple and 1 child	112.00	88.70	7.50	3.50	—	99.70	89.0
Married Couple and 2 children	130.70	88.70	15.00	8.50	—	112.20	85.8
Married Couple and 3 children	149.50	88.70	22.50	14.50	0.70	125.00	83.6
Married Couple and 4 children	168.20	88.70	30.00	20.50	3.20	136.00	80.9
Married Couple and 5 children	186.00	88.70	37.50	27.50	5.70	148.00	79.6
Married Couple and 6 children	204.10	88.70	45.00	34.50	8.20	160.00	78.4
Married Couple and 7 children	221.90	88.70	52.50	41.50	10.70	172.00	77.5
Single Parent	69.70	53.20	—	—	—	53.20	76.3
Single Parent and 1 child	89.30	59.20	7.50	3.50	—	70.20	78.6
Single Parent and 2 children	108.30	59.20	15.00	8.50	—	82.70	76.4
Single Parent and 3 children	127.00	59.20	22.50	14.50	—	96.20	75.7
Single Parent and 4 children	145.00	59.20	30.00	20.50	—	109.70	75.3

Notes: (i) The poverty lines assume that the head is at work and are updated to the March quarter 1979 when average weekly earnings were $231.40. (ii) The child allowances are assumed to be taxable for married couples, and not taxable for single parents. The guardian's allowance for single parents is assumed to be $6.00. (iii) The income tax calculations assume that the annual income is 52 times the weekly income shown. (iv) All figures have been rounded to the nearest ten cents.

increase of 31 per cent in the single rate. Since the major concern here is with the situation of children, attention will focus purely on possible improvements to the child-related allowances, rather than the basic pension and benefit levels, although the two changes should be seen necessarily as complementary.[25] Since family allowances are payable to all families with children, any increase would involve a considerable drain on revenue. A source of additional revenue is available however, since these allowances are currently not taxable. Child poverty could be reduced, and the equity of the tax-transfer system improved, if family allowances were to be made taxable and the resultant gain in revenue used to increase the value of family allowances. The allowances could be taxed in the hands of the highest income recipient in the family. Calculations by the author suggest that this proposal, if introduced in 1978–79, would allow family allowances to be increased by 50 per cent at an annual cost of less than $10 million—the income tax clawback would almost completely finance the higher allowances.[26] Families in which the highest income recipient paid the standard rate of income tax (33.5 per cent in 1978–79) would find the two changes offset each other, those on lower incomes would gain, whilst those on higher incomes would be worse off. This change would need to be accompanied by an increase in the rate of child allowance. A 50 per cent increase in these allowances would cost approximately $98 million in 1978–79. Combined with the higher family allowances, they would considerably improve the financial position for low income families with children, and thereby reduce child poverty, at an annual cost to revenue of less than $110 million. The net effects of the proposed changes is shown in table 5, which should be compared with table 4.

These changes would not eliminate child poverty in Australia, but they would reduce it considerably. Large two-parent families would remain relatively disadvantaged, as would single-parent families. A restructuring of the family allowance rates so that they were related to the age of the child, and not simply to the number of children in the family, would ensure that the allowances bore a closer resemblance to the costs of children. Such a change could be introduced at no additional cost, other than that required to administer a slightly more complex system. More generous increases along these lines, accompanied by upward adjustments in the pensions and benefits payable to single adults and married couples, could eliminate financial poverty in Australia at costs which are not prohibitive. The reward for these costs would be the immediate improvement in the living standards of many children, particularly the quarter of a million living below the poverty line. These improvements would in turn raise the contributions which these children could make in later life, from which all could benefit.

Table 5: Poverty lines and proposed social security provisions, April 1979 ($ per week)

Family Composition	Poverty Line	Basic Pension or Benefit	Child Allowance	Family Allowance	Income Tax Due	Net Income	Net Income as a Proportion of the Poverty Line (%)
Married Couple	93.30	88.70	—	—	—	88.70	95.1
Married Couple and 1 child	112.00	88.70	11.20	5.20	—	105.10	93.8
Married Couple and 2 children	130.70	88.70	22.50	12.70	4.90	119.00	91.0
Married Couple and 3 children	149.50	88.70	33.70	21.70	11.70	132.40	88.6
Married Couple and 4 children	168.20	88.70	45.00	30.70	18.50	145.90	86.7
Married Couple and 5 children	186.00	88.70	56.20	41.20	25.80	160.30	86.2
Married Couple and 6 children	204.10	88.70	67.50	51.70	33.10	174.80	85.6
Married Couple and 7 children	221.90	88.70	78.70	62.20	40.40	189.20	85.3
Single Parent	69.70	53.20	—	—	—	53.20	76.3
Single Parent and 1 child	89.30	59.20	11.20	5.20	—	75.60	84.7
Single Parent and 2 children	108.30	59.20	22.50	12.70	—	94.40	87.2
Single Parent and 3 children	127.00	59.20	33.70	21.70	—	114.60	90.2
Single Parent and 4 children	145.60	59.20	45.00	30.70	—	134.90	92.7

Notes: See *Notes* to table 4, p. 213.

Whilst proposals such as these are an essential component of any attempt to eliminate child poverty, they need to be accompanied by complementary commitments, particularly in the area of children's services. The downward trend in the real provision of services, which was noted earlier, must be arrested and reversed. One particular area which will be briefly considered is the provision of child-care facilities and the tax treatment of individual expenditures on child care. Whilst there has been a considerable growth over recent years in the provision of child-care centres—the Department of Social Security reported that by June 1978, 400 child-care centres had been given approval since the inception of the Children's Services Programme—the overall level of provision remains inadequate. This means that some mothers who would otherwise choose to join the labour force are unable to do so, whilst others who are forced into the labour force through economic circumstances must make private child-care arrangements. Since child-care expenses are a legitimate expense involved in family members joining the workforce, it can be argued that they should be an allowable deduction (or rebate) from income before calculating income tax liability. This view was supported by the Taxation Review Committee.[27] Such a concession, however, would benefit only those who avail themselves of child-care facilities for which a payment in cash is required.

An alternative approach, stressed by Apps, and Edwards, recognizes that all families with children incur child-care costs whether they take the form of cash payments to others, or are an implicit labour cost incurred by family members in the home.[28] Since child rearing within the household produces labour which is ultimately used in the industry sector of the economy, it should by rights receive monetary compensation, in the same way and for the same reasons that labour in the industry sector is remunerated. Whilst Apps argues that such payments could take the form of increased family allowances, it might be more appropriate to consider the payment of a clearly differentiated child-care allowance. This would allow a clear distinction to be made between family allowances, which would reflect the cost of the goods and services which contribute to the child's living standards, and the child-care allowance, which compensates for the labour services expended on child rearing.

Conclusion

This chapter has reviewed the available evidence on the costs and needs of children, the extent of poverty amongst children in

Australia, and the adequacy of existing income support provisions to families with dependent children. The major conclusion which emerges is that the existing provisions are neither sufficient to eliminate child poverty, nor to adequately compensate parents for the contributions which are implicit in their child-rearing activities. A necessary (but not a sufficient) condition for the attainment of the much-heralded goal of equality of opportunity is that all children are provided with a minimum standard of living. To deny them this, as we currently do in many cases, is to impose hardships which are intolerable and unacceptable. Social relationships, attitudes and institutions may serve to reinforce the sense of isolation and frustration felt by the poor, and ensure that poverty during childhood becomes lifetime poverty. It has been shown that the costs of the abolition of financial poverty amongst children need not be prohibitive. Such costs would be reduced in the longer run once the cycle of poverty was broken, whilst the improved life-chances given to children would be socially beneficial. The question is not whether we can afford the costs of the abolition of child poverty, but whether we can afford to tolerate its persistence.

Economic Relationships and Social Values

Barbara Spalding

It is often surprising for parents to find the very personal processes of childbirth and child rearing referred to in the vernacular of economists. Children are described as assets or liabilities. Consideration is given to whether their production and upkeep is an investment or consumption activity. Sometimes it is their immediate families' balance sheet which is being considered. Sometimes it is the national balance sheet. Sometimes our concern is with children and how much we are prepared to expend on them now—on their health, housing, education, recreation. Sometimes our concern lies with children in a more detached sense, as the instruments of population replacement, as the future labour force or in terms of their effect on the ratio of productive to dependent members of society.

Yet deliberating upon the economic relationship between children and the broader community is far from being the exclusive prerogative of economists. A quick scan of the press reveals an abundance of evidence that this is a popular preoccupation.

> Taxpayers who choose not to have children should not have to subsidize the indulgences of other people.
>
> Paying pensions to single mothers encourages promiscuity.
>
> Government should not have to pay out for families of deserting fathers until legal action has been taken to get maintenance out of the men responsible.
>
> People who make sacrifices to send their children to private schools should be assisted financially.
>
> The health status of Aboriginal children is a national disgrace.

Couples who don't have children are selfish.

Families must accept responsibility for their own unemployed young people.

Statements such as these are likely to be familiar to readers. Yet each contains assumptions about economic relationships between children and the broader community. More to the point, each reflects values of one sort or another about the private and public responsibilities of parenthood and the distinctions between the roles of the state and its social institutions on the one hand and of the family on the other. The provisions we as a community make for our children, through government auspice and through churches, voluntary organizations and community groups, reflect these values. It is not surprising therefore that one searches in vain for consistency. For the roles and responsibilities of families vis-a-vis the community at large are being reshaped constantly. They are an area of public policy which is particularly prone to conflicting ideologies.

It is useful to distinguish between our approach to children as children and to children as potential adults. In general, outlays on children as children are considered the private business of parents. As such they are not subject to official calculation and we do not impute any value to that type of expenditure in our national accounts. It is treated as an aspect of household consumption. On the other hand, public outlays on behalf of all children, as a special category of people within our population, tend to be regarded as a form of national investment in the next generation or as in the long-term interests of the community. As such these outlays are the business of the taxpayer who often feels disposed to enter into the debate about whether or not the community is getting value for money. This has been evident in recent years with respect to education. The claim has been made by some groups, including employers, that the outputs of the education system are not satisfactory. That is, as a form of investment in potential adults, this expenditure has had poor returns.

Unfortunately we are not clear about the potential adults we want. This results in confusion about goals. For example, is education primarily about meeting the developmental needs of the child as a child or is it about turning out the types of adults needed in the market place? The two are not necessarily consistent. In this context, Peter Saunders has drawn attention to those families who are deemed to need public assistance with the private area of responsibility for supporting children within households. He has outlined the array of provisions made, particularly through the social security system, to direct resources to some families with children. His account suggests that we are operating, albeit in a refined way, according to 19th century pauperism precepts based on identifying certain categories of 'needy' people and endeavouring to relieve their situation through the provision of subsistence incomes in the form of pensions and benefits. Our debates tend to focus around how we define 'need' and what level of help is adequate. With this approach there is a general presumption that poverty is absolute and therefore can be relieved by fixing some minimal level of income for people. At the same time, special programmes are mounted in education, welfare, health, housing and access to legal protection to ameliorate the more severe effects of economic disadvantage.

Yet our idea of need is far from absolute and is subject to continuing redefinition. During the 1970s new categories of need were recognized in the social security system. Responsibility for dependent children became an increasingly significant factor in this regard. Single mothers and subsequently lone supporting fathers became eligible for social security payments. Family allowances were introduced—ostensibly to assist families too poor to benefit from the previous system of child endowment plus tax concessions for dependent children. In similar vein, the decision to withhold indexation of benefits to unemployed people was not applied to beneficiaries with dependents. Still, some families on social security payments receive significantly less than others of similar composition but in different social security categories. For example, people on long-term Unemployment Benefit are discriminated against, creating a differential between them and most other social security recipients. These differentials are maintained by the application of a stringent income test. Children of people on long-term Unemployment Benefit are particularly disadvantaged by withholding fringe benefits granted to most other categories of recipients. These fringe benefits are calculated to be worth from $10.00 to $12.00 per week.

The caprices in our system of determining who will receive social security assistance and on what terms, has led to proposals for a guaranteed minimum income. These proposals have the advantage of including a comprehensive range of relevant variables in assessing need (such as family size, housing costs, actual income from all sources, etc.) and a uniform income standard which the community as a whole would accept as a minimum for its members. The guaranteed income schemes advanced to date vary; nevertheless they offer an efficient alternative to the current array of pensions and benefits. However they would involve readjustments which have received little support as yet from the main political parties.

If the issue of access to economic resources is cast in terms of relative deprivation, rather than as some form of absolute where some people have sufficient and others not enough, then the solutions must take on different dimensions. It opens up the question of inequality and why it is that some children have vastly different access to economic resources, both in their childhood and in their future life opportunities. The present system, and the various proposals for refining it and making it more efficient, will not remove the differentials. Despite a limited redistribution through progressive income tax, the *relative* position of people on lower incomes has worsened over the past five years. Changes in income tax, changed balances between income tax and regressive indirect taxes, the effect of wage-fixing mechanisms and the disproportionate burden of unemployment on low income people, have all contributed to this development.

As to the differentials that exist between children and their effects in influencing later life opportunities, it is unlikely that major changes can be expected. This is because the situation of children is inextricably linked with that of their families. A child's family circumstance is still the major source of inequality of access of economic resources. Goodnow and Burns discuss above the shifting alliances and changing patterns of responsibilities between children, their families and the state. This takes on special significance in economic relationships. The findings of the Australian Poverty Inquiry suggest that poverty is many-sided in its effects. It is shortsighted therefore to design policies to improve the position of disadvantaged children which focus solely on them and ignore the many other crucial dimensions affecting their lives, particularly the situation of their families.

If one does focus on the family financial dimension, then it is necessary to consider the distinction made earlier between those areas of financial responsibility for children which are treated as public and those which remain private.

Parents are regarded as having almost sole responsibility for the provision of goods and services necessary for the day-to-day wellbeing of children. These include food, clothing, shelter, etc. Family allowances provide a subsidy towards these costs but of a symbolic nature, unrelated to actual costs. The capacity of parents to meet these private costs depends on their command of resources through means which are unrelated to their parental responsibilities. Of these means, the principal ones are income earned through wages and salaries and control over capital resources through inheritance, investments, etc. But the costs of parenting vary with the number of children and the ages of the children. (For example, it is estimated that a fourteen-year-old costs three times as much to keep as a child in the first year of life.)[1] Thus it is in Australia that some children are more vulnerable than others. Children of large families, of female-headed families, of certain one-income families, and of families where the parents lack skills valued in the labour force are more likely to be at economic risk than others.

If public policy is to be reviewed in its role of assisting in the private sphere of parenting—and a review is urgently needed—then the assumptions it makes about functions within families need to be closely examined. The present system rests on the assumption that there is a breadwinner in the paid workforce sustaining the costs of supporting the children and a partner who provides unpaid child-care services.

An extension of this assumption has been made with respect to social security provisions. Where the breadwinner is absent or incapable of fulfilling this role the partner providing the child-care services and the children are supported instead by government through pensions and benefits. This acceptance of maternal and child dependency within households, when taken over by government, has been a significant cause of proverty amongst some children. Furthermore, it is a form of sex role stereotyping which is only recently being translated into provisions that accept the possibility not only of role modification but also of role reversal. Acceptance of the possibility of wives claiming husbands as dependents (e.g. for unemployment benefit in 1974) and introduction of supporting parents benefit for fathers in 1977 are two exmaples. As yet widowers with dependent children have not the same right as widows to a pension.

If the market remains the principal means for securing economic resources for parenting functions in the private domain, policies which support parenting by the provision of practical services and financial help while not discriminating against maternal workforce participation are likely to have different outcomes from policies which provide compensation for parenting costs but discourage maternal workforce participation. The failure to accept non-family child-care costs as work-related expenses for tax purposes while providing a tax concession for a dependent spouse is an example of the latter. Thus child-care services which have to be purchased out of taxable income are not allowed for tax purposes while domestic services provided free to a taxpayer from non-taxable sources by a dependent spouse attract a government subsidy, even where there are no children. These two are examples of social assumptions about private economic and social relationships within households which have been carried into public policy.

Two recent Australian studies show the inconsistency between public policy and assumptions about private behaviour and the reality. Elspeth Browne's recent study of fertility control in

Australia over the past century describes the complex reasons why Australians have progressively limited the size of their families, despite the long-prevailing official attitude towards population expansion in this country.[2] At the risk of oversimplifying her very point about complex reasons for family limitation, it is worth drawing attention to two factors. The first is acceptance of the ethic that the aged are not dependent on their children. Children are not now a form of personal economic investment for parents. Whatever rewards children bring, they are not economic. The second factor is a relationship between family size limitation and an increasing aspiration for economic well-being, associated with increased parental responsibility for the support of children. It might be said that parents these days generally expect to outlay more on their children for less return.

Harper and Richards' study of mothers at work and at home indicates not only that families are obliged increasingly to keep two parents at work to maintain these new high standards (of which housing is a major factor), but that this is becoming essential for the social and personal survival of many women—just as it has been customarily for men.[3] The economic and the social aspects of family behaviour cannot be separated. Family sociologists describe a different reality from the popular image and suggest that, while some trends in family behaviour are influenced by both family economics and national economic conditions, they have sufficient impetus from other factors to proceed apace anyway. Whether public policies support trends within families, ignore them or endeavour to reverse them is another issue.

In summary, as a general trend the thrust of our policy objectives is towards gradual acceptance of subsistence income as a minimum for all families with children. There are still notable exceptions. But the long term possibility of achieving poverty level support for all families is now commonly acknowledged as within our capacity, for example in reports of the Australian Council of Social Service, the Brotherhood of St Laurence, and the Poverty Inquiry. Although not yet endorsed by government, official policies already tend towards this outcome—albeit on a piecemeal basis.

This approach does not seriously disturb relativities between rich families and poor families. Rich parents can purchase privileges for their children, both in the present and longer term. This is considered to be virtuous in itself; hence government subsidy of private schools. Poor families have to use all their income in satisfying current consumption needs. Very poor families cannot even do that. They cannot invest in their children's futures because they have no surplus after they purchase necessities. This is the reality of poverty and one of the major reasons why the family itself will continue to be a vehicle for perpetuating inequality even if the goal of a poverty level income for all very poor families is reached.

Australia is moving slowly and in a fragmented way towards providing for the minimum consumption needs of the children of poor people. It has far to go. Whether it is prepared to face the issue of inequality is a question for the future. First it has the immediate problem of a generation of children now entering adulthood to whom it may not be able to offer a productive role. Many of them will be excluded from our economic life. The arrival of the children of these children will be a painful national testing time.

PART 8

Children and the Law

Richard Chisholm

There is considerable talk about children's rights these days, and, in the absence of the late W.C. Fields, everyone seems in favour of them.[1] But what *are* children's rights?[2] Lawyers ought to know; the law is supposed to be concerned with rights. But the law seems to have no sensible answer to this sensible question. It is not even clear what a 'child' is. Women can get married at 16 years of age, men at 18; they can both vote at 18; they can leave school at 15. If they are involved in a custody dispute between their parents, the court should normally follow their wishes if they are over 14. Children at 12 must consent to their own adoptions, but they acquire the dubious privilege of being able to commit crimes at the age of 10 in some states, 8 or 7 in others.

Our legal system does not contain any broad general statements about the rights of the child. It could, if any of our governments wanted to create it. The United Nations Declaration of the Rights of the Child, a unanimous resolution of the United Nations General Assembly, has no legal force in Australia. But it could be adopted as a statute by any of our state legislatures, and thus become part of the law of that state. Alternatively, our Constitution could be amended to include a Bill of Rights, which could include children's rights. In either case, we would then have a definition of children's legal rights.

There is another reason why it is very hard to say what are children's rights in law. Legal rules do not come neatly labelled under such categories as "children's rights", "children's disabilities", and "other". It is very much a matter of opinion which rules do and which do not promote children's rights. For example, many people consider that compulsory schooling laws promote children's rights; but there is an important stream of thought, whose most prominent spokesperson is Ivan Ilich, that believes these laws deny children their rights. It is easy to see that laws control children's lives in ways that adults would not tolerate, and it could be said that they therefore deny children such basic rights as freedom of movement. On the other hand, it can be argued that laws protect children from exploitation and give them an opportunity to get on in the world, and that it is inappropriate for children to have the same rights as adults. Whether we regard certain legal rules as promoting children's rights or not depends very much on our values. Where some see rights, others see oppression.

When people talk of children's rights, however, they usually mean more than just legal rights. A claim that children have a right to good health, or education, is not primarily concerned with law at all, but with the provision of services and opportunities. 'Children's rights' cannot be divorced from wider social problems such as unemployment and discrimination. Children are primarily members of society, affected by its strengths and weaknesses. This point can very easily be overlooked. Advocates of children's rights might argue in favour of more resources for children's homes and of foster care, correctly perceiving that many children are in need of alternative care. But the need for alternative care may itself spring from deeper problems as diverse as poor urban planning, unemployment and work patterns which disrupt family life, the lack of an adequate minimum income policy, the isolation of nuclear families, or inadequate education in family planning and parenthood. There is a danger that the 'children's rights' movement will be a positive disadvantage to children, by focussing on superficial issues while leaving untouched the deeper structural problems which constitute more serious threats to children's rights.

It follows that 'children's rights' is not a simple concept. It involves more than legal rules, and it cannot be divorced from other social issues. Nor does the law offer any clear guidelines as to what children's rights are or should be. This does not mean that all the recent talk of children's rights is meaningless, or cynical. It reflects a widespread concern to promote children's well-being and avoid injustice to them. This spirit was well expressed by the Family Court of Australia in 1976:

> A child has rights, a child has status. He is not another asset acquired by the parties during the marriage and available for distribution on breakup. He is not an award to an innocent party, he is not a weapon to be employed against the other spouse....

Law is one of the tools through which policy decisions are made about children. It is a powerful and complex tool, capable of doing harm in clumsy hands. Those who wish to enhance children's lives need to consider whether the law is a tool they should use, and if so, how.[3]

This chapter looks at some aspects of the law relating to children, with the aim of promoting an understanding of how it works, and at the relation between legal issues and issues of policy. It looks first at certain problems in child welfare law, which applies when for some reason children do not have adequate parenting; then at 'custody' law, which applies when a child's family breaks up; and finally, at the legal framework in which families are re-organized. While legal technicalities have been minimized, no attempt has been made to simplify the questions involved; indeed, it is intended to indicate the extreme complexity and difficulty of many of the issues, some of which have been obscured by existing legal categories. This discussion is based on the idea that an important function of the law is to allocate power over children's lives between a variety of adults, institutions, and the children themselves. From this point of view, the law will promote children's rights if it allocates power over their lives in the way most likely to promote their well-being. Getting the allocation right is the tough part.

Child welfare[4]

In November 1962 William Neyens went to the Child Welfare Department of the Australian Capital Territory and asked them for help in looking after his nine-month-old son. The mother, an unmarried woman who had lived with Mr Neyens for a year, had just left, and Mr Neyens, a farm worker on a low income, could not look after the child himself. However, he only wanted temporary assistance; he expected that he would be soon reunited with his wife, who would be able to help him care for his son.

The departmental officer arranged for Mr Neyens and the child to go before a children's court, and Mr Neyens agreed to this. The child was found to be 'destitute' and the children's court made an order that he be made a state ward. He was then transferred to the care of the New South Wales department, and placed in a babies' home. In December 1962 Mr Neyans was reunited with his wife, and asked for his son back. But the department refused.

After further efforts by Mr Neyens proved unsuccessful, he applied to the Supreme Court of the Australian Capital Territory for an order giving him custody of his son. The department did not argue about the welfare of the child. They argued about power. They said that the Child Welfare legislation[5] gave them total power over the child, since he was a state ward. Even the courts were not allowed to consider what was best for the child. The Supreme Court threw out this argument, found that the child's welfare would be promoted by being returned to his father, and said some harsh things about the department. It had long been established that custody should not depend on whether the father was married, but what order would promote the child's welfare. And in determining the child's welfare, the court easily found that a father who was suitable and able to bring up the child in a satisfactory home was preferable to foster care.

The department appealed to the High Court, still arguing that the Supreme Court had no jurisdiction to hear the case. As it turned out, the department knew more about its own power than about the child's welfare, because the High Court upheld the appeal.[6] The result of the case is that in the Australian Capital Territory and in New South Wales once a child becomes a state ward no court has any further jurisdiction. The department's power is absolute. And that is not all. In New South Wales the Child Welfare Act provides that a child can become a state ward without any court hearing at all, even the perfunctory hearing before the Children's Court which occurred in Neyens' case. The statute does not set out any procedures to be followed, or say who can apply for a child to be made a ward, or what criteria the department is to apply in deciding whether to make the child a ward. It has no obligation to notify anybody, or to give reasons for its decisions.

Origins and objectives

Neyens' case shows the law allocating almost total power over some children's lives to a government department. This pattern needs to be understood against the historical background.[7] The outlines of the child welfare laws were established in nineteenth-century England,and here we find a curious paradox, for that was a time when parental rights—more precisely paternal rights—were very prominent. Laws seeking to protect children against cruelty and exploitation were resisted on the grounds of family autonomy. At the same time, a quite different approach to family life was taken in relation to the poor. The offence of child neglect first appeared not as part of the ordinary criminal law, but in an amendment to the Poor Laws in 1868, and the prosecuting authorities were the Poor Law Guardians. Similarly, the first legislation authorizing the transfer of parental authority without a court order was a provision inserted into the Poor Laws in 1889 that the Poor Law Guardians could assume authority over a child maintained under the Poor Laws and deserted by the parents. Thus while the general law gave enormous authority to the father over his (legitimate) children, the special provisions governing poor people gave the relevant authorities unchecked power to intervene between parent and child.

A clue to this curious legal situation seems to lie in the association between 'child welfare' legislation and quite different objectives. The Poor Laws formed part of a very strict system of social and economic regulation, and the laws seeking to protect children went hand in hand with concerns to promote 'law and order' and exploit child labour. It is not possible here to unravel the complex background to the early legislation. It can only be noted that the 'parental rights' so dominant in the general law were replaced by almost total bureaucratic power over poor children. Complex connections between help and punishment, the relief of poverty and the manipulation of poor people, social welfare and social control, run through the old Poor Laws and early protective legislation. A sense of this history shows how wrong it is to assume that increased governmental power necessarily ensures the promotion of children's rights.

Australian reforms

Recent developments in Australian child welfare law can largely be seen as a retreat from the ideas and assumptions of its origins, manifested so strikingly in Neyens' case. At a judicial level, the High Court has made it clear that it regards the result of Neyens' case as quite unsatisfactory, and will do what it can to interpret child welfare legislation in a way that preserves the court's ultimate jurisdiction over state wards.[8] It has held that under the Queensland and Victorian legislation the state Supreme Courts retain their jurisdiction (the words of the legislation are slightly different from that of New South Wales and the Australian Capital Territory), so that in those states parents or foster parents who disagree with the department's views may challenge them in court.

Legislative changes have also occurred. Two recent amendments to the Victorian legislation[9] illustrate the direction of recent thinking, and (in the second case) the persistence of established patterns of power even where new concepts are introduced.

The first amendment may be illustrated by supposing that Mr Neyens approached the Victorian Department of Community Welfare Services in the same situation today. Mr Neyens would now apply for the child to be admitted to the department's care for a maximum period of twelve months. The child would be admitted by virtue of an 'agreement' between the Director General and the parent. This reflects quite a new perception of the parent: not as a threat to the child, but as a person who will continue to play a valuable part in the child's life, even while actual care is being provided by the department. Nevertheless, it may be that when a parent wishes the child to be returned the department may feel reluctant to do so because it considers that a return would put the child at risk. The new Victorian provisions respond intelligently to this problem. Either the parent or the department can 'terminate the agreement' on giving 21-days notice to the other. Thereupon, the director must either return the child within 14 days, or apply to the children's court for an order that the child be deemed to be in need of care and protection. This provision strikes a sensible balance between the powers of the parent and the department, recognizing the crucial distinction between voluntary and involuntary transfer of parental power.

The second amendment relates to a procedure which, although contained in child welfare legislation, is in many ways akin to the criminal law. Traditionally, parents (and the police or welfare authorities) may take children to the children's court for being 'uncontrollable', and the court may make orders quite similar to those it can make over children who commit criminal offences. Observers of children's courts have often mentioned that it is not easy to tell whether children are being dealt with for offences or as being uncontrollable, and critics say that 'uncontrollable' proceedings are sometimes used to overcome difficulties in proving a specific offence, or to take advantage of the lesser degree of proof required, or even to punish a child under the age of criminal responsibility.

The new Victorian provisions focus not on the child's behaviour but on the relationship between parent and child. The application is now to be brought by "any person having the care and custody of a child who believes that there is a substantial and presently irreconcilable difference between himself and the child to such an extent that his care and custody of the child are likely to be seriously disrupted". Consistently with the new focus, the child too may now make such an application. One would expect to find other changes. It would be appropriate to provide some form of preliminary conciliation procedure to try to resolve the irreconcilable difference. At least, it could be provided, as in the sections just considered, that the court should satisfy itself that the department has taken all reasonable steps to help the parties resolve the difference—there are various organizations that undertake family counselling, to which these cases could be referred. If the provision is to be part of the protection of children and advancement of their interests, the court should have to decide the case with a view to promoting the child's welfare. Finally, the court should have power to make orders relating to either of the parties to the difference—both parents and child.

Unfortunately, the new concept has not been fully worked out, for none of these provisions exist. In particular it remains true that the only orders the court can make are against the child, who can be placed on probation, committed to the care of the department, or released on conditions of 'good behaviour' if the case is adjourned. Until the new concept—a very interesting one—is accompanied by real changes in the distribution of power, it will have to be counted among the many cosmetic reforms which can so easily confuse and distract those who wish to see a child welfare law which really does promote the rights and welfare of children.

Foster care

Particularly difficult questions arise when a child has been in foster care for some time. It is instructive to examine this situation in the context of the law in New South Wales. Suppose Mrs A is a single parent who, because of poverty and ill-health, cannot manage to care for her baby daughter. She asks the department for help, and the child is made a state ward and placed in foster care. The child does very well with the foster parents, and has little contact with the mother, who remains depressed and ill, and feels guilty about having given up the child. After five years the mother's health and circumstances improve, and she lives with a man in a stable de facto relationship. She now wants the child returned. But the foster parents, who have come to love the child and regard her as one of the family, are unwilling to give her up and want to adopt her.

It is now established law that in this kind of situation the child's welfare is the 'paramount consideration'. The decision should not be made on the basis that it would be unfair to the mother not to return the child. Nor can it be made on the basis that the mother has not married the man she is living with. But what is for the benefit of the child is such a case? Opinions may differ. Some would say that the child should remain with the foster parents, who have become her 'psychological parents', and should not be subjected to the distress of a complete change of environment. Others would say that the child's long-term welfare would be promoted by being brought up by her mother, despite the temporary distress of the transfer. Even if the child is to remain with the foster parents, there may be different views about whether the mother should be allowed (or encouraged) to visit and form a relationship with the child, or whether she should remain permanently absent and the child should look exclusively to the foster parents for her family.

The legal issue is, who has power to decide these questions? We have seen in Neyens' case that, because the child is a state ward, Mrs A has lost her parental powers, and the New South Wales courts cannot review the department's decisions. Nor have the foster parents access to court. Even if Mrs A agrees that the child should be adopted by them, the foster parents cannot put this proposal to the court. This is because under the adoption law of New South Wales the application is not made by the foster parents, but by the department (or another agency) on their behalf. If for some reason the department places the child with some other persons and applies for them to adopt the child, neither the first foster parents nor Mrs A can put their own claims to the court. For even if the court decides that the child would be better off adopted by the original foster parents, or returned to Mrs A, its hands are tied. It can only choose between granting the adoption order in favour of the people nominated by the department or refusing it; and in the latter case, the child remains a state ward in the department's control.

In New South Wales reform of the law has been imminent for some years. In 1974 the Phibbs Committee recommended that a Wardship Review Tribunal be established, to consider such matters. In late 1978 the Minister published a Green Paper recommending a Community Welfare Tribunal which would have wider powers. Public submissions were called for and were considered in 1979 by yet another committee, the Legislative Advisory Panel. Its report takes a different approach. It argues that the philosophy of normalization, so prominent in relation to people with handicaps, should be applied to state wards. So rather than set up a special and separate tribunal for wards, we should have questions of custody and access determined by the ordinary courts, as they are with other children. From this point of view, state wards are seen as ordinary children whose guardian happens to be the Minister for Youth and Community Services: like the guardians of other children, the Minister should be subject to the ordinary jurisdiction of the courts.

Where should the power lie? To a large extent, it depends on whether we have more trust in courts or departments to make wise and fair decisions. But there are some considerations which suggest that a judicial process is desirable.

First, a judicial process involves the relevant people being given notice of the proceedings, and an opportunity to put their case. Second, the decision is made by someone who is impartial. In a sense, of course, the department is also impartial: its job is to find the best result for the child. But the department is involved in service delivery. It has decided already that the child had to be transferred to foster parents rather than supported in the care of the mother, and has selected and paid the foster parents. There may be subtle pressures to confirm earlier decisions, or loyalties to foster parents selected and paid by the department, or the tendency of any bureaucracy, and officers with a heavy case-load, to take the easier way. Whatever the accuracy of these speculations, it does seem likely that departmental decision making in such cases might be influenced by factors not directly related to the welfare of the child.

Third, a judicial process requires a reasoned decision, subject to review on appeal, and with the advantages that go with having to articulate acceptable reasons. Our situation is open to resolution on quite inappropriate criteria, e.g. that children should not be placed with people living 'in sin'. The articulated reasons of a judicial process may go some way to avoid decisions being made on such improper criteria, or being thought to be by the disappointed parties.

These are rather theoretical arguments. In practice, the performance of courts in these difficult cases is not easy to evaluate. In Neyens' case, the proceedings in the children's court, when the child was made a state ward, were quite unsatisfactory. There was no consideration given to the possibility of less drastic alternatives, and the finding that the child was 'destitute' is very questionable. But the Supreme Court decision was also worrying. The child's mother actually appeared and wanted the child back; but she was unrepresented, and only managed to say a few ineffectual words in her own defence. Yet part of Mr Neyens' case included serious allegations that she had ill-treated the child. The department never made it clear what plans they had for the child—at one stage they seemed to be arguing for him to be returned to the mother, but they had no evidence to offer on this point. The foster parents wrote a letter to the judge, but as we have seen, they had no right to appear in the case, and the department did not call them as witnesses; the judge felt obliged to disregard their letter. It is far from clear that the evidence enabled the court to make a proper evaluation of the child's welfare. The proceedings lend support to those who argue that the courts should adopt a more positive 'inquisitorial' role rather than the passive role required by the 'adversary' system.

The real problem with judicial determination of such matters therefore lies in the procedure, structure and jurisdiction of the courts themselves. Custody jurisdiction is sadly split between federal courts (the Family Court of Australia) and state courts (in most states, the Supreme Courts). The argument for judicial decision making would be much more persuasive if in practice the courts were better equipped to do the job. At present, the theoretical arguments for judicial review have to be set against the dismaying prospect of the cases being decided by judges who may have no special understanding of the issues or interest in the area, without the benefit of the conciliatory and advisory services performed by a counselling service attached to the court, and where the provision of legal aid is insufficient to enable all children to have the advantage of properly presented arguments from all sides. In this area as in others, real advancement of children's rights requires technical legal changes coupled with a resolution of the present jurisdictional mess and the provision of funds for the proper functioning of the judicial process.

The Family Law Act does provide that the Family Court may make orders over children who are state wards, and such orders will override the power of state welfare authorities. But this power is limited to 'children of a marriage' and can only be exercised in special circumstances, and is in any case of arguable validity. Its importance is mainly symbolic, foreshadowing the essential reform—which now seems likely—of the states referring to the Commonwealth their power over custody of ex-nuptial children.

Custody

Parents are equally guardians of their children, and entitled to their custody.[10] Any differences relating to the children are usually settled within the family when the parents are living together. But if the parents separate, they may each have different plans for the children. Each parent may want the children to live with him or her. Or it may be agreed that one parent should look after the children, but the second parent may have some particular wish about the children's upbringing, or insist on a greater degree of contact with the children than the first parent wishes.

It is sometimes said that these matters, concerning personal inter-relationships rather than property or 'rights' in the usual sense, should have nothing to do with the law or lawyers. But it is generally assumed that some system is desirable to settle disputes—otherwise the stronger, wealthier and more ruthless people will prevail. For most Australians, the law is the only available framework for the authoritative resolution of differences about children.

Our courts have decided 'custody' cases according to the usual 'adversary' procedures which characterize our legal system. The contesting adult parties, represented by lawyers, put their cases, and the judge, having passively heard them, determines the dispute on the basis of the evidence before him or her and the relevant rules of law. As we will see, the Family Law Act has modified this system in important ways, and if the system continues to diverge from the usual pattern of our courts, it will become increasingly questionable how far lawyers should play the dominant roles in arguing and deciding cases. But this debate lies mainly in the future, for even the most innovative forum for custody disputes, the Family Court, still relies on legal representation of the parties (and sometimes of the children), and judges still decide the cases. Non-legal expertise, though it now forms an essential part of the process, is used to provide information and advice to the judge (through family reports and expert evidence) and to counsel the people concerned and help them resolve the matter by agreement. Despite these important changes, to be mentioned later, the resolution of custody disputes remains firmly within the traditions of our legal system.

In Australia, some custody matters come under federal law (the Family Law Act) and some under the laws of the states. The division is most unfortunate. The Family Court of Australia, which is staffed by specialist judges and supplemented by counsellors attached to the court, can deal only with custody matters relating to 'children of a marriage'. Other children must be dealt with in state courts, under state law, usually without the benefit of specialist judges or adequate support staff. Step-children as well as ex-nuptial children are excluded. Thus, in a family where there is one child of the married couple, and a child of the wife from a previous marriage, if the couple separate and disagree about custody of the children, there must be two quite separate proceedings, in two separate courts, one for each child.

This problem arises because the federal legislation, the Family Law Act, is based on a provision in the Constitution giving the Commonwealth power to make laws about 'marriage'—it has no power to make laws about custody of children as such. Because it is so difficult to amend the Constitution—there must be a referendum—this problem is being tackled in a different way. The states are to give their power over custody of children who are not children 'of the marriage' to the Commonwealth. This 'reference of power' has been agreed in principle, but may take some time to implement.

Questions of custody can arise between people other than the parents—for example, foster parents may seek custody. But for reasons of space this chapter will deal only with custody disputes between parents.

The level of court adjudication

How does the court resolve arguments between separated parents about their children? The first issue is the extent to which the court should resolve disputes. At one extreme, the court could undertake to decide for itself any dispute about the child, even on such matters as diet or dress. Whenever one parent disagreed with a decision by the other, the court could be asked to resolve it. This would mean the maximum involvement of the court in decision making for the child. At the other extreme, the court could say, in effect: "The parents, who are jointly responsible for the children, cannot agree. The court will therefore decide which parent is better equipped to exercise the power, and will make that parent the child's sole guardian." This position was advanced by the authors of a controversial publication in 1973, *Beyond the Best Interests of the Child.*[11] They argued that the court's competence to regulate continuing relationships is limited. They said that the only criterion for choosing between parents should be which parent is the child's 'psychological parent'. The court should place total responsibility with the 'psychological parent', who could even decide that the child should have no contact at all with the other parent.

It seems unlikely that this argument will prevail in Australia. It is mentioned because it illustrates the need to see how different reform proposals would transfer power over children's lives. The authors see themselves as advocates for children's rights. But the closest the law has come to their position was in the nineteenth century and before, when the courts seemed more concerned with parental rights than children's rights. Although the early cases did not use the idea of the 'psychological parent', they did tend to decide cases by giving custody to one parent without attempting to regulate the continuing relationship of the parents with their child. The modern trend of the law, not only in Australia, is in the opposite direction: promotion of children's rights is thought to require more, not less, court control of relations between separated children and their parents. As in other areas, a commitment to children's rights does not necessarily lead to a simple answer to the difficult question how power over children's lives should be allocated.

The present law is somewhere between the two extremes. The parent with 'custody' may make most decisions about the child's life. If the other parent disagrees with a decision the court will not form its own view about that issue, but will support the decision of the custodial parent. On the other hand, the court will consider on its merits any claim by the other parent relating to contact with the child; the most common order is for one parent to have 'custody' and the other 'access'. Thus the court leaves it to the custodial parent to exercise parental authority, except that the relationship between the child and the other parent will be determined by the court if the parents do not agree. Custody and access orders are never final; they can be varied if the situation changes.

While this is the traditional position, recent trends seem to be towards the court making more detailed provisions about the child's life. It may be that the Family Court of Australia, augmented by its counselling staff, feels more confident than earlier courts in its ability to regulate the relations between child and parents.

Joint custody

Sometimes courts order that the parties have 'joint custody', with one having 'care and control' of the child. The difference between this and the usual custody-access order is that since the parents are joint custodians, equally entitled to make decisions about the child's life, it would seem that any dispute would be considered on its merits by the court. Thus a decision to make a joint custody order rather than a custody–access order means, among other things, that the court will play a potentially greater role in regulating the child's life. In practice joint custody seems to be ordered mainly where further disputes are unlikely, and serves the symbolic purpose of impressing on the parties their continuing role as parents. This example illustrates that the question of power requires careful analysis; for while in theory joint custody orders open up more potential disputes for the court's attention, in practice they may help the parents to accept their responsibilities for their children rather than litigate.

Criteria: the 'paramount consideration'

Most discussions about custody law have focussed on the issue: What criteria should the court apply in making custody decisions? Early custody decisions in our legal system were not based primarily on the court's evaluation of the child's needs. The rule was that the father was the guardian of his legitimate children, was entitled to their custody, and his judgement prevailed on all matters. The courts regarded the father's rights as 'sacred' and would deny them only 'in the utmost need and in the most extreme case'. One such case was that of the poet Shelley, who lost his children because of his atheism and immorality. This decision shows the other strong theme of the early cases, that custody would be denied to parents whose beliefs or behaviour was irreligious or scandalous. This was applied particularly to women and particularly to what was regarded as sexual impropriety.

Gradually, the child's welfare (as perceived by the court) came to prevail over such notions. In 1925 English legislation (soon copied in the Australian states) provided that in custody cases the court was to treat the child's welfare as 'the first and paramount consideration'. Yet the courts had considerable difficulty in understanding this apparently clear and emphatic directive. Sometimes, they said that the word 'paramount' indicates that other considerations are relevant, although somehow less weighty than the child's welfare. But now, after many hesitations, it seems settled that the statutory provision means that the court's job is to make whatever order will best promote the child's welfare. Parental vices and virtues are to be considered only if they are relevant to the child's welfare.

Determining the child's welfare

How do courts determine what order will be best for the child? In practice, they look at the whole case and do what they think is best. In doing so, they reflect the values and assumptions of the community, and of the particular judge. Sometimes certain assumptions or values gain wide judicial acceptance and take on special importance. For example, it is sometimes said that young children should normally go with their mothers, or that siblings should not be separated, or that children who are already in a satisfactory environment should not be moved. These ideas—rules of thumb, as it were—sometimes act as presumptions or tentative rules of law. The courts often point out that these approaches are not rules of law. But they often provide starting points in the difficult task of predicting what will be best for the child.

Changing values

Since 1976, the most important developments in custody law have taken place in the Family Court of Australia. In the many reported decisions, one can see changing social values and perceptions about children, to some extent modified by the individual approach of each judge. There have been a number of cases, for example, of lesbian mothers seeking custody. Formerly, judicial moralizing would have given them little chance. By contrast, in a recent series of cases the Family Court judges have looked at the evidence about the effect of a homosexual environment on children, and have awarded custody to a number of lesbian mothers, recognizing that people's sexuality is but a part of their life. They have drawn on an influential decision of the South Australian Supreme Court in 1975, where Bright J. said, "... I am influenced most by my strong belief in the mother's very great love for her children. I believe that herein lies the best safeguard for the children...."

Another example of changing approaches concerns statements that children, especially young children, were better off with their mothers. In its determinations the Family Court has preferred to examine the actual qualities of the parents, their relationship with the children, and all the other circumstances. Here too, myths and presumptions are giving way to a careful consideration of the facts. But the 'mother principle' can be easily understood in the context of the development of custody law. It represents a reaction to the earlier dominance of the father's rights, reflecting the displacement of a proprietary attitude to children by a concern for their healthy development. And the judges of a few decades ago were no doubt reflecting a society in which sex-roles were more strictly defined than today; few married women had jobs; few men accepted responsibility for the care of young children; and the literature on child development focussed particularly on the dangers of separating children from their mothers.

Access

One of the last bastions of parental rights was the question of access. Until the early 1970s the courts were describing access as the basic right of any parent. But in 1973 the English Court of Appeal pointed out that the logic of the 'paramount consideration' rule meant that access, as much as any other question, must be approached from the children's point of view. Access is now held to be the child's right to contact with the non-custodial parent, and it will be refused where the court does not feel it will benefit the child. Such is the theory; one cannot tell to what extent judges have parents' interests in the back of their minds when they decide (as they usually do) that children's interests will be best served by continuing contact with both parents.

In practice, it is access that is increasingly occupying the energies of judges and counsellors. The parent's separation is recognized as changing, but not ending, their parenting responsibilities. The challenge for the law is to provide a framework which will help them maintain the best possible relationship with their children. Crucial to this is that their own relationship, though it may be difficult, should be made as amicable as possible. The message is filtering from research and the counsellors' professional expertise to the judges and legal practitioners that the children's welfare often depends more on the success with which all parties negotiate the painful process of re-ordering their lives than the simpler notion of who wins the custody battle. This realization has long been obscured by the prominence in family law of primitive notions of fault, 'guilty parties', and proprietary rights in children. As these ideas give way to a recognition of the importance to children's development of the successful negotiation of changes in the family relationships, the procedural framework of the law, so long accepted as suitable for battles about fault, is being re-examined.

Procedures

Apart from contributing to such shifts of approach to the task of determining the child's welfare, the Family Law Act introduced a number of valuable changes in law and procedure. They can only be noted briefly. Firstly, counselling staff is attached to the court, helping the participants to negotiate the difficulties of reorganizing their lives, and providing family reports to the court to assist if the matter cannot be resolved by agreement. The wishes of the child have a new prominence: the court must normally follow the wishes of a child over 14 years of age, and may take into account the wishes of younger children. These wishes may be put to the court as part of the counsellor's report, or through the child's own legal representative (another innovation) or in a private interview with the judge. These and related changes involve a cautious movement away from the traditional 'adversary' system, towards more conciliation-oriented procedures. The new procedures are still in their formative years, but they constitute the major advance of recent years in the law relating to children. New procedures in the Family Court of Australia, especially the role of the counsellors, may show that the key issue in the next decades will not be rules of law but the process through which the law helps separated children and their parents re-arrange their lives, and the part to be played in that process by counsellors, lawyers, judges and other people.

Re-ordering relations between separated parents and children usually involves other people, for most parents form new family units, while retaining links with their existing family members. To this subject of family re-organization we now turn.

Family re-organization[12]

Fred and Ethel, who have two children, separate and obtain a divorce. Ethel is awarded custody of the children, and Fred obtains 'reasonable access'. Later, Ethel marries Jack. The law continues to recognize Fred's relationship with his children. Even though he does not have custody, he is still (jointly with Ethel) their guardian. Consequently, his consent is required before the children can be adopted, and he retains other powers associated with guardianship (precisely what these are is a matter of some difficulty which cannot be pursued here). Depending on the financial circumstances, he may be required to pay maintenance for the children. If he dies without a will, the children will share in his estate. If he makes a will and leaves them inadequately provided for, the courts have a discretionary power to order a fair portion of the estate to be paid to the children. He may be able to persuade a court to order that the children retain his surname.

Step-children: a legal vacuum

But a new family unit has been formed: mother (Ethel), step-father (Jack) and the children. As time goes by Jack may become like a father to the children. To what extent does the law recognize this new family? In particular, what is the legal relationship between Jack and his step-children?

State legislation provides that Jack may come under an obligation to pay maintenance to the children if he has accepted them as part of his family. But in the eye of the law, Jack is largely a 'stranger' to his step-children, for the law has traditionally ignored step-relationships. Apart from difficulties about the children's surname, few problems may arise while Jack and Ethel are living together. But if Jack dies without a will the children take no share of his estate, nor does the court have power to make an order in their favour if he leaves them nothing. If Ethel dies, or leaves, Jack's position is precarious. Ethel cannot make him guardian during her life, although she may effectively do so in her will. Because he is not the children's guardian, or entitled to their custody, there may be doubt about a host of matters. For example, his consent is not required for the children's adoption, and there may be serious doubts about whether he can consent to medical treatment for the children, commence legal proceedings on their behalf, or prevent them being taken into care by child welfare authorities. Thus although the law may require step-parents to pay maintenance for their step-children, it does little to encourage them to take on a parenting role, even where no other parent is available.

Adoption as a solution: nuptial children

In the light of these problems, it is not surprising that many step-parents wish to regularize their relationships with their children. The most effective way of doing so is by adoption, which transfers all parental rights and responsibilities to the adopting parents. In 1973–74, about a quarter of all Australian adoptions were of this kind. Is adoption, then, the solution for Jack and the children?

Under the state adoption laws, Fred's consent is required, if he is still alive, although the court has power to dispense with it in certain circumstances and allow the adoption to proceed over his protests. The grounds on which such orders can be made mainly concern situations where the father has, through abandonment or ill-treatment of the child, been thought to have forfeited his rights. But the court can also dispense with consent where to do so would promote the child's welfare (there are significant variations between the states on this point). In general, the courts are reluctant to allow adoption where it will have the effect of cutting off the children from a father who has retained an interest in them, particularly if he has supported them financially.

Ex-nuptial children and their fathers

Let us now vary the example: assume that Fred and Ethel did not marry, but had a stable de facto relationship. Although they felt as committed to each other and the children as married couples generally do, they had idealogical objections to marriage. But after ten years the relationship breaks down and they separate. Ethel marries Jack, and they wish to adopt the children. Fred objects; he wants a continuing relationship with his children, although he accepts that they will be in the custody of Ethel and Jack. Can he do this, or will Jack and Ethel be able to obtain an adoption order and shut Fred out of the children's lives?

Adoption law has hardly recognized the relationship between an unmarried father and his children, regardless of the actual relationship between them. Fred's consent is not required for the adoption; there is no need even for him to be notified. If he does discover what is happening in time, however, he may ask the court, as a matter of discretion, to allow him to oppose the adoption.

He might want to take the initiative himself and apply for custody or access. Until recently, this was difficult, since state custody legislation did not generally allow unmarried fathers to apply for custody: the word 'father' was interpreted to refer only to married fathers. But recent legislation has sought to remove discrimination against children born outside marriage, and one aspect of this is a greater recognition of their relations with their fathers. Today, therefore, Fred could apply for custody or access under state legislation. Formerly, he would have to apply to the Supreme Court in its ancient 'parental' or 'wardship' jurisdiction for a custody or access order.

By the late 1970s, Australian states had passed legislation seeking to eliminate discrimination against ex-nuptial children: at the heart of this is the legal recognition of the relationship between these children and their fathers. As a result of the Acts, children born outside marriage now inherit equally with nuptial children when their father dies without making a will. The legislation also helps children establish paternity in certain circumstances, e.g. where the father was cohabiting with the mother when the child was conceived.

Adoption continues to pose problems.[13] While it is clearly desirable to recognize the interest of fathers in their children, it is also important not to frustrate or seriously delay adoptions where the connection between the child and the father is minimal and the child's needs require speedy finality. The first serious attempt to tackle this problem is contained in recent South Australian legislation, under which the consent of a father who has been legally recognized as such may be required. While the details of the Act have drawn some criticism, this legislation may be seen as a step towards the desirable objective of protecting the link between father and children if in fact there is a real relationship between them.

Adoption: a crude solution

It has been have shown that in determining whether Fred should have a continuing relationship with his children, the law has until recently been preoccupied not with the child's welfare as such but with Fred's marital status. As a husband, he could normally keep in touch with his children; as a mere father, however loving, he could not. Recent reforms, however, have re-directed attention to the child's welfare, and to the substantial and difficult issue: whether the law should maintain the children's links with their original family, or should, by adoption, bind the child exclusively to the new family unit. There is an emerging view that doubts the wisdom of adoption in these cases. In England, the Houghton Committee took the view that 'the legal extinguishment by adoption of the child's links with one half of its own family was inappropriate in most cases'. Consequently, legislation in 1975 explicitly preferred the use of guardianship and custody orders rather than adoption in these cases.

The present law is crude. If Jack does nothing, the law treats him as almost a stranger to the children. If he adopts the children, the law recognizes him, but to the total exclusion of Fred and Fred's relatives. It is too little, or too much. The emerging view is that the law should recognize both families, and here orders relating to guardianship, names, custody and access provide a more sensitive instrument than adoption. Nevertheless, there are difficult questions of policy involved, for example in the areas of maintenance and property. At what point, if ever, should the responsibility for the children's maintenance shift from the father to the step-father (jointly, of course, with the mother)? Should the children be able to inherit from the step-father, or the biologial father, or both? What about inheritance from other relatives through the father and step-father? How far should these questions turn on the particular facts of each case? The more flexible approach suggested here requires fundamental reconsideration of these and related questions.

The need for the law to recognize the complex relationships between children and other members of their 'families' is reflected not only in a new questioning of the use of adoption, but in the nature of adoption itself. It has been recognized for many years as good adoption practice to encourage adopters to tell the children that they have been adopted. A further development is the now familiar and powerful lobby on behalf of adopted people who wish to trace their origins, or even establish contact with their biological relatives. Cracks are even appearing in the legal wall that separates adopted children from their biological relatives. In two recent English decisions, adoption orders were made subject to access orders in favour of the biological father. In a technical variant on the same theme, the court used its wardship jurisdiction to grant access to a father immediately after the adoption order had been made. This last case is of potential importance in Australia, because although our adoption legislation does not seem to contemplate conditional adoptions orders, there is no technical impediment to a disappointed father seeking access by an application to the wardship jurisdiction of the Supreme Court after the adoption order has been made. This may be of special interest in Queensland, where adoption orders are not made by a court at all, but by the Director of Children's Services.

It is perhaps not too optimistic to see the developments noted here as the beginnings of a systematic recognition that children may have a variety of important relationships with adults. This recognition is particularly important, for example, where there are ethnic differences between the children and their new 'parents'. In this the law seems only a little behind research into child development, which has in recent years been moving away from preoccupation with mothers towards a respect for the richness and complexity of children's relationships with other people. If so, we can expect a reconsideration of some apparently 'fundamental' legal notions. Adoption, based as it is on a rather idealized notion of the isolated nuclear family, is perhaps the clearest example. Law books have usually treated custody, adoption, maintenance of children, and so on as separate topics, each with its own history and values. If the trends noted here are indicators for the future, we might expect to see such categories as 'family re-organisation' appear in legal texts, and the law might become more closely linked to actual patterns of family life than to traditional stereotypes, many of which were formed in times when adult concerns about property and proprieties tended to overwhelm children's interests.

Underlying these developments is the view that the law should recognize the importance of a variety of people in children's lives, not only those who are labelled 'parent' or 'guardian'. This view may be linked with many factors, including the implications of a pluralistic society (e.g. where members of a child's family have different ethnic origins); the pressure for the rights of those whose family life departs from the conventional norm, such as single parents, unmarried couples and homosexuals; and the way child development theory has moved beyond preoccupation with mothers towards a recognition of the importance of other relationships in children's lives. The challenge will be to find new legal categories and procedures which match the actual patterns and values of Australian society. The questions that are now emerging are difficult, but may indicate that the complex world of children is being taken rather more seriously.

The changes that we have seen in the law are not simple responses to social changes; they are partly the result of political choice. Those who participate in these choices should understand (among other things) the law's role in allocating power over children. Thus we saw in child welfare how a correct perception that children's needs sometimes require state intervention led to a disastrous conclusion that the answer was to give largely uncontrolled power to state welfare department; and how today's reformers are trying to devise a system that protects children, yet respects the rights of those involved, including the child, to participate in decisions about their lives. In custody law, we saw the Family Court of Australia playing a very active role in re-organising parenting roles after family breakdown, but through the counselling service and the emphasis given to the children's wishes and to proper representation of their interests, seeking to do so in a way that encourages the people concerned to work out their own solutions. And in re-organized families we saw the law beginning to share power more widely among significant adults in children's lives, rather than concentrate it in the hands of those adults falling within technical categories such as 'guardian' or 'parent'.

Throughout, we may detect a theme: that in the increasingly changing and pluralist Australian society the law should, while retaining a protective framework, place considerable power in the hands of the children and the adults who are closely involved in their lives. But this still leaves open many questions: the respective power of courts and government agencies such as schools; the respective merits of various types of procedures; the roles of professionals and community representatives; the place of minority beliefs about child rearing; and many others. Children's rights, and those of adults, will be advanced to the extent that we address these issues with wisdom and humanity.

Afterword: Policies for Children

R.G. Brown

What emerges most consistently from the papers, written from their various viewpoints, is the emphasis on change and uncertainty—the belief by the writers that we are going through a time of instability in which, while we may be adding to our stock of knowledge and information about people and society, we are not necessarily doing so well in adding to our capacity to use that knowledge and information in the best interests of the individual and the community so far as these are reconcilable.

We cannot say that the effects of change on people are greater now than they have ever been—we do not know, for example, whether change was felt to be less rapid and pervasive by people during the industrial revolution in England in the eighteenth century—but we may agree that there have been times of relative stability and times of change and that the present is a time of rapid and extensive change. That change has its material and non-material aspects. Materially the sources of change have been the continuing economic and physical development whose effects can be seen in industrialization and urbanization. These are apparent to individuals in the growth in size and complexity of the political, social and economic institutions with which they have to deal, which may be influential in their lives, but over which they may feel they have little control.

Associated with these changes have been changes in the status of children and in the relations into which children customarily enter. There has been a more careful prescription of the rights of children and an increasing willingness to see them assume more responsibility for themselves at younger ages. In terms of the relations most central to this book, there has been increasing uncertainty about the rights, responsibilities and roles respectively of the child, the family and the state.

The contributors to this book set out to explore these relationships; to try to put down from their knowledge, experience and particular expertise what is generally known about children in their relations with family and community; to consider, for example, whether the status of children is changing, whether our understanding of children is changing, and what assumptions are determining our attitudes to children and the ways we respond to them. And they have set out to do this with particular reference to the work of the *human services*, to whom society has delegated some of its responsibilities for children.

The book has not attempted to deal with the technical problems of the public response to children. It does not say how in particular the human services could respond better to children on behalf of society. It deals instead with the substance of what that response does. It asks what we know and think about children, what status we ascribe to childhood, what meaning we give to it; and then it considers what that tells us about the nature of the response that the human services could make on behalf of society, particularly with respect to relations between the young, dependent child, the family and the state.

Children, families and the state: changing relations

It is a truism that the family has changed. We can be more certain about the nature of some changes than about others. Thus those that have occurred during the lives of the present generations of children and adults have been written about extensively. They are what we have been most concerned with here.

We may also be moderately sure about changes that took place many centuries ago in the old societies from which most European Australians draw their ancestry. These changes occurred when simple, pre-literate, tribal societies began to give way to urban societies in the process of early economic development. Then there were well-defined patterns of family and kinship which determined the rights and responsibilities of each person in the community, usually a tribe, clan or similar group, to others in that community. All members of the community were in direct, face-to-face contact, and children knew to whom in the community they were responsible and what the responsibilities of others were to them. The range of people, in effect of 'aunts' and 'uncles' who might not necessarily be blood relatives, who were responsible for a child was much greater than it is now, and their responsibilities, for example on the death of a child's mother, were clear, specific and mandatory.

We can be reasonably sure about the nature of the changes in family and community life in such societies in the past because social anthropologists have given accounts at first hand of changes in what are believed to have been similar societies in more recent times, as these societies have moved from a subsistence agricultural economy based on barter of goods and exchange of services to one based on cash payment for goods and services. Those changes saw the breakdown of the traditional exchange of rights and responsibilities through the institutions of family and kinship and the beginnings of replacement of the personal responsibility of kin-group by the public responsibility of community and state. With the specialization of division of labour in a cash economy based on a domestic system of production began the division of labour in what we now call the human services, and many responsibilities once discharged by kin were taken up by society, first by religious and other community groups and later by the state.

We can be less sure about changes that occurred more recently but beyond the range of our personal experience. Historians have begun only recently to take an interest in the social life of 'the common people' in earlier times and the sources to which they can turn are fragmentary. What they have said about societies like our own some two centuries ago, at the beginning of the industrial revolution in Europe which set the pattern for modern economic and social life, is that more people then lived in extended families. Families of three generations and of other extended kin were more common in all social strata, and in the middling classes a kind of extended family of immediate relatives, distant relatives, servants and apprentices might be found under the same roof. Children were likely to be seen as little adults, as workers, and therefore almost as property. Children had few rights; parents had almost complete rights of control over their children; and so did parent-surrogates—whether nannies, school mistresses, or masters in employment.

It may be less important to know about family and community life before the industrial revolution than to understand what changes are taking place today, what forces are influential now in determining the status of children, and what effect this may have on their lives. Our consideration of children in family and community life might therefore begin with what we know from our own experience to have been so, particularly in those relations in which we are most interested—those between child, family and state.

In the past it was mainly changes in economic life and their associated demographic and social changes that altered the relations of children with their family and community. More recently these relations have been affected by social changes whose origins are less clear—changes in attitudes to authority, including parental authority; an increasing emphasis on individual rights, including an uncertain but influential emphasis on the right to personal fulfilment; and changing notions of civil rights. These appear to be part of powerful social movements over which children, families and indeed the state may have little influence. There is no evidence to suggest that they will be halted or reversed in the near future, and it seems that relations between children, families and the state will continue to change in ways that may be hard to predict.

Changes in family and community have been reflected in changes in attitudes to children and in the laws affecting them. When children were more firmly within their family and kin-group, when the institutions of family and kinship were more directly the source of children's education and health care and the arbiter of their place in society, and when in return through much of their lives children were economic contributors to their families, then parents and guardians were seen as having a kind of natural right to their children. The state only interfered if there was manifest neglect or corruption of them. With industrial development and urban growth there has been a separation of functions within the family and, in response to that, changes in law and administration affecting children's relations with families and with public institutions.

In this century the minimal notion of the rights of children has slowly given way, and in the last quarter century in particular there has been a quickening recognition of them. Children have entered in their own right into new relations with public institutions such as schools and welfare departments and other human service organizations. In recognizing this, law and public administration have had to undertake the difficult task of weighing the rights of children against the rights of parents and the responsibilities of public institutions. In the last decade more particularly they have had to question the assumption that parents and guardians necessarily represent the best interests of children. There has been a move toward recognition of children as legal persons, not only legally independent of parents at earlier ages through formal recognition of lower ages of adulthood, but also, and perhaps more problematic, through formal and informal recognition of much earlier ages at which children, though still legally children, could act or ask public institutions to act on their behalf independent of parents and guardians.

Whatever the means by which it came about, the modern family has usually been described as a nuclear family, notionally a two-generation family of parents and children, in which the husband is the breadwinner, the wife the homemaker. They are bound together in a marriage contract that assumes a permanent union within which the children are nurtured through a relatively long period of economic and personal dependency. In that situation the primary task of the family was to nurture the child and to ensure his development in ways that were consistent with the demands of the larger society.

Many other tasks that once might have been performed by the family—formal education and vocational training, for example—had become the responsibility of the state.

There were always differences from that general pattern of family life, but today the differences have become more common. There are more families with two parents working outside the home. More women, more married women, and more women with pre-school and school-age children are working outside the family. Divorce, and remarriage, are more common; single-parenthood is more common. Nevertheless, almost all children grow up in a nurturing relationship with one or more adults—in what we are still prepared to call a family. Within families these days there may be more changes from time to time, as parents move into and out of employment, and as families form and reform. But it is still true, and appears likely to be so for as far as we can think ahead about the future of family life, that most children will grow up in families. Since many responsibilities for children have been delegated to the state, one of the first considerations is what the relation shall be between the state, the family and the child in meeting those obligations.

If families are to continue to be the primary source of economic and personal support for children, then probably it would be agreed that the business of the state should be to support the family and not to supplant it except in unusual circumstances. And that may well be the first assumption on which public policy rests with respect to children. The task of determining what that might involve in practice would be hard enough in times of relative stability. It has been made more difficult by changing attitudes to children and families which may be more influential in affecting public policy than changes in families themselves.

Relations between family members have become more uncertain, and these uncertainties are more likely to be acknowledged publicly as involving conflicts between the rights of the different parties. Attitudes to the rights of children and of parents may be in conflict, and these in turn may not be reconcilable with changing attitudes to the status of women. Nevertheless, the state may be expected to balance the interests involved. Children and parents may see themselves as less clearly bound to each other and as more entitled to seek personal fulfilment even at the cost of marital and family bonds; and the state may be expected to legislate to deal with the personal and family difficulties this creates and to administer public services that can respond to them. These complex assumptions about personal and familial rights and responsibilities may be compounded by the public expression and advocacy of rights groups, who may be effective not only in determining standards of behaviour but also in influencing the nature of the state's response to the situations that are then created.

These uncertainties are further compounded by influences outside the family, such as from some institutions of business and commerce and of the media and popular culture, which may influence the assumptions on which people live and the standards by which they behave. These assumptions and standards are not always consistent with what may be publicly acknowledged as desirable. Directly and indirectly, through commercial advertising, through the kinds of life-styles that are given prominence and sometimes approval in the media, and through a multitude of other influences, they may put before people aspirations, life-styles, values and assumptions that are at odds with the conventional assumptions by which it is expected people will live and which it is assumed the family and the state are reinforcing. The resources available to these other institutions to determine life-styles and standards of behaviour may far exceed those available to the state to respond, through its human services, to the adverse effects that may be created by these uncertainties. At the same time as these complexities have increased, the state is expected to be more effective in response to them. Law and administration are expected to enter into more complex and uncertain personal, familial and social situations with more sureness.

These changes are continuing. When they have run their course a new set of certainties may emerge based on more stable relations between children, families and the state and the other institutions of society that influence them. We cannot be sure of this, for at least three reasons. We have no ground for assuming that there is any obviously stable set of relations that can emerge from the clashes of personal, group and institutional interests affecting the family. Nor can we assume that the conflicting demands with which people are faced by the many interests outside the influence of family and state will become less forceful. And there are few signs that we can develop the knowledge and the capacity in the human services to deal with these complexities at costs the country is willing to pay. In these circumstances the state, in attempting to discharge its responsibilities for children, may not even be able to see clearly what those responsibilities are, let alone to decide surely and fairly what it should do with respect to them.

Changing public response

Australian experience has been similar to that of other Western industrial societies. Three phases can be seen in the history of our public response to children: a period of minimum state action based on acceptance of the rights of parents over children and a belief in the virtues of individual and voluntary endeavour; a gradual shift toward more state intervention but on relatively simple assumptions about the right of the state to interfere in the relations between parents and children; and, more recently, a period of greater uncertainty in which a belief in a more positive role for the state in its relations with families and children has not been matched with as much assurance about the assumptions on which that intervention should rest or as much certainty about whether the conditions for it are achievable.

The early antecedents of public responsibility for social welfare in Australia were the English poor laws. Although poor laws as such were never enacted in the Australian colonies, as for example they were in the comparable period of the history of the United States, assumptions derived from them were nevertheless influential in our early colonial experience and elements of poor law attitudes remain today. With hindsight we may say that poor law thinking lacked an understanding of the complex social and personal causes of problems and hence was harsh and discriminatory in its response to troubled people, since it neither understood why they were in trouble nor what would assist them out of it. It was largely a policy of what today is called 'blaming the victim'. We may not be much the better for believing that. Our greater understanding of the complexities of personal and social life may not be of as much practical value as it might seem. We may be no nearer, for example, to resolving the old poor law dilemma of 'how to relieve destitution without encouraging idleness', which in more sophisticated form still appears to lie at the centre of much thinking about Australian social policy, and probably accounts for some of what has come to be called the welfare backlash of the 1970s.

Characteristic of poor law thinking and practice in early Australia as elsewhere was its failure to distinguish causes of need and to respond differently to different causes. Coupled with assumptions about the rights of parents and the limits of responsibility of the state, this meant that the public response to children was primarily a response to those most in trouble—to those who were severely physically neglected, grossly abused or manifestly corrupted. In less serious situations interference with the rights of parents was minimal; but when it did occur it usually took the form of the state assuming parental rights, sometimes for long periods. More subtle notions of public responsibility were not considered, not only because the knowledge on which they might rest had yet to develop, and because ideas of a positive developmental role for the state in social policy had yet to emerge, but also and perhaps more important because problems of gross physical deprivation were what most obviously confronted the state.

That kind of thinking began to give way with a growing recognition of the need for more individual responses to children and a growing acceptance of a more active role by the state. The state might now act not only more quickly and in response to less severe problems but it might also consider acting preventively in situations of assumed need. That was a large step beyond the beliefs that had guided public responsibility in the past. Thus began the move toward greater public involvement in the affairs of children, but on assumptions that did not clarify the rights and responsibilities of children, of families and of the state. There was more acceptance of public responsibility for children but it was not backed by an understanding that could inform action, and public action in child welfare was still largely founded on the belief that the state could abrogate the rights of parents but need not consider the rights of children. It is the questioning of those assumptions that perhaps most characteristically marks the present phase of public response to children, and it is the failure to resolve those issues to the public satisfaction and to the satisfaction of the parties and interests involved that probably accounts for much of the uncertainty that surrounds current policies with respect to children.

These changing attitudes to the role of the state with respect to children and families coincided with far-reaching changes in law and social administration which have come to be known as 'the welfare state'. During and after the Second World War the assumption was widely made that the state through legislation and administration could shape economic and social life to produce a more just society. In many Western societies the quarter century following the war saw much social legislation which sought to achieve two objectives. The first was to secure for all citizens an adequate minimum standard of living sufficient to assist them to withstand the major uncertainties of life such as unemployment or disability over which they may have little control. The second objective, which went beyond that minimum standard, was to assist people to secure more equal access to resources, such as health care and education, so that they could better themselves and, it was hoped, better contribute to the enhancement of their community and the advancement of their society.

More recently these ideas of individual betterment and social advance were joined in an assumption that the state, through social policy-making and social planning, could be involved in social development just as it is involved in economic development with economic policy-making and planning. These far-reaching assumptions about the developmental role of the state in social affairs had hardly begun to be explored in theory and had little significance in practice when they were overtaken by a world-wide economic recession which left much uncertainty about the future of the state in social provision.

The movement toward the welfare state provided some of the rationale on which positive policies of public responsibility for children could be based. Thus in child welfare the modern conception of the state as the mediator between parents and children in which the rights of both have to be respected and related to the interests of the larger society in its future citizens has grown alongside the idea of the state as the arbiter of general welfare. What began with the need to help particular children in trouble, and grew into more general responses to social problems affecting children, and remained thus for the greater part of the history of children's welfare, now aspires to be assertive social policy-making about as yet unclear, and for the present at least unachievable notions of social development.

This has led to assumptions that the state should achieve balanced and comprehensive policies for children and families that would contribute to the enhancement of individual and social life. These are large endeavours. We may know what we want in terms of those general goals, but it is not clear that we understand how to translate them into specific objectives for programmes, that we can reach agreement about the means by which particular objectives are to be achieved, or that we can readily summon the knowledge and expertise needed to devise the means. Thus there may be general agreement with the view that the human services should be concerned with assisting children to develop their potential physically, intellectually and emotionally and to become responsible citizens. But it is more difficult to reach a working understanding between the people and interests involved about what that means in practice, for example in guiding the determinations of family courts about the care of children in broken marriages.

Some substantial problems face the human services in these endeavours. First, attitudes to welfare provision are now less favourable than they have been for some time. Resources are tight in a world-wide economic recession, and partly because of this but also partly for less tangible reasons there is a resistance to further expansion of social services. While some of this may spring from a proper desire to know where we are going with welfare provision on the scale that it now is, some of it appears to stem from less laudable motives. Thus, however technically competent we may now be, for example in designing income maintenance or health-care systems to serve children better, there is little indication that the will exists amongst the more fortunate to share the costs of the burden that now falls on the less fortunate—a goal well below the notion of social development and closer to that of minimum adequacy with which we emerged from the Second World War.

Issues such as these are not likely to go away. If the present economic downturn is reversed, we may not return to the prosperity of the last quarter century and may not expect the same support for child welfare policies. Even if we do return to earlier levels of general prosperity, technological and structural unemployment may be high. Some in society will bear the burden of this economic adjustment disproportionately and some children, perhaps large numbers of children, may grow up in deprivation, as the children of some particularly poorly favoured groups such as Aboriginals already do. If these children are to have a decent future the will must be found to share the burdens of economic change more equitably—a goal well below the equality of opportunity to which we committed ourselves following the Second World War.

Even if greater agreement could be reached about the particular intentions of society for children through the agency of its human services, for example if we could achieve more understanding about what we mean by rehabilitative juvenile justice programmes, we should still be faced with deficiencies in the expertise that has to be brought to bear. The range of expertise required in the human services is enormous. It includes policy-making and planning, development of programmes to implement policies, administration of organizations capable of providing programmes, supervision of and provision of services, and monitoring and evaluating all those tasks. Two related problems have to be faced in the design of implementable programmes: sometimes the expertise is inadequate for the problems—there may be no socially acceptable technical solution to a particular problem, at least at costs the community is prepared to pay; sometimes the expertise is adequate but its efficacy is blunted by the social and political uncertainties within which it has to be applied—a technical solution may be available but the political will to achieve it may not be.

An example of the first kind of problem, where technical capacity may be weak, is the difficulty in devising welfare initiatives that can bring together resources from the different levels of government and the non-governmental sector in coordinated programmes that reduce duplication and gaps in services but do not face the consumer with unresponsive monolithic service structures. There is the difficulty, for example, in relating central planning, direction and supervision of services to the demand for decentralized and localized operation of them with substantial elements of worker participation and consumer involvement. These issues are further complicated in Australia by the federal system of government. But even without the added uncertainty of the politics of Australian federalism, the difficulties are considerable in maintaining a child welfare system that is strong enough centrally to be capable of implementing the policy directives of the responsible Minister in Cabinet and is flexible enough locally to be responsive to the diversity that confronts it.

The second kind of difficulty, where technical capacity is blunted by uncertainties about how it should be used, can also be seen in the provision of children's services. We disagree, for example, about whether children's services should be mainly remedial and rehabilitative and concerned mostly to palliate the more serious effects on children and families of the problems they face in coping with modern life in all its complexities, or whether the services should assume a more developmental and preventive stance aimed at reducing the incidence of those problems in industrial society. Our intention moves between these goals and at best maintains an uneasy compromise between them. Our laws and the administration of services reflect these doubts. Resources are consumed in the human services in clarifying uncertainties to achieve a working compromise that is publicly acceptable. Thus, not only are resources drawn away from the technical task of providing better services, but even when good solutions to welfare problems are available there may be no clear mandate for them.

Finally, however laudable may be our intentions with respect to children, they may not be realizable by the family and the state through its human services, because they face strong interests which may not support their intentions. Materialist interests outside the influence of the family, and in a market economy largely outside the control of the state, may create uncertainty in the minds of children and even of adults about what are desirable values by which to live, what are worthwhile goals for which to strive, and what are proper means for achieving them. Thus the environment in which the family and the human services work is made uncertain by a lack of consistency and at times an antitheses between their intentions and the activities of other influences in society that may be more powerful and pervasive. In the face of this, many actions by parents and many interventions by human service organizations are relatively ineffective aspects of the world of their children.

The task of the human services in their response to children and families is difficult. Aspirations are high, but the means and the will to achieve them may not be there. The prosperity of the last 25 years had led to high expectations, not only that there will continue to be higher general standards of living, but also in the assumption that social problems ultimately are solvable and that the resources will be available for their solution. It is hard to say how much of that is now realizable. For the present at least we can expect fewer resources for welfare purposes, at best a more slowly growing welfare budget. Even if the real value of resources for the care of children is maintained, we cannot be sure that they will be used better until our intentions for child welfare services are made more clear. There are differences, reasonable enough, between the various interests involved—the rights of families, of children, of women, for example, are not necessarily reconcilable. There are covert conflicts between publicly stated goals for children and families and the at least indirect influence of other interests. In that climate of uncertainty the problems facing the human services in performing better with possibly fewer resources are formidable. Their task is enormous in developing the expertise needed to produce thoughtful policies for children that can come to terms with conflicting values about children and families, and that can devise strategies to implement those policies in a publicly accountable manner, so as to be seen to be working toward generally accepted goals while responding flexibly to the diversity of local conditions and particular problems with which they are faced in practice.

Policies for children

The 250 years since the beginning of the Industrial Revolution, and in particular the last 50 since the onset of the Second World War, have seen great economic and social changes. These have altered the lives of children and the relations between children and families and the social institutions, such as the agencies of the state, with which increasingly they have had to deal. Many of these changes are part of larger economic and social movements outside the control of individuals and perhaps little influenced even by governments. These changes are continuing, and there are few signs of how they will end. We may expect therefore that the status of children and families will continue to be uncertain and a matter for sometimes contentious debate, and that the state's responsibilities for children in relation to parents and others will be ill-defined, stated equivocally in legislation, and difficult to determine administratively.

In these circumstances, we may lose sight of the assumptions on which we had been working and which have provided the mandate for the human services. It is important, therefore, that we should think again about those assumptions and the aspirations we have adopted in response to them; and we should either re-affirm them or alter them so that we may acknowledge publicly what our goals are and can get on with the task of achieving them in an ethos less uncertain than the present one. For our purposes the propositions on which the human services have rested can be considered to be of two kinds: those which concern welfare policies generally and those which concern children's policies in particular.

As to welfare policies generally, there were certain assumptions which emerged from the heightened sense of corporate responsibility generated by the experiences of the world-wide depression of the 1930s and the Second World War. They reflected a considerable change in thinking about public responsibility, and the agreement about them was a significant influence in the development of the so-called 'welfare state', the name by which loosely we have come to describe the welfare legislation with which we attempted to express those assumptions.

Foremost was a recognition that individualism and the free play of market forces would leave some, perhaps substantial, groups in conditions not tolerable by the standards of the times, and that therefore some collective action would have to be taken on their behalf. This was seen to be so not only for the good of those who would be the direct beneficiaries but also for the good of the wider society, both because the humanitarian sensibilities of that society were affronted by what had emerged about inter-war social conditions and because it feared the consequences to the maintenance of the social order from the continuation of those conditions. This experience led to a general acceptance of public responsibility for ensuring adequate minimum standards of living for people and beyond that to providing them with the opportunity of access to the means for their betterment—in their own interests and in the interests of the wider society.

Most people in Australia benefitted from the combination of economic growth and social legislation in the 25 years following the Second World War, but the full aspirations of the post-war were never realized. The Australian Government Commission on Poverty assessed the nature and magnitude of the problem in the 1970s. On the most conservative interpretation of their estimates, there is a sizeable problem of at least relative poverty in Australia. Even with the favourable economic experience of the post-war, which may not be repeated, there were identifiable, and in some cases large, groups of people who could not achieve acceptable minimum standards of living through their own efforts, and who therefore were entitled to public support according to the assumptions that then ruled.

Secondly, somewhat later, and perhaps less forcefully, there was a recognition that, beyond the failure of the market to ensure an adequate minimum standard for all, the price of economic progress may be borne unfairly by some, perhaps substantial, classes of people—the poorly endowed, the poorly educated, the vulnerable and minority groups. And there was a realization that some readily identifiable categories of people—those in large families of low skill, low income wage earners, for example—were the losers in urban-industrial societies in countless continual ways. For them it meant little to speak of equality of opportunity in access to health, education and other such resources that might secure their betterment, since by the very depths and nature of their disadvantage they were unable to make the most of the opportunities that might be available in ways more familiar to the established, articulate, endowed middle classes.

Something more than a notional equality of opportunity was needed to break the enduring cycle of disadvantage from which they suffered, and for a time in the late 1960s there was talk of positive discrimination and some moves in that direction, for example in education. But if the aspiration to achieve a basic minimum standard of life for all was difficult to achieve, even more was the goal of equality of opportunity, not merely because the technical initiatives were difficult to devise but because the political will and the public agreement, which had never been great, evaporated quickly in the face of the costs that were thought to be involved. The Australian Government Royal Commission on Human Relations documented the plight in the 1970s of some of the most disadvantaged people in Australia, and more recently, with respect to children and families in particular, the evidence has been assessed by the Australian government's Family Services Committee. There is little doubt from these and other authoritative sources that we have fallen short of the aspirations we set ourselves 25 years ago. The task of the human services in making up the lost ground is the greater in the face of the current economic uncertainties and the evident retreat from post-war idealism. The existence of these barriers is the more reason for renewing efforts to determine what our goals now are and to what extent and by what means they are achievable.

These general assumptions of the last quarter century about social welfare policy, if they are to apply, of course apply to children. They bear with particular force on some groups of disadvantaged children—Aboriginal children, children of some ethnic origins, children in poverty, children with emotional, intellectual and physical handicaps. They apply with great force to young children generally, because of their helplessness and vulnerability in the face of the personal and social forces with which they have to deal and because of their importance to society as future citizens. The basic civic minima which it was once assumed economically advanced societies could guarantee would then be the birthright of all children. Further lies the expectation, still remote, that particularly disadvantaged children will receive some form of positive discrimination to try to break their cycle of disadvantage and to achieve for them at least equality of opportunity, if not a greater measure of actual equality—a goal now receding in the face of prevailing attitudes to the less fortunate in Australia.

Beyond these general welfare assumptions, which may be seen on both humanitarian and utilitarian grounds to apply with great force to children, there have been particular assumptions of policy with respect to children which also were based upon beliefs about their special situation—their vulnerability and their claim as future citizens. Translated into general policy aspirations for children they require, beyond the guarantees of opportunities for economic betterment implied in general welfare policies, that no child should suffer preventable physical or social deprivation, and that all children should be provided with as close to optimal conditions for their development as is achievable.

These are large assumptions, at present apparently unrealizable. Nevertheless, if they are still our ultimate aspirations for children, they should be publicly acknowledged as such, so that they can be re-affirmed in the face of the current economic stringency and social uncertainty, so that governments and political parties can be expected to say to what extent they endorse them as general goals and what are their explicit proposals for moving toward them. This means that the machinery should be established, in and out of government, to determine how many of these objectives are realisable, by what means, in what time. The data and information and the proposals based upon them should be public knowledge, available alike to governments at all levels, federal, state and local, to all political parties, and to non-governmental bodies and citizens' groups concerned with the rights and the welfare of children.

Determining specific objectives within such broad policy assumptions and translating them into achievable proposals in the technical and the political senses are tasks beyond the scope of this book. They require substantial resources not generally available to individual researchers. At most one can establish some preliminary desiderata. The baseline provision for any social policy for children requires, within some acceptable range of inequality in living standards, that people responsible for children should share equally in the fruits of economic output, and that they should bear the costs of economic development only within limits that are considered fair; so that all who are responsible for children achieve at least an acceptable minimum economic standard through work or from income security provisions, and so that the burden of risks such as unemployment and disability, which are apparently inescapable features of industrial society, is shared equitably.

It may seem that these are unrealizable goals in the present economic and social climate. Yet they are well below the level of the fundamental social rights for children to which the greater part of the energy of the International Year of the Child was directed. They are minimum inescapable goals for economically advanced societies in the twentieth century. Without them the greater aspirations of the International Year are unlikely to be achieved. The task is less to determine their general worth than to re-affirm them as publicly accepted goals for the last quarter of the century—economic security for children, their freedom from deprivation, and the means for their betterment. The task then is to secure a firm public commitment to them, to strengthen the flagging political will needed to secure the resources for them, and then hopefully in a more favourable ethos to get on through the human services and in other ways with ironing out the technical complexities in the way of their achievement.

On this economic base there should be adequate access to resources for betterment so that, for example through maintenance of standards of public and personal health and of education, families will be able to provide children with opportunities for their advancement and hopefully the advancement of the wider society. Beyond this there should be provision of resources to help people overcome special difficulties—positive discrimination in favour of the least personally and socially favoured.

These proposals are based on assumptions that the years of child rearing have become the period of greatest financial hardship for many families, that the effects of failure of basic income support for families with children can have serious long term effects on the future lives of children and therefore on the future of the society of which they are a part, and that the economic and social situation of families is the largest single determinant of the opportunities open to children and hence should be the largest component of a policy of investment in children and in the future society to which they are heirs.

References

Children and Society

1. This chapter owes a great deal to a larger work: A. Burns and J.J. Goodnow, *Children and Families in Australia* (George Allen & Unwin, Sydney, 1979). It also owes much to the setting provided by Derek and Caroline Lucas (Kangaroo Valley) and to the enthusiasm of a student (Max Morrisey) who brought to our attention the writing of McKellar and the 1929 discussion of child endowment.
2. John Locke, 'Report for the Reform of the Poor Law, 1697', cited in *Children in English Society*, I. Pinchbeck and M. Hewitt (Routledge & Kegan Paul, London, 1969), vol. 1, pp. 310–11.
3. L.L. Robson, *The Convict Settlers of Australia* (Melbourne University Press, Melbourne, 1965), pp. 170–71.
4. K. MacNab and R. Ward, 'The Nature and Nurture of the First Generation of Native-Born Australians', *Historical Studies of Australia and New Zealand* 10, no. 39 (1962): 289–308.
5. P. McDonald, *Marriage in Australia*, Australian Family Formation Project Monographs, no. 2 (1975), p. 29.
6. Ibid., p. 36.
7. Pinchbeck and Hewitt, *Children in English Society*, p. 167.
8. Ibid., p. 162.
9. J.F. Cleverley, *The First Generation: School and Society in Early Australia* (Sydney University Press, Sydney, 1971), p. 11.
10 Historical Records of Australia, 1805, cited by Burns & Goodnow, *Children and Families in Australia* pp. 21–22.
11. K. Windschuttle, 'Evangelism and Philanthropy: The Public Roles of Ruling Class Women in Colonial Australia 1788–1850', *Women and Labour Conference Papers* (Australian Radical Publications, Glebe, Sydney, 1978), p. 57.
12. M. Horsburgh, 'Child Care in NSW in 1870', *Australian Social Work* 29, no. 1 (1976): 3–24.
13. C. Judge and F. Emmerson, 'Some children at Risk in Victoria in the 19th Century', *Medical Journal of Australia* 1 (1974): 490–97.
14. K. Daniels, K. Murnane and A. Picot, *Women in Australia: An Annotated Guide to Records*, 2 vols. (Australian Government Printing Service, Canberra, 1977), p. 55.
15. Report of the Royal Commission on Child Endowment or Family Allowances, (1929), p. 71.
16. Horsburgh, 'Child Care in NSW in 1870', p. 8.

17. C.H. Kempe, 'Keynote Address', in *The Battered Child*, Proceedings of First National Australian Conference (Department for Community Welfare, Perth, Western Australia 1975), p. 7.
18. Windschuttle, 'Evangelism and Philanthropy', p. 57.
19. L. Soccio, 'A family in Italy and Australia', in *Melbourne Studies of Education*, ed. S. Murray-Smith (Melbourne University Press, Melbourne, 1977), p. 21.
20. A. Ellis, *Sydeny Morning Herald*, 11 June 1979, p. 3.
21. C.S. Dweck and T.E. Goetz, 'Attributions and Learned Helplessness', in *New Directions in Attribution Research*, ed. J. Harvey, W. Ickes and R. Kidd (Hillsdale, New Jersey, 1978), pp. 157–77.
22. Burns & Goodnow, *Children and Families in Australia*.
23. Report of the Royal Commission, p. 71.
24. Pinchbeck and Hewitt, *Children in English Society*.
25. K. Porter, 'The Old Order', in *The Leaning Tower and Other Stories* (Signet, New York, 1963), p. 31.
26. R. Twopenny, *Town Life in Australia* (Penguin, Melbourne, 1973), p. 101.
27. A. Summers, *Damned Whores and God's Police* (Penguin, Melbourne, 1975).
28. Report of the Royal Commission, p. 71.
29. D.L. Gurry, 'The Doctor as Detective' in *The Battered Child*, Proceedings of First National Australian Conference.
30. J. McCaughey and W. Chew, 'The Family Study', in *Who Cares?*, ed. J. McCaughey, S. Shaver, H. Ferber et al. (Sun Books, Melbourne, 1977), p. 127.

Children and the State

1. Opinions expressed in this paper do not necessarily reflect those of the Department of Community Welfare Services in Victoria, where the authors are employed.
2. C. Lasch, *Haven is a Heartless World: The Family Under Siege* (Basic Books Inc., New York, 1977), pp. 183–89.
3. James L. Paul and G.R. Neufeld, *Child Advocacy within the System*, Syracuse Special Education and Rehabilitation Monograph Series, no. 11. (Syracuse University Press, New York, 1977), p. 14.
4. Ibid., pp. 22, 26.

Children and Families

1. W. Hetznecker and M.A. Foreman, *On Behalf of Children* (Grune & Stratton, New York, 1974).
2. *Final Report of the Royal Commission on Human Relationships*, vol. 4 (Australian Government Printing Service, Canberra, 1977).
3. L. DeMause, 'The Evolution of Childhood', *Historical Childhood Quarterly* 1 (1974): 503–74.
4. P. Aries, *Centuries of Childhood: A Social History of Family Life* (Knopf, New York, 1962).

5. E.M.R. Lomax, *Science and Patterns of Child Care* (W.H. Freeman & Co., San Francisco, 1978).
6. E.J. Anthony, 'Child Therapy Techniques', in *American Handbook of Psychiatry*, ed. G. Caplan, 2nd ed., vol. 2 (Basic Books Inc., New York, 1974).
7. E.J. Anthony, 'A New Scientific Region to Explore', in *The Child in His Family*, vol. 4, *Vulnerable Children*, ed. E.J. Anthony, C. Koupernik and C. Chiland (John Wiley & Sons, New York, 1978).
8. J. Tizard, 'Nursery Needs and Choices', in *Human Growth and Development*, ed. J.S. Bruner and A. Garton (Clarendon Press, Oxford, 1978).
9. Family Services Committee, *Families and Social Services in Australia: A Report to the Minister for Social Security*, vols. 1 and 2 (Australian Government Printing Service, Canberra, 1978).
10. P. Eisen, 'In the Shadows of Their Lives: The Search for Opportunity, Development and Care for Children', *Australian and New Zealand Journal of Psychiatry* 12 (1978): 255–61.
11. A. Toffler, *Future Shock* (Pan Books, London, 1974).
12. E.H. Erickson, 'Foreward: Reflections on Historical Change', in *The Child in His Family*, vol. 5, *Children and Their Families in a Changing World*, ed. E.J. Anthony and C. Chiland (John Wiley & Sons, New York, 1978).
13. G. Caplan, 'Family Support Systems in a Changing World', in *The Child in His Family*, vol. 5, *Children and their Families in a Changing World*.
14. R. Wernick et al. *The Family* (Time-Life International, Nederland, 1976).
15. Report of the Royal Commission on Human Relationships, vol. 4.
16. World Health Organization, *Statistical Indices of Family Health*, Technical Report Series, no. 587 (Geneva, 1976).
17. F. Elkin and G. Handel, *The Child and Society: The Process of Socialisation*, 3rd ed. (Random House, New York, 1978).
18. T. Lidz, 'The Family: The Developmental Setting', in *American Handbook of Psychiatry*, ed. S. Arieti, 2nd ed., vol. 1 (Basic Books Inc., New York, 1974).
19. M.K. Pringle, *The Needs of Children* (Hutchinson, London, 1974).
20. P. Eisen, 'The Rights of Children: Some Assumptions and Questions', *Social Security Journal* (in press).
21. Law Reform Commission, *Child Welfare: Children in Trouble*, Discussion Paper no. 9 (Sydney, 1979).
22. L. Foreman, *Children or Families*? (Australian Government Social Welfare Commission, Canberra, 1975).
23. World Health Organization, *Child Mental Health and Psychosocial Development*, Technical Report Series, no. 613 (Geneva, 1977).
24. P. Eisen, 'Children Under Stress', *Australian and New Zealand Journal of Psychiatry* (in press).
25. P. Eisen, 'Stress within Families: Some Questions and Possibilities', *The Australian Journal of Family Therapy* (in press).
26. E.A. Strommen, J.P. McKinney and H.E. Fitzgerald, *Developmental Psychology: The School-Aged Child* (Dorsey Press, Homewood, Illinois, 1977).
27. A.J. Sameroff, 'Early Influences on Development: Fact or Fancy?', in

Annual Progress in Child Psychiatry and Child Development 1976, ed. S. Chess and A. Thomas (Brunner/Mazel, New York, 1977).
28. J. Bowlby, *Attachment* (Basic Books Inc., New York, 1969).
29. E.H. Erikson, *Childhood and Society* (Norton, New York, 1950); H.S. Sullivan, *Conceptions of Modern Psychiatry* (Norton, New York, 1950).
30. Z.J. Lipowski, 'Physical Illness, the Patient and His Environment: Psychosocial Foundations of Medicine', in *American Handbook of Psychiatry*, ed. M.F. Reiser, 2nd ed., vol. 4 (Basic Books Inc., New York, 1975).
31. M. Rutter, 'Early Sources of Security and Competence', in *Human Growth and Development*, ed. J.S. Bruner and A. Garton (Clarendon Press, Oxford, 1978).
32. J. Goldstein, A. Freud and A.J. Solnit, *Beyond the Best Interests of the Child* (Free Press, New York, 1973).
33. Ibid.
34. J.S. Wallerstein and J.B. Kelly, 'The Effects of Parental Divorce: The Adolescent Experience', in *The Child in His Family*, vol. 3 *Children at Psychiatric Risk*, ed. E.J. Anthony and C. Koupernik, (John Wiley & Sons, New York, 1974); J.S. Wallerstein and J.B. Kelly, 'The Effects of Parental Divorce: Experiences of the Pre-School Child', *Journal of the American Academy of Child Psychiatry* 14, no. 4 (1975): 600–616; J.S. Wallerstein and J.B. Kelly, 'The Effects of Parental Divorce: Experiences of the Child in Early Latency', *American Journal of Orthopsychiatry* 46, no. 1 (1976): 20–32.
35. M. Bohman, 'A Study of Adopted Children, their Background, Environment and Adjustment', *Acta Paediatrica, Scandinavia* 61 (1972): 90–97; L. Cunningham, R.J. Cadoret, R. Loftus and J.E. Edwards, 'Studies of Adoptees from Psychiatrically Disturbed Biological Parents: Psychiatric Conditions in Childhood and Adolescence', *British Journal of Psychiatry* 126 (1975): 534–49.
36. R.E. Helfer and C.H. Kempe, eds., *The Battered Child* (University of Chicago Press, Chicago, 1968); A.H. Green, 'A Psychodynamic Approach to the Study and Treatment of Child-Abusing Parents', *Journal of the American Academy of Child Psychiatry* 15, no. 3 (1976): 414–29; A.H. Green, 'Psychopathology of Abused Children', *Journal of the American Academy of Child Psychiatry* 17, no. 1 (1978): 92–103.
37. W. Goldfarb, R.L. Spitzer and J. Endicott, 'A Study of Psychopathology of Parents of Psychotic Children by Structured Interview', in *Annual Progress in Child Psychiatry and Child Development 1977*, ed. S. Chess and A. Thomas (Brunner/Mazel, New York, 1977); E.J. Anthony, 'From Birth to Breakdown: A Prospective Study of Vulnerability', in *The Child in His Family*, vol. 4, *Vulnerable Children*.
38. P. Eisen, 'Parent-Child Fit and its Significance for Later Development', *The Australasian Nurses Journal* 7, no. 4 (1977): 25–27; A.J. Costello, 'Deprivation and Family Structure with Particular Reference to Twins', in *The Child in His Family*, vol. 4 *Vulnerable Children*; A.J. Sameroff, 'Infant Risk Factors in Developmental Deviancy' in *The Child in His Family*, vol. 4, *Vulnerable Children*.
39. J. Henry, *Pathways to Madness* (Vintage Books, New York, 1965).

40. P. Eisen, 'Do Children Need Parents?', *Mental Health in Australia* 1, no. 5 (1976): 147–55.
41. E.J. Anthony, 'A New Scientific Region to Explore', in *The Child in His Family*, vol. 4, *Vulnerable Children*.
42. P. Eisen, 'Children's Rights to Psychotherapy', Proceedings RANZCP Section of Child Psychiatry, 1978.
43. P.L. Adams, 'Functions of the Lower-Class Partial Family', *American Journal of Psychiatry* 130 (1973): 200–203.
44. *Report of the Royal Commission on Human Relationships*, vol. 4.
45. P. Eisen, 'Children under Stress'.
46. J. Harper and S. Williams, 'Adopted Children and Psychiatric Care', *Australian Journal of Social Issues* 11, no. 1 (1976): 43–53.
47. Elkin and Handel, *The Child and Society*.
48. R.M. Kanter, ed., *Communes: Creating and Managing the Collective Life* (Harper & Row, New York, 1973).
49. B. Bettelheim, *Children of the Dream* (Macmillan, New York, 1969).
50. E.J. Anthony, 'Naturalistic Studies of Disturbed Families', in *Explorations in Child Psychiatry*, E.J. Anthony (Plenum, New York, 1975); D.W. Winnicott, 'The Effect of Psychotic Parents on the Emotional Development of the Child', in *The Family and Individual Development*, (Travistock, London, 1965).
51. Family Services Committee, *Families and Social Services in Australia*.
52. P. Eisen, 'Children under Stress'.
53. P. Eisen, 'Stress within Families: Some Questions and Possibilities'.
54. R.S. Kalucy and P. Eisen, 'Dependence as a Psychological Mechanism in the Urban Setting' (unpublished).
55. A.J. Solnit, 'Change and the Sense of Time', in *The Child in His Family*, vol. 5, *Children and their Families in a Changing World*.

Every Girl's Dream

1. This answer was given by a woman in a survey of families in Melbourne in 1976. The survey is reported in Lyn Richards, *Having Families: Marriage, Parenthood and Social Pressure in Australia* (Penguin, Harmondsworth, 1978).
2. See Richards, *Having Families* and Jan Harper, *Mothers and Working Mothers* (Penguin, Harmondsworth, 1979).
3. Quoted in B. Ehrenreich and D. English, *For Her Own Good: 150 Years of the Experts' Advice to Women* (Anchor Press, New York, 1978), p. 207.
4. Adrienne Rich, *Of Woman Born: Motherhood as Experience and Institution* (Bantam Books, New York, 1977), pp. 282–83.

Ethnic Children in Australia

L. Claydon, T. Knight and M. Rado, *Curriculum and Culture* (George Allen & Unwin, Sydney, 1977).

J.I. Martin, *The Migrant Presence* (George Allen & Unwin, Sydney, 1978).

School's Commission Committee on Multicultural Education, *Education for a Multicultural Society* (Australian Government Printing Service, Canberra, 1979).

J.J. Smolicz, *Culture and Education in a Plural Society* (Curriculum Development Centre, Canberra, 1979).

Aboriginal Children

1. I wish to thank the Australian Institute of Aboriginal Studies and the Commonwealth Department of Aboriginal Affairs for supporting research in south-east and south-west Queensland for the three years between 1970 and 1972. From 1974–76 research in south-west Queensland was fully funded by the Australian Istitute of Aboriginal Studies.
2. E.H. Erikson, *Childhood and Society* (W.W. Norton & Co., New York, 1963); R.W. White, 'Competence and the Psychosexual Stages of Development', in *The Causes of Behaviour*, ed. W. Allinsmith and J.P. Williams (Allyn & Bacon Inc., Boston, 1972); A.H. Maslow, *Motivation and Personality* (Harper Row, New York, 1970).
3. H.W. Maier, *Three Theories of Child Development* (Harper International, New York, 1969).
4. There are numerous accounts of this period of Australian history. Among the better chronicles are: R. Evans, K. Saunders and K. Cronin, *Exclusion, Exploitation and Extermination: Race Relations in Colonial Queensland* (ANZ Books, Sydney, 1975); C.D. Rowley, *Outcasts in White Australia: Aboriginal Policy and Practice*, vol. 3 (ANU Press, Canberra, 1971); J. Woolmington, *Aborigines in Colonial Society* (Cassell, Australia, Melbourne, 1974).
5. An excellent analysis of nineteenth century western philosophy and 'scientific' thought and their effect on European perceptions of Aborigines is found in: A. Chase and J. von Sturmer, 'Mental Man in Social Evolutionary Theory', in *The Psychology of Aboriginal Australians*, ed. G.E. Kearney, P.R. de Lacey and G.R. Davidson (John Wiley, Sydney, 1973).
6. E. Goffman, *Asylums* (Pelican, Victoria, 1961).
7. J. Cawte, *Medicine Is the Law: Studies in Psychiatric Anthropology of Australian Tribal Societies* (University Press of Hawaii, Honululu, 1974).
8. 'Yumba' is the Gungari word for 'camp'.
9. For a detailed analysis of economic patterns in the region see A-K. Eckermann, 'Employment Patterns Among Aboriginal People in Rural Town S.W. Queensland', *Australian Economic Papers*, 1979.
10. For a full account of this research, its methodology and results see A-K. Eckermann, 'Contact: An Ethnographic Analysis of Three Aboriginal Communities including a Comparative and Cross-Cultural Analysis of Value Orientations' (M.A. Thesis, University of Queensland, 1973).
11. L. Lippmann, *Words or Blows, Racial Attitudes in Australia* (Penguin, Victoria, 1973), p. 152.
12. R. Taft, 'Attitudes of Western Australians towards Aborigines', in *Attitudes and Social Conditions*, ed. R. Taft, J.L.M. Dawson and P. Beasley (ANU

Press, Canberra, 1970), p. 39.

13. K. Gilbert, *Living Black* (Penguin, Victoria, 1978); C. Perkins, *A Bastard Like Me* (Ure Smith, Sydney, 1975).
14. Commission of Inquiry into Poverty, F. Gale & J. Binnion, *Poverty Among Aboriginal Families in Adelaide* (Australian Government Printing Service, Canberra, 1975), p. 1.
15. See the following references:-
16. Commission of Inquiry into Poverty, J.W. Brown, R. Hirschfeld & D. Smith, *Aboriginal and Islanders in Brisbane*, (Australian Government Printing Service, Canberra, 1974); Commission of Inquiry into Poverty, R.T. Fitzgerald, *Poverty and Education in Australia*, Fifth Main Report, (Australian Government Printing Service, Canberra, 1976); Gale & Binnion.
17. National Population Inquiry, *Population and Australia: A Demographic Analysis and Projection*, vol. 2 (Australian Government Printing Service, Canberra, 1975).
18. A-K. Eckermann, 'Employment Patterns Among Aboriginal People in Rural Town, S.W. Queensland'.
    C.D. Rowley, 'The Aboriginal Householder', *Quadrant* 7, no. 6 (1967): 90–96; J.N. Lickiss, 'Aboriginal Children in Sydney: The Socio-Economic Environment', *Oceania* 61, no. 31 (1971): 201–28; P. Beasley, 'The Aboriginal Household in Sydney', in *Attitudes and Social Conditions*, ed. R. Taft, J.L.M. Dawson and P. Beasley pp. 133–86; Y. Kitaoji, *Contemporary Aboriginal Families in the Lower Macleay Valley*, Preliminary report on fieldwork (Canberra, 1971); A-K. Eckermann, 'Contact'; H.M. Smith and E.H. Biddle, *Look Forward, Not Back* (ANU Press, Canberra, 1975).
19. Rowley, *Outcasts in White Australia*, p. 312.
20. Gale and Binnion, *Poverty Among Aboriginal Families in Adelaide*.
    A full discussion of the methodology employed and the results obtained are found in: A-K. Eckermann, 'Half-Caste/Out-Cast: An Ethnographic Analysis of the Processes Underlying Adaptation Among Aboriginal People in Rural Town, South-West Queensland' (Ph.d. Thesis, University of Queensland, 1977).
21. W. Goldschmidt, 'Areté: Motivation and Models of Behaviour', in *The Interface Between Psychiatry and Anthopology*, ed. I. Galdston (Brunner/Mazel, London, 1971), pp. 55–87.
22. White, 'Competence and the Psychosexual Stages of Development'.
23. G.E. Simpson and J.M. Yinger, *Racial and Cultural Minorities: An Analysis of Prejudice and Discrimination* (Harper & Row, New York, 1965).
24. C.H. Cooley, *Human Nature and the Social Order* (Free Press, New York, 1956).

Children and Values

1. M. Rokeach, *The Nature of Human Values* (Free Press, New York, 1973), p. 5.
2. Ibid., p. 25.

3. A.J. Ayer, *Language, Truth and Logic* (Gollane, London, 1948), ch. 6.
4. C.L. Stevenson, *Ethics and Language* (Yale University Press, New Haven, 1944).
5. R.M. Hare, *The Language of Morals* (Oxford University Press, Oxford, 1952).
6. W. Temple, *Nature, Man and God* (Macmillan & Co., London, 1934), p. 183.
7. N. Smart, *The Religious Experience of Mankind* (Charles Scribner's Sons, New York, 1969), ch. 1.
8. D. Little and S. Twiss Jr., 'Basic Terms in the Study of Religious Ethics', in *Religion and Morality*, ed. G. Outha and J. Reeder Jr. (Doubleday, New York, 1973), pp. 60–61.
9. P. Musgrave, *The Moral Curriculum: A Sociological Analysis* (Methuen, London, 1978).
10. J. Piaget, *The Moral Judgement of the Child* (Routledge & Kegan Paul, London, 1932).
11. N. Bull, *Moral Education* (Routledge & Kegan Paul, London, 1969), p. 6.
12. L. Kohlberg, 'Stage and Sequence: The Cognitive-Developmental Approach to Socialisation', in *Handbook on Socialisation, Theory and Research*, ed. N. Goslin (Rand McNally, Chicago, 1969).
13. L. Raths, M. Harmin and S. Simon, *Values and Teaching* (Chas. E. Merrill, Colombus, Ohio, 1966); J.S. Stewart, 'Clarifying Values Clarification: A Critique', *Phi Delta Kappan* 57 (1975): 686; R. Kirschenbaum, 'Clarifying Values Clarification: Some Issues', in *Moral Education: It Comes with the Territory*, ed. D. Tempel and K. Ryan (McCutchan, Berkely, 1976), pp. 116–25.
14. R. Goldman, *Religious Thinking from Childhood to Adolescence* (Routledge & Kegan Paul, London, 1964).
15. M. Grimmitt, *What Can I Do in R.E.?* (Mayhew-McCrimmon, London, 1973).
16. I. Ramsey, *Religious Language* (Student Christian Movement, London, 1967).
17. V. Madge, *Children in Search of Meaning* (Student Christian Movement, London, 1963).
18. The limitations of the chapter do not allow space for inclusion of the work of James W. Fowler on the development of faith. Readers are referred to J. Fowler and S. Keen, *Life Maps: Conversations on the Journey of Faith* (Texas Word Books, Texas, 1978).

Children's Health

1. Dr. Graham Vimpani wishes to thank the Minister of Health in the South Australian government, Mrs Jennifer Adamson, for permission to submit this article. The authors wish to thank Graham Andersen, Terry Dwyer, Peter Millier and Neil Wigg for their constructive comments and criticism.

2. B. Gandevia, *Tears Often Shed: Child Health and Welfare in Australia from 1788* (Pergamon, Sydney, 1978).

3. T. McKeown, *The Role of Medicine: Dream, Mirage or Nemesis* (Nuffield Provincial Hospitals Trust, London, 1976).
4. F.J. Stanley and M.S.T. Hobbs, 'Factors Associated with Improved Neonatal Outcome', *Australian Paediatric Journal* 14 (1978): 197.
5. T. McKeown, 'Validation of Screening Procedures' in *Screening in Medical Care*, Nuffield Provincial Hospitals Trust, London, 1968.
6. A.F. North, 'Screening in Child Care', *American Family Physician* 13 (1976): 85–95.
7. Editorial, 'The Abhorrence of Stillbirth', *Lancet* 1 (1977): 1188–90.
8. D. Nortmand, 'Parental Age as a Factor in Pregnancy Outcome and Child Development', *Reports on Population and Family Planning No. 16*, 1974.
9. W.H. Baldwin, 'Adolescent Pregnancy and Childbearing: Growing Concerns for Americans', *Population Bulletin* 31 (1977): 1–34.
10. U. Bronfenbrenner, *The Ecology of Human Development* (Harvard University Press, Cambridge, Massachusetts, 1979).
11. American Academy of Paediatrics, Committee on Adolescence, 'Statement on Teenage Pregnancy', *Paediatrics* 63 (1979): 795–97.
12. G. Rooth, 'Socioeconomic Aspects of Perinatal Medicine', in *Proceedings of European Congress of Perinatal Medicine* (Upssala, 1976): 11–14.
13. P.H. Bennett, C. Webner and M. Miller, 'Congenital Anomalies and the Diabetic and Pre-Diabetic Pregnancy', *Excerpta Medica* (Amsterdam, 1979); J. Pederson and L. Molsted-Pederson, 'Congenital Malformations: The Possible Role of Diabetes Care Outside Pregnancy', *Excerpta Medica* (Amsterdam, 1979).
14. M. Wynn and A. Wynn, *The Protection of Maternity and Infancy: A Study of Services for Pregnant Women and Young Children in Finland* (Council for Children's Welfare, London, 1974).
15. 'A Look at Antenatal Care', *Lancet* 1 (1979): 1307.
16. I. Illich, *Medical Nemesis: The Expropriation of Health* (Marion Moyass, London, 1975); R.J. Carlson, *The End of Medicine* (Wiley, New York, 1975).
17. C.A. Cox, J.S. Fox, P.M. Zinkin and A.E.B. Matthews, 'Critical Appraisal of Domiciliary Obstetric and Neontal Practice', *British Medical Journal* 1 (1976): 84–86.
18. Senate Standing Committee on Social Welfare, *Through a Glass, Darkly: Evaluation in Australian Health and Welfare Services* (Australian Government Printing Service, Canberra, 1979).
19. A.B. Bergman et al., 'Sudden Infant Death Syndrome', *Proceedings of the Second International Conference on Causes of Sudden Death in Infants* (University of Washington Press, Washington, 1970).
20. E. Watson, 'The Inner North London Study of Sudden Infant Death and Its Relevance for the Community Services', *Medicine, Science and the Law* 18, no. 4 (1978): 271–77; R.G. Carpenter, A. Gardner, P.M. McWeeney and J.L. Emery, 'Multistage Scoring System for Identifying Infants at Risk of Unexpected Death', *Archives of Diseases in Childhood* 52, no. 8 (1977): 606–12; R.G. Carpenter, A. Gardner, E. Pursall, P.M. McWeeney and J.L. Emery, 'Identification of Some Infants at Immediate Risk of Dying Unexpectedly and Justifying Intensive Study',

Lancet 2 (1979): 343–46; D.J. Scott, P.S. Gardner, J. McQuillan, A.N. Stanton and M.A.P.S. Downham, 'Respiratory Viruses and Cot Death', *British Medical Journal* 2 (1978): 12–13.

21. M. Holden, 'Sudden Infant Death Syndrome: A Current Assessment', *Highlight* no. 36 (National Children's Bureau, London, 1979).
22. I.K. Zola, 'Healthism and Disabling Medicalisation' in *Disabling Professions*, ed. I. Illich, J. McKnight, I. Zola et al. (Marion Boyass, London, 1977).
23. E. Freidson, *Profession of Medicine* (Dodd Mead & Co., New York, 1970).
24. J. Powles, 'On the Limitations of Modern Medicine', *Science, Medicine and Man* 1 (1973): 1–30.
25. J.W. Staines, *You and Your Baby* (Oxford University Press, Melbourne, 1978); J. Chapman, R. Harrington, A. Lowendie and K. O'Connor, 'An Intensive Support Unit for Parent–Infant distress', *Medical Journal of Australia* 2 (1977): 632–35; M. Griffen, 'Training Parents of Retarded Children as Behaviour Therapists: A Review', *Australian Journal of Mental Retardation* 5 (1979): 18–27.
26. U. Bronfenbrenner, 'Is Early Intervention Effective?', in *Handbook of Evaluation Research*, vol. 2, ed. M. Guttentag and E.L. Struening (Sage Publications, Beverley Hills, California, 1975).
27. J. Bowlby, *Attachment and Loss*, vol. 1, *Attachment* (Hogarth Press, London, 1969); J. Bowlby, *Attachment and Loss*, vol. 2, *Separation: Anxiety and Anger* (Penguin, Harmondsworth, 1975).
28. R.K. Oates, A.A. Davis, M.G. Ryan and L.G. Stewart, 'Risk Factors Associated with Child Abuse', *Australian Paediatric Journal* 15 (1979): 195; M.A. Lynch, J. Roberts and M. Gordon, 'Child Abuse: Early Warning in the Maternity Hospital', *Developmental Medicine and Child Neurology* 18 (1976): 759–66.
29. D.P. Davies, V. Haxby, S. Harbert and A.S. McNeish, 'When Should Preterm Babies Be Sent Home from Neonatal Units', *Lancet* 1 (1979): 914–15.
30. M.H. Klaus and J.H. Kennell, 'Mothers Separated from Their Newborn Infants', *Pediatric Clinics of North America* 17 (1970): 1015–37; B. Lozoff, G.M. Brittenham, M.A. Trause, J.H. Kennell and M.A. Klaus, 'The Mother Newborn Relationship: Limited of Adaptability, *Journal of Paediatrics* 91 (1977): 1–12.
31. R.B. Cairns, 'Beyond Social Attachment: The Dynamics of Interactional Development', in *Attachment Behaviour*, ed. T.A. Alloway, P. Pliner and L. Krames (Plenum, New York, 1977).
32. R.D. Parke, 'Perspectives on Father–Infant Interaction', in *The Handbook of Infant Development*, ed. J.D. Osofsky (John Wiley & Sons Inc., New York, 1979).
33. A. Wynn, 'Health Care Systems for Preschool Children', *Proceedings of the Royal Society of Medicine* 69 (1976): 340–43.
34. G.V. Vimpani, A.F. Vimpani, S.J. Pocock and J.W. Farquar, 'Differences in Physical Characteristics, Perinatal Histories and Social Background Between Children with Growth Hormone Deficiency and Constitutional Short Stature', *Archives of Diseases in Childhood* (1979).
35. P.A. Silva, 'Intervention for Preschool Children with Developmental

Language Delays: The Need for Diversity and Evaluation', Paper delivered at the Institute of Developmental Disabilities Conference, Adelaide, 1979.

36. U. Bronfenbrenner, 'Is Early Intervention Effective?'.

37. J.A. Mawdsley and G.D. Graves, 'A survey of Behaviour Problems in School Children to Aid Planning for Change in Service Delivery', Paper presented at the 9th International Congress of the International Association for Child Psychiatry and Allied Professions, 1978.

38. M. Rutter, J. Tizard and K. Whitmore, *Education, Health and Behaviour* (Longman, London, 1970).

39. P. Eisen, personal communication.

40. J. Bowlby, *Child Care and the Growth of Love* (Penguin, Harmondsworth, 1953); J. Robertson, *Hospital and Children: Parents Eye View* (Gollancz, London, 1962); Central Health Services Council, *Report of the Committee on the Welfare of Children in Hospital* (HMSO, London, 1958).

41. J. Barbalet, *The Adelaide Children's Hospital 1876–1976* (Adelaide Children's Hospital, Adelaide, 1976).

42. D.A. Howell, 'A Child Dies', *Journal of Paediatric Surgery* 1 (1963): 2–7.

43. L. Burton, *The Family Life of Sick Children* (Routledge & Kegan Paul, London, 1975).

44. V.B. Tisza, 'Management of the Parents of the Chronically Ill Child', *American Journal of Psychiatry* 32 (1960): 53–59.

45. L. Zoppa and M. Goskin, *Final Report of the Northern Area Co-ordinating Team*, Intellectually Retarded Services Division (South Australian Health Commission, Adelaide, 1979).

46. J.A. Haller, 'A Healthy Attitude towards Chronic Illness', in *The Chronically Ill Child and His Family*, ed. M. Debusky (Charles Thornes, Springfield, Illinois, 1970).

47. G.V. Vimpani, A.F. Vimpani and J.H. Pearn, 'Preschool Drowning: Has Recent Legislation Been Effective?', *Community Health Studies* 3 (1979): 141.

48. B.S. Hetzel, 'A Model for Public Learning in Health Care: Administrative Application of Epidemiology and Health Statistics in Australia', in *Epidemiology as a Fundamental Science*, ed. K.L. White and M.H. Henderson (Oxford University Press, New York, 1976).

49. J. Nixon and J.H. Pearn, 'The Use of Public Media as a Preventive Strategy in Childhood Drownings', *Community Health Studies* 3 (1979): 133.

50. S. Sandels, *Children in Traffic* (Elek Books, London, 1975).

51. C. Baker, 'Preventive Options', Paper presented at the International Year of the Child National Conference on Childhood Accidents and Prevention, Brisbane, 1979.

52. T. McKeown, *The Role of Medicine*; J. Powles, 'On the Limitations of Modern Medicine'.

53. B.S. Hetzel, *Health and Australian Society* (Penguin, Victoria, 1974).

54. M. Gracey, 'Nutritional Problems in the Australian Community', *Medical Journal of Australia* 1 (1978): 202–5; G.M. Maxwell and R.B. Elliot, 'Nutritional State of Australian Aboriginal Children', *American Journal of Clinical Nutrition* 22 (1969): 716–24; B.S. Hetzel, 'Nutritional Problems in the Australian Community', *Medical Journal of Australia* 1 (1978): 197–99; J.M. Cox, 'Growth Characteristics in Preschool Aboriginal Children', *Australian Paediatrics Journal* 25 (1979): 10–15;

P.M. Moodie, *Aboriginal Health* (Australian National University Press, Canberra, 1973).

55. J.M. Court, M. Dunlop, M. Reynolds, J. Russell and L. Griffiths, 'Growth and Development of Fat in Adolescent School Children in Victoria, Part 1', *Australian Paediatric Journal* 12 (1976): 296–305.
56. J.M. Court, G.J. Hill, M. Dunlop and T.J.C. Boulton, 'Hypertension in Childhood Obesity', *Australian Paediatric Journal* 10 (1974): 296–300.
57. J.B. Hickie, J. Sutton; J. Ruys and E.W. Kraegen, 'Serum Cholesterol and Serum Triglyceride Levels in Australian Adolescent Males', *Medical Journal of Australia* 1 (1974): 825–28.
58. M. Gracey, 'Nutritional Problems in the Australian Community'.
E.N. Owles, 'A Comparative Study of the Nutrient Intakes of Migrant and Australian Children in Western Australia, *Medical Journal of Australia* 2 (1975): 130–33.
59. C.L. Williams, C.B. Arnold and L. Wyndere, 'Primary Prevention of Chronic Disease Beginning in Childhood', *Preventive Medicine* 6 (1977): 344–57.
60. T. Dwyer, W.E. Coonan, A. Worsley and D.R. Leitch, 'An Assessment of the Effects of Two Physical Activity Programmes on Coronary Heart Disease Risk Factors in Primary School Children', *Community Health Studies*, 2 (1979): 196–202.
61. U.S. Senate Committee on Nutrition and Human Needs, *Dietary Goals for the United States* (Government Printing Office, Washington, D.C., 1977).
62. K. Ringen, 'The Norwegian Food and Nutritional Policy', *American Journal of Public Health* 67, no. 6 (1977): 550–51.
63. B.S. Hetzel, 'Diet and Health: Food as a Health Hazard', *Medical Journal of Australia* 2 (1979): 12–14.
64. D.C. Jarvis, *Folk Medicine* (Fawcett, Greenwich, Connecticut, 1957).
65. S. Chapman, 'Health Education and Social Class', *New Doctor* 13 (1979): 35–38.
66. T.G.C. Murrell and J. Moss, 'Health Care for Infants and Mothers', in *Family Planning and Health Care for Infants and Mothers*, Commission of Inquiry into Poverty, Social/Medical Aspects of Poverty Studies (Australian Government Printing Service, Canberra, 1977).
67. S.M. Booth and R.K. Oates, 'Immunisation Status of Children Attending Royal Alexandra Hospital for Sick Children', *Australian Paediatric Journal* 15 (1979): 191; M. Nowotny and P.J. Stretton, 'The Health of the Preschool Child', *Medical Journal of Australia* 2 (1979): 289–91; P. Wedge and H. Prosser, *Born to Fail* (Arrow Books, London, 1973).
68. M. Wynn and A. Wynn, *The Right of Every Child to Health Care: A Study of Protection of the Young Child in France* (Council for Children's Welfare, London, 1974).

Children's Health, Parents and the Community

1. S.K. Clarren & D.W. Smith, 'The Foetal Alcohol Syndrome', *New England Journal of Medicine*, 298, no. 19, 1975: 1063–7.
2. R.G. Hausfeld, 'The Social Prediction of Self-Perceived Morbidity',

Medical Journal of Australia, 2, 1973: 975–78.
3. D.A. Grimes & W. Cates Jr., 'Complications from Legally Induced Abortion: A Review', *Obstetrical and Gynecological Survey*, 34, no. 3 1979: 177–91.
4. *Second National Morbidity Survey*, United Kingdom, 1970–71.
5. P.M. Zinkin & C.A. Cox, 'Child Health Clinics and Inverse Care Laws: Evidence from Longitudinal Study of 1878 Pre-School Children', *British Medical Journal*, August 1976, no. 2: 411–3.
6. *Final Report of the Royal Commission into the Non-Medical Use of Drugs* (Gillingham Printers, Adelaide, 1979).

The Child and Education

1. Nan Hawkey, Clare Hughes, Wendy Edgar and other members of staff of the Curriculum Development Centre assisted in the collection and organization of materials for this chapter.
2. G. Kelly, *A Theory of Personality* (Norton, New York, 1963).
3. E.H. Erikson, *Childhood and Society* (Norton, New York, 1963).
4. L. Kohlberg, *Stages in the Development of Moral Thought and Action* (Holt, Rinehart and Winston, New York, 1969).
5. M.J. Angus, T.M. Beck, P.W. Hill and W. McAtee, *Open Area Schools*, draft copy, Research Branch of Western Australia Education Department, Perth, 1978).
6. P. Gammage and C. Woodhead, 'The Integrated Day Approach to Primary Education', mimeographed (University of Bristol).
7. M. Schwebel and J. Ralph, eds., *Piaget in the Classroom* (Routledge & Kegan Paul, London, 1974).

The Unending Challenge

1. P.E. Jones, *Education in Australia* (Nelson, Melbourne, 1974), p. 20
2. G. Hass, J. Bondi and J. Wiles, *Curriculum Planning: A New Approach* (Allyn and Bacon, Boston, 1974), part 1, section 3.
3. B. Jacka, *Directions in Primary Education* (Melbourne University Press, Melbourne, 1974), ch. 6.
4. Education Department of South Australia, *Secondary Division Building Committee Report* (Government Printer of South Australia, 1970), p. 5 ff.
5. J.S. Bruner, 'Structures in Learning', *National Education Association Journal* 52, no. 3 (1963): 26.
6. B. Jacka, *Directions in Primary Education*, p. 34.
7. J.S. Bruner, 'The Process of Education Revisited', *Phi Delta Kappan* 53, no. 1 (1971): 18.
8. B. Jacka, *Directions in Primary Education*, ch. 4.
9. J. Dewey, *The Child and the Curriculum*, and *The School and Society* (University of Chicago Press, Chicago, 1943).
10. N. Bennett, *Teaching Styles and Pupil Progress* (Open Books, London, 1976), p. 4.
11. Education Department of New South Wales, *Aims of Primary Education*

(New South Wales Government Printer, 1977), p. 14; Education Department of South Australia, *The Schools Curriculum 1* (Government Printer of South Australia, 1976), p. 36; Technical Schools Division, *Curriculum Policy Statement, Years 7–11* (Education Department of Victoria, 1979), para. 3.1.

12. E. Bowker, 'The Commonwealth and Education, 1901–69', in *Australian Education in the Twentieth Century: Studies in the Development of State Education*, ed. J. Cleverley and J. Lawry (Longman, Victoria, 1972), ch. 6, p. 153.
13. D.A. Jecks, ed., *Influences in Australian Education* (Carroll's, Perth, 1974).

The Economic Costs of Children

1. T.W. Schultze, 'The Value of Children: An Economic Perspective', *Journal of Political Economy*, Supplement 81, 1973, pp. S2–S13.
2. M. Wynn, *Family Policy: A Study of the Economic Costs of Rearing Children and their Social and Political Consequences* (Penguin, Harmondsworth, 1970).
3. P. Apps, *Child Care Policy in the Production-Consumption Economy* (Victorian Council of Social Services, Collingwood, 1975).
4. B.S. Rowntree, *Poverty and Progress* (Longman, London, 1941); *Social Insurance and Allied Services*, Cmnd 6404, HMSO, London, 1942.
5. M. Rein, 'Problems in the Definition and Measurement of Poverty' in P. Townsend (ed.), *The Concept of Poverty* (Heinemann, London, 1970). Rein notes the inevitable circularity implicit in basing the poverty line definitions on the observed expenditure patterns of the poor.
6. S.J. Prais & H.S. Houthakker, *The Analysis of Family Budgets* (Cambridge University Press, Cambridge, 1971); N. Podder, 'The Estimation of an Equivalent Income Scale', *Australian Economic Papers*, 10, 1971, pp. 175–87; N.C. Kakwani, 'Household Composition and Measurement of Income Inequality and Poverty with Application to Australian Data', *University of NSW, School of Economics Discussion Paper*, no. 19, June, 1976; L.D. McClements, 'Equivalence Scales for Children', *Journal of Public Economics*, 8, 1977, pp. 191–210.
7. For details of the model and the methods used, see Kakwani, pp. 4–6,
8. S. Richardson, 'Income Distribution, Poverty and Redistributive Policies' in F.H. Gruen (ed.), *Surveys of Australian Economics*, vol. 2 (George Allen & Unwin, Sydney, 1979).
9. Australian Bureau of Statistics, *Household Expenditure Survey 1974–75* (A.B.S., Canberra, 1978).
10. Commission of Inquiry into Poverty (First Main Report, Prof. R.F Henderson, Chairman), *Poverty in Australia*, vol. 1 & 2 (Australian Government Printing Service, Canberra, 1975).
11. R.F. Henderson, A. Harcourt, & R.J.A. Harper, *People in Poverty: A Melbourne Survey* (Cheshire, Melbourne, 1970).
12. It should be noted that the relativities implied in the Henderson poverty lines are similar to those used overseas in official studies of poverty. As indicated in a recent Organisation for Economic Co-operation and

Development (OECD) report, *Public Expenditures on Income Maintenance Programmes* (OECD, Paris, 1976), table 26, the poverty line for a four-child family expressed as a proportion of the poverty line for a two-child family, is 1.40 for Australia, 1.40 for Canada, 1.56 for France, 1.37 for the United Kingdom and 1.52 for the United States.

13. Priorities Review Staff, *Possibilities for Social Welfare in Australia* (Australian Government Printing Service, Canberra, 1975); H. Pritchard & P. Saunders, 'Poverty and Income Maintenance Policy in Australia—A Review Article', *The Economic Record*, 54, 1978: 17–31; Richardson.
14. Henderson, *Poverty in Australia*, vol. 1, pp. 198–99.
15. Kakwani; Commission of Inquiry into Poverty, N. Podder, *The Economic Circumstances of the Poor*, Research Report (Australian Government Printing Service, Canberra, 1978).
16. In a study of poverty amongst large families in the centre of Sydney, Halladay found 18.4 per cent below Henderson's poverty line. (A. Halladay, 'The Extent of Poverty among Large Families in the Heart of Sydney', *The Economic Record*, 48, December 1972, p. 487). This figure is comparable to Henderson's shown in table 2, although it is based on a quite different sample of families.
17. L. Bryson, 'Poverty', *Current Affairs Bulletin*, 54, no. 5, 1977: 4–17.
18. J. McCaughey & W. Chew, 'The Family Study' in J. McCaughey, S. Shaver, H. Ferber and others, *Who Cares? Family Problems, Community Links and Helping Services* (Sun Books, Melbourne, 1977).
19. McCaughey, Shaver, Ferber and others; P. Hollingworth, *Australians in Poverty* (Nelson, Netley, 1979).
20. C. Jencks and others, *Inequality: A Reassessment of the Effect of Family and Schooling in America* (Penguin, Harmondsworth, 1975), p. 143.
21. *Budget Speech, 1979–80*, Statement no. 3 (Australian Government Printing Service, Canberra, 1979), pp. 94–95.
22. P. Saunders, 'Equity, Income Redistribution and the Australian Direct Tax-Transfer System', *Economic Papers*, 62, November 1979: 53–68.
23. Department of Social Security, *Annual Report, 1977–78* (Australian Government Printing Service, Canberra, 1978), p. 33.
24. The current Federal government announced the abolition of the maternity allowance as from 31 October 1978 in the 1978–79 Budget.
25. Saunders in 'Equity, Income Redistribution and the Australian Direct Tax-Transfer System' considers increases in the adult pension and benefit rates.
26. Saunders. op. cit.
27. Taxation Review Committee, *Full Report* (Australian Government Printing Service, Canberra, 1975), para. 7.69.
28. Apps; M. Edwards, 'Proposals for a Child Care Allowance', *Social Security Quarterly*, Summer 1975–76: 19–23; M. Edwards, 'The Tax-Transfer Treatment of Married Couples', The *Australian Quarterly*, 51, no. 2, June 1979: 46–53.

Economic Relationships and Social Values

1. Margaret Wynn, *Family Policy* (Michael Joseph, London, 1970).

1. Elspeth Browne, *The Empty Cradle* (University of New South Wales Press, Sydney, 1979).
2. J. Harper and L. Richards, *Mothers and Working Mothers* (Penguin, Harmondsworth, 1979).

Children and the Law

1. Since this chapter is not primarily intended for Lawyers, detailed citation of legal sources is omitted. Most of them can be found in Richard Chisholm, 'Children and the Law', in A. Burns & J. Goodnow, *Children and Families in Australia* (George Allen & Unwin, Sydney, 1979).
2. On children's rights, see John Holt, *Escape from Childhood* (Penguin, 1975); Richard Farson, *Birthrights* (MacMillan, New York, 1974); *The Rights of Children*, Harvard Educational Review, Reprint Series no. 9, 1974; Beatrice Gross & Ronald Gross (ed.), *The Children's Rights Movement* (Anchor Books, New York, 1977).
3. There are now several introductory books on Australian law. See, for example, R. Chisholm & G. Nettheim, *Understanding Law*, revised edition (Butterworth, Sydney, 1978); Geoffrey Sawer, *The Australian and the Law* (Penguin, Victoria, 1972); S. Ross & M. Weinburg, *Law for the People* (Penguin, Sydney, 1976).
4. There is no satisfactory Australian text on child welfare, but for discussion see Commission of Inquiry into Poverty (Second Main Report, Professor R.H. Henderson, Chairman) R. Sackville, *Law and Poverty in Australia* (Australian Government Printing Service, Canberra, 1975); Australian Law Reform Commission, Discussion Paper no. 9, *Child Welfare: Children in Trouble* (Australian Law Reform Commission, Sydney, 1979); *Juvenile Justice: Before and After the Onset of Delinquency*, Sixth U.N. Congress on the Prevention of Crime and the Treatment of Offenders, Australian Discussion Paper Topic 2 (Australian Government Printing Service Canberra, 1979) (in which there is an extensive bibliography). There is an excellent discussion of child welfare in John Eckelaar, *Family, Law and Social Policy* (Weidenfeld & Nicolson, London, 1978).
5. 'Child Welfare Act' 1939 (NSW) and 'Child Welfare Ordinance' 1957 (ACT) as amended.
6. 'Minister for the Interior' v. 'Neyens' (1964) 113 CLR 441.
7. For historical background see I.M. Pinchbeck & M. Hewitt, *Children in English Society* (Routledge & Kegan Paul, London, vol. 1, 1969, vol. 2, 1972); Eckelaar.
8. 'Carseldine' v. 'Director of Children's Services' (1974) 4 ALR 195; 'Johnson' v. 'Director of Social Welfare' (1976) ALR 343; 'Director of Child Welfare' v. 'Ford' (1976) 12 ALR 577.
9. 'Community Welfare Services Act' 1978 (Vic) as amended.
10. For a general discussion of custody see H.A. Finlay, *Family Law in Australia*, 2nd edition (Butterworth, Melbourne, 1978). The operation of the Family Law Act and the case law is exhaustively treated in M. Broun & S. Fowler, *Australian Family Law and Practice* (Commerce Clearing

House, Australia Ltd., 1978) (looseleaf service).

11. J. Goldstein, A. Freud & A. Solnit, *Beyond the Best Interests of the Child* (Free Press, New York, 1973).

12. "Family reorganization" is not a recognized legal category and legal texts on family law, such as Finlay, discuss the issues under the headings "adoption", "custody" and the like.

13. For discussion of adoption law in Australia see Cliff Picton (ed.), *First Australian Conference on Adoption*, Melbourne, 1976 and Second Australian Conference on Adoption, 1978, and Royal Commission on Human Relationships (Report, Justice Elizabeth Evatt Chairman), vol. 4 (Australian Government Printing Service, Canberra, 1977).

Index

abandoned and delinquent children, 24
Aboriginal: Affairs, 104–6; children, 86–106; Medical Services, 103–4
Aborigines: needs and rights of, 25; nutritional problems, 160; schools, 185; self-determination, 103, 106, 112; white man's relationship with, 110
access, 238–9; order, 236
accidents, childhood, 138, 156–60
accommodation, in learning, 181
adolescent pregnancy, 142–3
adoption, 241–4; and attachment, 151; law, 231
adoptive families, 55–6
advocacy, child, 38–9
ambivalence towards children's needs, 44
ante-natal medical advances, 143–7
assimilation in learning, 181
attachment: importance of, 150; theory, 28
attitudes about natural properties of people, 29–33
authority, challenges to, 114

baby farming, 24
behaviour problems, 138, 154–5; research, 172
bi-lingualism, 109
birth rates, 142
births: home, 146; illegitimate, 142
boundary situations 119, 120, 128

change, 246; affecting families, 59–61; in community life, 247–8; in contemporary education, 175–6; effects of, 41; in families, social, 63, 248–9; world, 44, 52
child care: allowance, proposed, 216; facilities, 169, 216; inadequate provisions, 206
child rearing, 51, 261; basic attitude towards, 52–4; cost of time, 198; lack of clarity and direction, 179
child welfare, 227; legislation, 36; *see also* welfare
chronic illness, 141; social effects of, 155–6
church: role in religious education, 130–1; transmitting values, 134
cognitive development, 180–1, 191
colour discrimination, 100–1
communal families, 56–7
community: children's health, 166–72; involvement in the nurture of children, 65; life, changes in, 247; participation in education, 176, 185–7; *see also* government; state
Community Welfare Tribunal, 232
competence, 178
congenital defects, 138
continuity, cultural, 39–40
court, courts, 233; counselling service attached to, 233, 239; family, 234; level of adjudication, 235–6; uncontrollable children, 230; *see also* law; legislation
cultural: diversity, children's attitudes, 79–81; transmission, ineffective, 83
cultures, maintenance and development of ethnic, 67
curiosity, 178
curriculum development, 195; reform movement, 194
custody 18, 234; joint, 236; jurisdiction, 233; law, 227, 237–8, 239–40

dependency, 50
development: children's intellectual, 177–81; disturbances in child, 147–50; influences on child, 150; screening for delayed, 152–4

developmental: assessment, 170; difficulties, 138
disadvantaged children, 259
discrimination: against children born outside marriage, 242; colour, 100–1
Discrimination Act, Racial, 103
diversity, 114; affecting families, 59–61; cultural 73, 107–8; children's attitudes, 78–81; effects of, 41; of family structures, 62
duality of Aboriginal children's environment 89

economic costs of children, 197–217
education: Aboriginal, 105; aims, 193–4, 219; balance between labour and, 21; child and, 173–89; child development, 149; development of early, 23; for a multicultural Australia, 84–5; health, 139, 163; research into, 172; moral 121, 122–7; parental involvement in, 66; poverty and, 207; religious 130–1
educational: developments for Aboriginals, 102; policies, lack of clarity and direction, 179
effectiveness, development of, 40
employment for Aboriginals, 93
endowment, child, 25, 30; effect on fathers, 32
environoment: Aboriginal-Australian's 88–91; negative influence of a materialist, 256
ethnic children in Australia, 67–85
experience, education through, 182

families: Aboriginal, 96; children and, 41–61; financial support for children, 207, 212; in early Australia, 20–1; poverty amongst single-parent, 204; relativities between rich and poor, 223; roles, tasks and rights of, 46; with children at economic risk, 222
family: allowances, 207–10, 211–12; difference in patterns of life, 69–71; equivalence scales, 200–3; extended, 71; impact statements, 38; influence on moral development, 120, 126; influence seen as negative, 23; law, new legislation, 37 life and poverty, 205–7; nuclear, 45, 63, 249–50; re-organization, 240, 244; role in religious education, 130; roles, 41; uncertainty about, 246; size, 223; and poverty, 204; stability of, 44; structure, 45–6; diversity of, 62; special types of, 54–8; support services programme, 207; see also fathers; mothers; parents
Family Court of Australia: developments in custody law, 238, 239–40
Family Law Act: custody and, 234–5; state wards, 233
fathers: nurturing role of, 151; properties expected of, 31; state and, 32 *see also* families; family; mothers; parents
foster care, 231–4

goals for children, differing, 18
government influence on Aboriginal children, 102–6, 111

handicapped members, families with, 57–8; benefits for, 207–10
health, 27, 40, 138–65, 166–72; Aboriginals, 103; care and poverty, 206
Henderson Report, 202
historical roles of children within families, 42–5
hospitalization, 141; effects on child development, 155
housing for Aboriginals, inadequate, 94–6, 104

identity: among Aboriginals, 99–102; Australian, 108; ethnic, 71
Ilich, Ivan, 225
immunization, 140
income: scales, equivalent, 200–3; support, 197, 211; failure of basic, 261; tax, 221
individualism, 178
individuality, development of, 176
infant mortality, 138, 145; Aboriginal, 103
institutions, 28; nineteenth-century, 24; residential, 23
intellectual development, children's, 177–81

kindergarten movement, 24
Kohlberg, Lawrence, 123–4

labour: children as source of, 19; past traditions of, 21
language: Australian schools and ethnic, 81–5; differences, 68–9; English as a second, 77, 109; moral, 116; primary school teaching, 109; religious, 128
law: acting for children, 249; Australian

reforms, 229; child welfare, 227; children and the, 225–45; custody, 227; discriminating against Aboriginal people, 102; morality and, 116–17
learned helplessness, 178
learning: active, 182; as accumulation of information, 191; processes, 182; situations, devising appropiate, 180; skills and facts, 181
Legal Aid, Aboriginal, 102, 104
legal representation, child's own, 239; insufficient, 233
legislation: about children and family, ambiguous, 47; for the protection of children, 36; *see also* law
low-birthweight infants, 144, 150, 167

malnutrition, 206
mass media, influence on development of values, 121
mastery, sense of, 178
maternity allowances, 207–10
minority groups, needs of, 34
monism, 73; hybrid, 73
moral: development, 122–7, 180; values, 114, 123; acquiring, 120–2
morality, 116–18
mothering, 64–5
mothers: expectations and practices of Aboriginal, 97–9; major responsibility for children, 63; properties expected of, 31; *see also*, families; fathers; parents
multiculturalism, 74, 81, 108, 188; official policy, 75

needs 44: Aboriginal children's, 96–9; children's, 87–8; conflicting, 26; continuing redefinition, 220; in jeopardy, 25; lack of consensus about children's, 62; order of priority, 27–9
neglect, child, 228
nutritional disorders, 138, 160–3

obesity, 138, 161
obstetric care, 167–8
open education, 183–5

parental: authority and the law, 228–30; rights and access, 238–9
parenting: costs of, 221–3; effective, 169
parents, 17–18, 29; apparent role conflict, 63; children's health, 166–72; custody 234; law, 229; properties expected of, 29–33; training, 171; transmitting values, 133, 134; *see also* families; fathers; mothers
perception, 178–9
perinatal care: medical advances in, 143–7; problems of, 141
personal development, 177
Piaget, Jean, 127, 178, 180; moral development, 122
pluralism, 74
poor laws, 252; legislation concerning, 228
poverty, 63, 258–9; among Aboriginals, 93–6; attempts to relieve, 220; child, 197, 203; alternative measures of, 205; family life and, 205–7; line, 203–4; social security provisions, 212, 213, 215; measuring, 200
Poverty in Australia, Commission of Inquiry into, 202
Poverty Reports, Aboriginals and, 93
pregnancy, 166; adolescent, 142–3; some factors in early, 167
prematurity, 169
prevention of health problems: primary, 139–40; secondary, 140–1; tertiary, 141
progressive education, 180, 184
properties expected of children, 29–33
protection, children in need of, 51
protective factors, 50, 52
public response to children, changing, 251–7

racial attitudes towards Aboriginals, 91–3
relativism, 114, 115; moral, 125, 127
religion, 118–19; diversity in, 114; role in moral education, 126
religious: development, 127–31; differences among ethnic groups, 71–3; philanthropists, nineteenth-century, 24; values 114; acquiring, 120–2
rights: children's 51, 225; social issues and, 226; uncertainties about, 246; conflicting, 26, 52; family, 46–7; forfeited, 26; in jeopardy, 25; increasing emphasis on individual, 248; order of priority, 27–9; parents, 51

School of Industry, 23
schooling: aims, 193–4; compulsory, 17, 64, 225; nature of, 182; public accountability, 175; theory and research on development 181–3
schools, 192: cultural transmission,

75–7; influence on development of values, 121; "integrated day" primary, 185; role in moral education, 126; role inreligious education, 130–1; role in society, 174–7, 194
segregation of Aboriginal people, 90–1
self-esteem, Aboriginal, 112
services, 226; access to health, 164; children's, 216, 247; assumptions of, 53–4; funding, 207–10; expertise required in, 255; for special types of families, 54–8; health 170–2; information about, 66
SIDS, 147
single-parent families, 55
social: development, 177; growth of children, 192; interactions among ethnic groups, 79–81; values and economic relationships, 218–24
social policies, 34; developmental, 38; economic, 222; objectives for children, 40, 257–61; predictions for formulating, 58–61; unresolved issues, 62–3; welfare backlash, 252–3
Social Security, Department of, 207
social services: early development, 20; resistance to further expansion, 254; social security payments, 220, 222
social welfare *see* welfare
socialisation, 39; Aboriginal children's, 96–9, 110; changing patterns, 37; through school, 175
society: children and, 17–34, 247; nineteenth century, 36
stability of child-family relationships, 49–50
state: children and the, 35–40; relations between family, child and, 250–1; uncertainties about, 246; *see also* community; government
state wards, 18, 227; court jurisdiction, 228, 229; foster care, 231
step-children, 240
stigmatizing, 39
stress, 48–9; affecting families, 59–61; coping strategies, 41, 49; effects of, 41; family-centred, 41; specialtypes of families and, 54–8
Sudden Infant Death Syndrome (SIDS), 147
Sydney Orphan School, 23

teachers unions, 195–6
teaching: child-centred, 183; methods, 191

United Nations Declaration of the Rights of the Child, 225

values: children and, 114–31; clarification, 124–6, 135–6; conflicting, 133; education, 132, 134–7

wards of the state *see* state wards
Wardship Review Tribunal, 232
welfare: determining the child's, 237; movement, infant, 24; policy, 259; state, 253–5; system, child, 256–7